Ethnic Politics

Also by Milton J. Esman—

Management Dimensions of Development

Local Organizations: Intermediaries in Rural Development (coauthor)

Ethnic Conflict in the Western World (editor)

Ethnicity, Pluralism, and the State in the Middle East (coeditor)

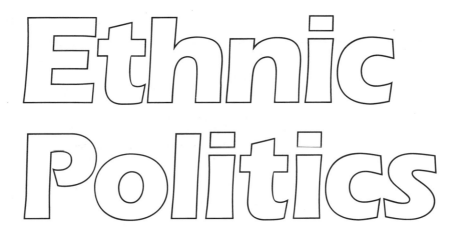

Ethnic Politics

MILTON J. ESMAN

CORNELL UNIVERSITY PRESS ▪ ITHACA AND LONDON

First published 1994 by Cornell University Press.

Library of Congress Cataloging-in-Publication Data
Esman, Milton J. (Milton Jacob), 1918–
Ethnic politics / Milton J. Esman.
p.   cm.
Includes bibliographical references and index.
ISBN 0-8014-3010-0
1. World politics—1945–   2. Ethnic relations.   I. Title.
D842.E83   1994
909.82—dc20   94-14440

Printed in the United States of America

∞ The paper in this book meets the minimum requirements of the American National Standard for Information Sciences—Permanence of Paper for Printed Library Materials, ANSI Z39.48-1984.

To Danny, Elizabeth, Emily, and Sarah

Contents

Acknowledgments

Over a quarter century as an ethnic politics watcher, observing, reading, researching, interviewing, conferencing, visiting and residing abroad, I have accumulated heavy obligations, some that I can no longer recollect, many more than I can specifically acknowledge. In addition to many people whose works I cited in this book, I list some to whom I am especially indebted and grateful for information about particular areas:

On Canada, Gerald Alfred, Lise Bisonette, Kenneth Bush, Edouard Cloutier, Denise Daoust, the late Davidson Dunton, Daniel Latouche, Kenneth McRae, Morris Miller, the late Donald Smiley, Arnaud Sales.

On Israel/Palestine, Meron Benvenisti, Naomi Chazan, Ibrahim Dakak, Daniel Elazar, Elias Freij, Emmanuel Guttman, Aziz Haidar, Dan Meridor, Joseph Olmert, Gabriel Sheffer, Itamar Rabinovich, Sammy Smooha, Shibley Telhami, Saadia Touval.

On Malaysia, the late Tun Abdul Razak, Rama Ayer, Elyas Omar, Ghazali Shafie, Donald Horowitz, Jamil Rais, the late Kadir Shamsuddin, Diane Mauzy, Stephen Milne, Musa Hitam, James and Mavis Puthucheary, Thong Yaw-hong, Unku Aziz, Karl Von Vorys.

On South Africa, Karel Boshof, David and John Bridgmen, H. C. Marais, Johan Olivier, Barend du Plessis, Nic Rhoodie, R. E. Vander Ross, Robert Schrire, Philip Smit, Helen Suzman, David and Virginia Welsh.

My thanks to Valerie Bunce for helpful comments on an earlier version of this manuscript.

Janice has shared all these experiences and contributed more than I could ever acknowledge.

M. J. E.

Ithaca, New York

Note to the Reader

The pace of events in South Africa and Palestine has outstripped the
publishing schedule for this book. For this reason I have cut off the
recording of events at January 1, 1994. The recent accession of Nelson
Mandela to the presidency of the Republic of South Africa and the withdrawal of Israeli forces from Gaza and Jericho are dramatic and consequential events, yet the reality of mobilized ethnic pluralism among
these peoples continues. Ethnic politics persists.

Ethnic Politics

1

Ethnic Solidarity as a Political Force: The Scope of the Inquiry

Glance at headlines in the early 1990s: pitched battles between Serbs, Croats, and Muslims in Bosnia, between Sinhalese and Tamils in Sri Lanka, between Muslims and Christians in northern Nigeria. Read of IRA bombings in London, of threatened genocide by Arabs against Dinka in Sudan, of riots involving African-Americans, Whites, and Koreans in Los Angeles. The ethnically defined successor states of the defunct Soviet Union contain restive minorities whose competing claims and status must be confronted and managed. Canada is threatened with the peaceful secession of Quebec, led by the French-speaking majority, now "masters in their own homeland"; India is coping with a violent Sikh secessionist movement in the Punjab; the minority Sunni Arab regime in Iraq struggles to maintain control over rebellious Kurds and Shia Muslims; Belgium has periodically been without a government for weeks at a time pending tedious negotiations between representatives of its Walloon and Flemish peoples; French and German public affairs are roiled by conflicts over the status of large immigrant diasporas. The catalog of brutally violent and of more or less civic manifestations of ethnic conflict includes all continents.

Ethnic identity, ethnic solidarity, and ethnic conflict are by no means new phenomena. From the dawn of history communities organized on putative common descent, culture, and destiny have coexisted, competed, and clashed. Thirty-five hundred years ago the Israelites demanded freedom and self-determination from the Pharaohs. In the nineteenth century the main preoccupation of the rulers of the Austro-Hungarian Empire was to maintain a viable coexistence between the state and the refractory mi-

norities of their multiethnic polity.[1] What distinguishes the current era is
not the existence of competitive ethnic solidarities but their global political salience. As other scholars have demonstrated, of the 180 territorial
states that make up the political map of the contemporary world, more
than 90 percent are multiethnic, containing two or more ethnic communities of significant size.[2] These communities tend to be organized, legally
or covertly, on behalf of their common interests. In multiethnic or multinational federalized states such as India, Russia, Switzerland, and Spain,
they may exercise autonomous control over designated territories; in some
states they compete for influence and attempt to impress their needs and
preferences on the central government; in others they struggle for separation and independent statehood. These patterns, diverse and complex,
will be described, analyzed, and explained in this book.

The fundamental reality is that of ethnic pluralism within the boundaries
of the great majority of political systems in the contemporary world. From
this fundamental reality emerge the central problems—relationships and
terms of coexistence, coercive or consensual—that are shaped and maintained by these ethnic communities and the rules and practices enforced by
the political authorities that govern these states. Ethnic pluralism establishes the need for ethnic politics that range from civic to violent. It does
not, however, explain why and how ethnic solidarities have become so politicized in modern societies that they preoccupy, even to the point of obses-
sion, statesmen, political entrepreneurs, and informed observers. Indeed,
since the end of the Cold War, ethnic conflict has emerged as the principal
source of destabilization and organized violence around the world, producing massacres, destruction of whole communities, and pathetic streams of
refugees.

Conquest, Colonization, Immigration

Ethnic pluralism can be traced to three factors. The first is conquest and
annexation, when a people is defeated and brought under the rule of the

[1] An ethnic community that aspires to political self-rule usually designates itself a "nation." French Canadians in Quebec (Québecois) call themselves a nation, though they
disagree on whether self-rule should be realized as a province within the Canadian polity
or as a separate and independent state. The various aboriginal communities, Indians and
Eskimos (Inuit), seek a measure of self-rule and call themselves nations. The Ukrainians,
Chinese, Jewish, and Italian diasporas in Canada constitute mobilized ethnic communities
with common interests that they attempt to impress on the state, but they do not seek self-
rule and thus do not claim to be nations in the Canadian context.

[2] Walker Connor, "The Politics of Ethnonationalism," *Journal of International Affairs*
27:1 (1973): 1-24.

victor. Thus the Russian tsars incorporated dozens of ethnic minorities in the vast territories they overran during the three centuries preceding World War 1. The second is the process of European colonization and decolonization, which assembled within administrative boundaries established for the convenience of colonial powers peoples who had no mutual affinity and were often traditionally hostile. In the process ethnic communities were often split among two or more states governed by different colonial masters. The postcolonial successor states inherited these ethnically arbitrary boundaries. Let it be said, however, in fairness to conquerors and colonists, that settlement patterns among the world's many peoples are often so intricate and intermixed that no cartographer could conceivably produce maps that would leave even the majority of states ethnically pure. Minorities and, inevitably, ethnic pluralism would always exist.[3]

The third main contributor to ethnic pluralism is population movements. From the beginning of recorded history, individuals have crossed political boundaries in search of economic opportunity or religious and political freedom. At times whole communities have moved and settled in areas already inhabited or claimed by indigenous peoples. People have been transported as slaves or as indentured laborers; others have been refugees fleeing war, famine, or persecution; communities have been expelled en masse as undesirables or as alleged subversives. Because of relatively cheap, reliable transportation, the twentieth century has witnessed an unprecedented volume of migration from poor to rich countries, creating large ethnic diasporas, permanent settlements of ethnic minorities in receiving countries.

Self-Determination and Its Consequences

Conquest, colonization and decolonization, migration—these have been the main sources of ethnic pluralism. But why has this pluralism so often generated intense ethnic conflict during the past two centuries? For centuries, even millennia, peoples with distinctive cultures, social organization, and collective identities—ethnic communities—were ruled by political authorities, often dynasties, which extracted revenues and deference but in most respects let their subjects alone as long as they caused no problems for the regime. Despite occasional rebellions, people gen-

[3]This was the substance of the eloquent argument against self-determination elaborated by the historian Alfred Cobban after World War II: *The Nation State and National Self-Determination*, rev. ed. (New York: Thomas Y. Crowell, 1969).

erally acceded to authority unless it became unduly oppressive. Minorities were rarely organized for collective action; where they did maintain some degree of collective solidarity, their notables attempted to negotiate the most favorable terms possible for themselves and their communities. Government was for the most part a remote presence that impinged only slightly on the daily lives of its mostly peasant subjects; ethnic communities, usually unmobilized, accepted foreign rule as inevitable. Seldom were rulers troubled by normative doubts about their moral right to dominate their subjects, including alien peoples.

The French Revolution ushered in the era of political democracy and the associated ideology of political nationalism.[4] The dominant version of this ideology endowed all peoples, all self-declared nations, with the right of "self-determination." Foreign rule was inherently unjust, therefore illegitimate. Every state should be the living expression and embodiment of a single constituent nation. It thus became the duty of state elites to build a united, indivisible nation by assimilating or eliminating ethnic minorities. At the same time, every aspiring nation enjoyed the inalienable right to self determination, to mobilize politically and to struggle for self-government. Thus ethnic nationalism and the doctrine of national self-determination stimulated and legitimated unprecedented activism among previously passive and compliant ethnic communities. National self-determination, first the rallying cry for numerous hitherto subordinated peoples in Europe—Irish, Poles, Italians, Czechs, Serbs, Finns—then spread globally to areas of European colonization in Asia, Africa, the Middle East, and the Caribbean. It became the main justification for anticolonial struggles that culminated in universal success in the decades following World War II. The doctrine of national self-determination still justifies the breakup of larger states into smaller, more homogeneous political units. It spawns numerous secessionist movements, from the successor republics of the Soviet Union to the Québecois in Canada, the Kurds in Iraq and Turkey, the Tibetans in China, and

---

[4]The intellectual father of ethnic nationalism was the German philosopher Johann Gottfried von Herder who, in the late eighteenth century, proclaimed the right of every people to enjoy and develop its distinctive gifts and traditions. See Robert E. Ergang, *Herder and the Foundations of German Nationalism* (New York: Octagon Books, 1966). Among the classics in the vast literature on nationalism are Hans Kohn, *The Idea of Nationalism* (New York: Macmillan, 1945); Elie Kedourie, *Nationalism* (London: Hutchinson, 1960); and John Armstrong, *Nations before Nationalism* (Chapel Hill: University of North Carolina Press, 1982). For a schematic summary of various and competing "building blocks" of theory, see James G. Kellas, *The Politics of Nationalism and Ethnicity* (New York: St. Martin's, 1991), 171–73.

the Slovaks in former Czechoslavakia. We should note, however, that the achievement of self-determination by one group seldom inspires tolerance on its part for the claims of ethnic minorities that remain within the boundaries of a newly independent or autonomous polity. Asians in Uganda, English-speakers in Quebec, Russians in Estonia, South Ossetians in Georgia, and Tamils in Sri Lanka can attest that ethnic grievances and ethnic politics do not end when one kind of self-determination has been realized; only the parties and the alignments change. Yesterday's victims become tomorrow's oppressors.

During the heyday of state nationalism, in the century and a half preceding World War II, members of ethnic minorities, whether indigenous or of recent immigrant origin, were expected to assimilate as individuals into the nation represented by the state in which they resided. Minority status implied dual loyalty, a challenge to the security of the state and the legitimacy of the social order. Minorities were therefore discouraged, often by intimidation, from political and even cultural self-assertion. As the duty of state elites was to build a united and homogeneous nation, the duty of ethnic minorities was to assimilate; the only acceptable alternative to assimilation was passivity.

The ideology of state nationalism has experienced a notable decline since World War II, especially in Europe and North America. French, German, and Italian youth are now moved more by sentiments of membership in a European community than by the gut patriotism of previous generations. This development has opened political space, especially for indigenous ethnic minorities but also for immigrant diasporas, to mobilize for political action and to make claims on the state. The activation of ethnic minorities has, in turn, generated countermobilization by nativists who feel threatened or offended by these demands and whose leaders aspire to build political constituencies by exploiting these anxieties. Paradoxically, the erosion of the ideology of state nationalism has stimulated ethnic politics without diminishing the potency of self-determination as a spur to ethnic activism. Nothing on the horizon of world affairs appears likely to diminish the salience or the intensity of ethnic politics either in the industrialized West, in Third World areas, or in the territories of the former Soviet Union.

The disintegration of the multinational Soviet and Yugoslav states has, since 1990, precipitated intense ethnic conflicts. Those regimes, which had attempted with some success to delegitimate and repress ethnic claims and antagonisms, eventually collapsed. These developments have attracted widespread academic interest and public concern, though indeed they recapitulate many processes of European decolonization in Asia and Africa during the decades after World War II. For example: The boundaries of the former Soviet republics were often arbitrarily drawn; weak successor states, unprepared for the burdens suddenly thrust on them, possess little legitimacy or coercive capacity but generate fears and anxieties among their restive minorities; political entrepreneurs are available to exploit these fears. The fate in these states of 26 million previously privileged Russians, now regarded by many among the ethnic majorities as foreigners and ex-colonialists, remains to be determined. Lethal ethnic-based violence has broken out in Azerbaijan, Georgia, Moldova, and Tadjikistan, while militant secessionist demands from Tatars, Chechyns, and other mobilized regional minorities confront the weakened Russian Federation. External intervention by other states and by international organizations has occurred or is threatened in several instances. Though I do not focus on Eastern Europe and the former Soviet Union in this book, the dynamics of these conflicts accord with processes identified and analyzed in this and other recent studies of ethnic politics, and the eventual management of these conflicts will likely be governed by similar logic.

Manifestations of Ethnic Pluralism: Homelands and Diasporas

Though every instance of ethnic pluralism has distinctive features, for analytical purposes these can be conveniently grouped into two general types: homelands societies and immigrant diasporas.

Homelands societies claim long-time occupancy of a particular territory. Native status implies that the land belongs exclusively to them and that they possess the moral right to rule. Their interests in that land override any claims by a central government controlled by an alien people or any claims to equal treatment by immigrants. Place names reflect the people's long association with the land where generations of ancestors labored, cleared the land, constructed homes and towns, and lie buried. Historical claims are reenforced by archaeological data and by myths constructed to vindicate disputed claims to homeland status. These historic rights are expressed in the doctrine of ethnic nationalism, which legitimates their right to independent statehood and privileges natives over all other claimants to political, cultural, or economic rights on their ancestral territory.

Homelands peoples insist on control over their territory. Immigrants may be tolerated but must adjust to rules established by the native majority. Where homelands peoples are a minority in a multiethnic or multinational state, their demands may range from territorial autonomy to secession and independent statehood. Autonomy usually includes the right to select officials and control significant areas of public affairs, preferential access by natives to economic opportunities, and privileged or exclusive status for the ethnic language in education and government transactions. In federalized systems territorial minorities may also demand equitable participation in the affairs of the central government and fair shares in the state's allocations of valuable resources. Problems or disputes may arise over who, indeed, are the authentic natives. Is Palestine the exclusive homeland of Jews or of Arabs? How long must a people control a territory before they can legitimately claim it as their exclusive homeland? What of the claims of earlier native peoples that they displaced? Are French-speaking Caucasians after 350 years the authentic homelands people of Quebec, entitled by right of self-determination to separate from Canada? Or must their claims yield to Algonquins, Mohawks, and other Indian nations who were there many centuries earlier?

Homelands-based ethnic communities may be privileged over other regional claimants to the patronage dispensed by governments. For instance, although by economic criteria Scotland and the north of England are about equally disadvantaged, Scots as an ethnic/national community have been more successful than the nonethnic northerners in extracting public investments and concessions from the British government. Distinctive ethnicity legitimates regional claims for special treatment. In the hope that this might legitimate and buttress their demands, regional entrepreneurs in the south of France attempted during the 1960s to reconstruct a vanished Occitanian collective identity.

A consequence of migrations, diaspora communities are formed in the receiving country. Whether they have moved to escape oppression or to improve their economic prospects, immigrants are inclined to maintain their distinctive collective identities and customs, in part because they are excluded by virtue of these differences from participation and membership in the host society. Diaspora communities often organize to provide mutual assistance in a strange environment and to maintain elements of their culture while they adapt to local conditions. Normally they maintain material and sentimental links with the country from which they migrated. They may find it necessary or advantageous to deploy their organizational strength politically in defense or promotion of their collective interests.

There are three types of ethnic diasporas. The first are groups of settlers, like the Norman invaders of Britain, who arrive in such numbers and with such military and technological superiority that they soon subordinate, exterminate, or expel the existing inhabitants and take effective possession of the territory. They soon claim the status of native sons, making the transition from an immigrant diaspora to a homeland people. For practical purposes we treat such dominant settler societies as homelands people.

The diasporas that remain minorities fall into two major categories.[5] Bourgeois diasporas are immigrant communities that move to host societies with educational or economic skills equal or superior to those that prevail among the indigenous people. In some cases, like that of Jews in the Ottoman Empire, they are welcomed by the local authorities. More commonly they encounter obstacles and discrimination of various kinds but succeed in establishing beachheads in the local society that ensure economic power and political access. Middleman minorities— Chinese in Southeast Asia, Indians in East Africa—are examples of this phenomenon.[6] Because they are conspicuous, unassimilated, and relatively prosperous, bourgeois diasporas often attract the envy of indigenous economic competitors and nationalist intellectuals. Marginal to their host society, economically strong but politically powerless, they hold a precarious status and are vulnerable to scapegoating.

Labor diasporas are the most common type in the current era, a result of large-scale migration from poor, overpopulated, labor-surplus countries to prosperous labor-scarce economies. These voluntary movements of workers and their families supplement the involuntary movements of African slaves and indentured Asians that formed some earlier labor disaporas. Because migrant workers tend to be relatively uneducated and unskilled, they enter the lowest strata of the labor market in their host countries, poor, culturally marginal, and politically powerless, often targets of formal or informal discrimination. The eventual political mobilization of labor diasporas to articulate, promote, and defend their collective interests in less than hospitable environments depends on the

[5] See John Armstrong, "Mobilized and Proletarian Diasporas," *American Political Science Review* 70 (June 1976): 393–408.
[6] See Edna Bonacich, "A Theory of Ethnic Antagonism: The Split Labor Market," *American Sociology Review* 37 (1972): 547–59.

openness of the host society to the organized expression of minority group interests.

Bourgeois and labor diasporas, recent arrivals who are normally concentrated in urban areas, cannot credibly claim control over territory. What they normally demand is nondiscriminatory participation as individuals in public affairs—voting, office holding, access to justice—plus nondiscriminatory access to education, employment, housing, business opportunities, and public services; and official recognition of their right to maintain institutions that perpetuate elements of their inherited culture. Because these aspirations may offend or generate resistance from segments of the indigenous society or from representatives of the state, diasporas find it necessary to mobilize politically to press their claims, provoking, in turn, hostile countermobilization within the majority society.

Most academic attention to ethnic relations has focused either strictly on homelands peoples or strictly on immigrants, resulting in two separate streams of literature that seldom intersect.[7] In this book I attempt to accommodate conceptually both the homelands and the diaspora dimensions of ethnic politics.

Ethnic Solidarity: Essence and Existence

Ethnic solidarity with its tendency to become politicized is so palpable a reality in public affairs that many observers are inclined to regard it as an existential fact of life. The human species is composed of different peoples; though not immutable, their differences persist over time. What interests them are such questions as the conditions under which and the processes by which ethnic identities and solidarities become activated and converted to political conflict, the kinds of issues such transformation raises for ethnic competitors and for the state, how conflicts thus engendered are waged, and how their outcomes can be mitigated, managed, and eventually settled. To these observers ethnic solidarity is a pervasive consequential reality whose various manifestations deserve careful examination and analysis so that the phenomenon can be both better understood and more wisely regulated by public policy.

---

[7]See Milton J. Esman, "Two Dimensions of Ethnic Politics: Defense of Homelands, Immigrant Rights," *Ethnic and Racial Studies* 8 (July 1985): 438–40.

Many social scientists, however, find this existential approach super-ficial. They wish to probe the essence of ethnicity, its origins, underlying properties, and function in human affairs. The principal debate within the essentialist camp has been between "primordialists" and "instru-mentalists."[8] The former hold that ethnicity as a collective identity is so deeply rooted in historical experience that it should properly be treated as a given in human relations. A few argue that ethnicity is at root a biological phenomenon, an expression of the powerful drive to extend genetic endowments into future generations.[9] Others contend that as in-dividuals are born and socialized into an ethnic community, they imbibe from their earliest experiences the unique identity, collective memories, language, and customs of their people. They learn as birthright and ob-ligation the historical myths of common ancestry that bind them to their people. They locate security, welfare, and trust in their own community, which shares common beliefs and meanings forever denied to outsiders. They learn the critical distinction between us, the insiders, and them, the outsiders—who are at best different, at worst (and often) hostile. Thus individuals are bonded early in life to their ethnic community and these bonds tend to be perpetuated intergenerationally as distinctive peoples, tribes, or nations. When necessary, ethnic communities adapt their func-tions to changing conditions, but the community persists. Social scien-tists who hold the primordialist view tend to attach high value to historical continuity, group sanctions, and social solidarity as determi-nants of human behavior.

Instrumentalists, conversely, argue that ethnicity is not a historical given at all, but in fact a highly adaptive and malleable phenomenon. In response to changing conditions, the boundaries of an ethnic collec-

---

[8] James McKay, "An Exploratory Synthesis of Primordial and Mobilizational Ap-proaches to Ethnic Phenomena," *Ethnic and Racial Studies* 5 (October 1982): 395–420. For examples of the primordialist position see Harold Isaacs, *Idols of the Tribe: Group Identity and Political Change* (New York: Harper and Row, 1975) and Anthony Smith, *The Ethnic Origin of Nations* (Oxford: Blackwell, 1986). Among instrumentalists see Paul Brass, "Ethnic Groups and the State" in Brass, ed., *Ethnic Groups and the State* (London: Croom-Helm, 1985), 1–58; and Fredrik Barth, "Introduction" in Barth, ed., *Ethnic Groups and Boundaries: The Social Organization of Cultural Differences* (Boston: Little, Brown, 1969), 9–38. In the U.S. context, contrast Michael Novak's primordialist statement *The Rise of the Unmeltable Ethnics* (New York: Macmillan, 1971) with the work of the extreme instrumentalist Stephen Steinberg, *The Ethnic Myth: Race, Ethnicity, and Class in America* (New York: Atheneum, 1981). For a balanced treatment see R. A. Schermerhorn, *Com-parative Ethnic Relations: A Framework for Theory and Research* (New York: Random House, 1970).

[9] Pierre Van den Berghe, *The Ethnic Phenomenon* (New York: Elsevier, 1981).

tivity can expand or contract, individuals move in and out and even share membership in more than one community. The very content, symbols, and meaning of a particular collective identity can and do evolve. In effect, ethnicity is a dynamic, not a fixed and immutable element of social and political relationships.

Other instrumentalists are even more skeptical about the integrity of ethnic identity and solidarity. They argue that ethnicity is primarily a practical resource that individuals and groups deploy opportunistically to promote their more fundamental security or economic interests and that they may even discard when alternative affiliations promise a better return. Among the instrumentalists are adherents to the rational actor or public choice schools, who attempt to explain all behavior as the rational pursuit of individual, mainly economic values. To them ethnicity is valuable only as it benefits the individual with more security, prestige, or material returns than available alternatives. That ethnicity is a cynical myth or expression of "false consciousness" is argued by some Marxist-oriented scholars intent on demonstrating the primacy of material and class values over cultural values as motivators of behavior, especially in modern capitalist societies. Thus, according to instrumentalists, ethnicity is either an ideology that elites construct and deconstruct for opportunistic reasons or a set of myths calculated to mobilize mass support for the economic or political goals of ambitious minorities.

Before addressing this controversy, however, it would be useful to explore some of the properties of ethnicity and its treatment by recent writers. Among social scientists the hostiles and the skeptics have greatly outnumbered the believers. The majority of mainline academics in the social sciences have had difficulty coming to terms with the frequency and intensity of ethnic conflict in recent years. Many tend to ignore it or dismiss it as an aberrant or transient phenomenon. The choice to avoid the issue derives largely from the assumptions of the most prominent and influential theories through which scholars construct and interpret their social universe. None of these theories allots a central position to ethnic solidarities.

Liberal theory, dominant in the West for nearly three centuries, regards the individual as the main unit of social value and predicts that progress will inevitably break down artificial barriers based on parochial, ascriptive allegiances. In the emergent society, free of ascriptive or communal constraints, people would participate and compete as self-determining individuals valued and rewarded according to their individual contributions and performance. No preferences, no discrimination—

a level playing field for every individual. Ethnicity would survive only as nostalgic vestiges of an earlier and less enlightened stage of historical development. The influential modernization variant of classical liberalism argues that voluntary associations based on occupational and other "rational" interests would supplant status groups based on particularistic and parochial solidarities. In the wake of economic development and nation building, ascriptive loyalties would lose their social function and gradually wither away.[10] More recently, neoclassical economic concepts and logic have invaded the broader field of social theory, combining methodological individualism with rational actor notions to produce "public choice" theory. That world of atomized individuals maximizing personal, principally economic, preferences provides little space for group solidarities, especially those based on ascriptive bonds. Meanwhile, even the vigorous and sophisticated school of social scientists who focus on social movements pays virtually no attention to ethnic movements.[11]

Although Marxist writers are troubled by the persistence of ethnic loyalties—which some attribute to inherent contradictions in latter-day capitalism and others to calculated ruling class strategies—they confidently predict their eventual demise in the face of working class solidarity. The inevitable triumph of socialism will eliminate economic exploitation, the principal cause of antagonistic social conflict. Lenin's historic compromise with national sentiments in the formation of the USSR was no more than a necessary tactical concession to a retrograde phenomenon that is destined to be swept away by the inevitable advance of proletarian internationalism.[12] Despite fundamental disagreement on most issues, liberals and Marxists alike denigrate and delegitimate ethnic

[10]Talcott Parsons, "Some Theoretical Considerations on the Nature and Trends of Change of Ethnicity," in Nathan Glazer and Daniel Patrick Moynihan, eds., Ethnicity: Theory and Experience (Cambridge: Harvard University Press, 1975); Karl Deutsch, Nationalism and Social Comunication: An Inquiry into the Foundations of Nationality (Cambridge: MIT Press, 1953); Benjamin Akzin, State and Nation (London: Hutchinson, 1964).

[11]See, for example, Aldon D. Morris and Carol McClung Muller, eds., Frontiers of Social Movement Theory (New Haven: Yale University Press, 1992); Bert Klandermans, Hanspeter Krossi, and Sidney Tarrow, eds., International Social Movements Research (Greenwich, Conn.: JAI Press, 1988), vol. 1; and Doug McAdam, John D. McCarthy, and Mayer N. Zald, "Social Movements" in Neil J. Smelser, ed., Handbook of Sociology (Beverly Hills, Calif.: Sage, 1988), 695–739.

[12]For a review and analysis of this doctrine and an excellent bibliography, see Walker Connor, The National Question in Marxist-Leninist Theory and Practice (Princeton: Princeton University Press, 1984).

solidarity, predicting its waning relevance in capitalist and postcapitalist societies. The force of this attitude has helped to persuade many scholars in Third World societies that politicized ethnicity (such as "tribalism") in their countries is an unfortunate residue of backwardness, certain to diminish in the wake of economic development and therefore of little interest to forward-looking social scientists.

Though dominant, liberal and Marxist ideas have not gone unchallenged. A loosely knit group of academics identified as pluralists have been observing, analyzing, and writing about ethnic phenomena, about empirical expressions of cultural, social, and structural pluralism and their implications for modern society.[13] Their work has not been disciplined by rigorous, deductive theory, but they all understand ethnic pluralism as a pervasive phenomenon that severely strains many contemporary societies and governments and that may precipitate widespread injustice, violence, and human suffering. Whereas some scholars relate ethnic pluralism to processes of stratification and domination, others draw attention to segmental structures and speculate on methods to achieve consensual and peaceful coexistence.[14] These diverse authors share the recognition of ethnic solidarity as a free-standing and enduring phenomenon that needs and deserves to be examined and understood on its own terms.

Ethnicity as politics is meaningful only in a relational framework. As a collective identity ethnicity is shaped not only by self-definition but also by constraints imposed by outsiders. Thus the internal "we" must be distinguished from the external "they." Where no relevant others exist, the need for solidarity disappears and society fragments on the basis of internal differences.[15] The need for ethnic solidarity arises only when strange, threatening, competitive outsiders must be confronted. Only then are distinctions between "us" and "them" noted, explained,

[13]See, inter alia, Leo Kuper and M. G. Smith, eds., *Pluralism in Africa* (Berkeley: University of California Press, 1969); Glazer and Moynihan, "Introduction," *Ethnicity: Theory and Experience*; Schermerhorn, *Comparative Ethnic Relations;* Joseph Rothschild, *Ethnopolitics: A Conceptual Framework* (New York: Columbia University Press, 1981); Crawford Young. *The Politics of Cultural Pluralism* (Madison: University of Wisconsin Press, 1976).

[14]For emphasis on structural stratification, see Michael Hechter, *Internal Colonialism: The Celtic Fringe in British National Development, 1536–1966* (London: Routledge and Kegan Paul, 1975); also Philip Mason, *Patterns of Dominance* (London, Oxford University Press, 1970). On segmentation, see Arent Lijphart, *Democracy in Plural Societies: A Comparative Exploration* (New Haven: Yale University Press, 1977).

[15]In ethnically homogeneous Somalia, for example, society has been riven by mobilized and hostile factions based on extended kinship and lineage.

and evaluated to reinforce internal coherence and to signal and explain differences with outsiders and competitors. Only then does the need for internal solidarity and discipline become evident.

Ethnicity is thus shaped by environment, by the threats and the opportunities it affords. Seldom is ethnicity invented or constructed from whole cloth: a cultural and experiential core must validate identity and make solidarity credible to potential constituents. Yet problems posed by the external environment are as likely as the historical experiences and collective aspirations of the group to determine its dynamics—its definition of problems, needs, and strategies. The polar extremes of primordial givens and of instrumental opportunism seldom account for the real behavior of ethnic communities.

The concept of ethnic identity and solidarity that informs this study is drawn from both the primordialist and the instrumentalist positions. Ethnicity cannot be politicized unless an underlying core of memories, experience, or meaning moves people to collective action. This common foundation may include historical experiences, such as struggles against outsiders for possession of a homeland, or cultural markers, especially language, religion, and legal institutions that set one community apart from others. Ethnic solidarities are also contextual, adaptable to and activated by unexpected threats and new opportunities; they can be oriented to fresh goals, and they can be infused with new content. Historical myths can be shaped from imagined pasts to legitimate current goals; boundaries can expand and contract. Thus every ethnic collectivity and solidarity can be located on a spectrum between (primordial) historical continuities and (instrumental) opportunistic adaptations. This observation applies both to homelands and to diaspora communities, though the former are more likely to tilt to the primordial and the latter to the instrumental poles; either way, the solidarities are authentic, not imagined, constructed, or fantacized.[16]

---

[16]The notion that collective identities, including ethnic identities, are "socially constructed" has attracted a large following among social scientists. To the extent that "socially constructed" implies that ethnic solidarities are the product of sheer perception or cynical manipulation with no objective reality, I find the paradigm incompatible with the evidence of experience. To the extent that social construction implies that collective identities are objective phenomena that, however, are interpreted and reinterpreted, adjusted, and adapted to changing circumstances, threats, and opportunities, I find it a useful and valid concept. Ethnic boundaries can be redefined; so can the content and meaning of collective identity, the labels that designate them (from French Canadian to Québecois, from Colored to Negro to Black to African American), as well as goals, strategies, and

This approach allows for the variability of ethnic solidarities, past as well as present, and regards ethnicity as one of several collective identities that can motivate individual behavior. Under some stimuli, the individual may attach more or less priority to ethnicity as a motivator of behavior than to class, occupational, regional, ideological, or still other sources of collective identity. At any time two or more sources of identity, loyalty, obligation, or interest may compete to determine the individual's behavior. A person cross-pressured in this way attempts to reconcile these competing claims in order to avoid painful choices or cognitive dissonance. Ethnicity is not, however, normally only one of several equal choices. The more politicized ethnicity becomes, the more it dominates other expressions of identity, eclipsing class, occupational, and ideological solidarities. Ethnicity normally taps deeper layers of socialization, experience, emotion, and pride than collective identities that are more instrumental to the individual. Thus, individual and collective identity become fused; when the community is threatened, so is the individual, while the success of a community enhances its members' sense of self-worth. Instinctive loyalty, as well as considerations of personal and family security and of group sanctions, tie individuals to their ethnic community, especially under conditions of intergroup tension and conflict.

The literature contains narrow and broad definitions of ethnic identity and solidarity.[17] The narrower definition denotes a community that claims common origin, often including common descent or fictive kinship; that possesses distinctive and valued cultural markers in the form of customs, dress, and especially language; and that traces a common

---

tactics. But underlying interpretation and adaptation (construction) are the objective phenomena of real communities that retain the allegiance of their members, while competing, often warring, with outsiders over real values. Efforts to construct collective ethnic identities from inchoate materials for opportunistic reasons, such as the "Occitanian" movement in southern France, are likely to experience hard going or to fail entirely because they are not credible to the constituencies they are trying to mobilize. On the meaning of social construction, see William A. Gamson, "The Social Psychology of Collective Action," and Bert Klandermans, "The Social Construction of Protest and Multiorganizational Fields" in Morris and Muller, *Frontiers of Social Movement Theory*. For an application of social construction methods to an ethnic conflict, see Virginia R. Dominguez, *People as Subject, People as Object: Selfhood and Peoplehood in Contemporary Israel* (Madison: University of Wisconsin Press, 1989).

[17]For competing definitions of ethnicity, see Glazer and Moynihan, "Introduction," *Ethnicity: Theory and Experience;* Donald L. Horowitz, *Ethnic Groups in Conflict* (Berkeley: University of California Press, 1985), chapter 1; Schermerhorn, *Comparative Ethnic Relations*, 12–14.

history and expects to share a common destiny. Persons born into such a community generally share a collective identity and constitute a distinct people.

The broader characterization of ethnicity incorporates other ascriptive solidarities such as race, religion, and nationality. Although some authors use the term "communal" to designate this broader concept of ascriptive solidarity, this usage conflicts with other meanings of that term that are inapplicable here. Rather than invent still another term, I employ the concept ethnicity in its broader meaning to include any collective identity and solidarity based on inherited culture, racial differences, belief systems or sentiments of common nationality. In Lebanon, communities identify themselves and are defined by outsiders along religious or confessional lines—Maronites, Druze, Orthodox, Shiia. Similarly, in Northern Ireland, the disputes between Catholics and Protestants do not in fact concern theological issues but the relative power, status, and resources available to each community. In Canada, the main cleavage is defined as cultural-linguistic—Anglophone versus Francophone— though in the nineteenth century it contained an important religious element, Catholic versus Protestant. Today, the claims of Canada's aboriginal peoples introduce racial as well as cultural differences. In Malaysia, the differences between Malays and Chinese include racial and religious as well as cultural dimensions. And although the parties in South Africa have been defined by race, the majority Black society encompasses highly mobilized peoples differentiated by distinctive cultures and institutions. The word "ethnic" as used in this book is thus a useful shorthand for communities whose collective identities and solidarities are based on ascriptive criteria. Ultimately, the critical consideration is ethnic pluralism—two or more ascriptive solidarity groups, us and them, coexisting under a single political authority.

Actors and Structures

The participants in ethnic disputes are, of course, organized and mobilized ethnic communities. The mere existence, however, of two or more ethnic communities under the same political authority does not imply that ethnicity will become politicized. Ethnic communities that continue to perform their normal functions of providing security, mutual assistance, and symbolic meaning for their members may nevertheless eschew politics. Perhaps they deem participation in politics unnecessary for their survival and well-being; perhaps they feel such engagement unduly risky for the uncertain benefits it might yield. Ethnic groups may forego political action because they harbor no major grievances, because they are reasonably satisfied with the status quo, because they prefer to remain relatively inconspicuous, or because they consider themselves too few or too weak to make a political impact. Such ethnic communities prefer to adapt to the realities they encounter by remaining on the fringes of political struggles or by acquiescing in the assimilation of their members into the dominant society.

The last century, especially the period since World War II, has witnessed the expansion and proliferation of ethnic-based political action. This phenomenon has been explained as a political consequence of the process of modernization, marked by the spread of manufacturing technologies, commercialization of agriculture, urbanization of living patterns, secularization of culture, speeding of communications and transportation, and consequent rising mass expectations for material improvement and political participation.

Yet the first academic response to the impact of modernization predicted the decline of ethnicity as a political force in the belief that modernization tends to homogenize contemporary societies.[18] With industrialization and urbanization, persons of all ethnic backgrounds and affiliations tend to pursue the same material and social values; rewards are distributed according to individual performance or achievement by universal, objective, competitive standards rather than by ascriptive status or group membership. The associated processes of nation building and rapid communications further undermine parochial allegiances. As ethnicity loses its utility to individuals and society, the argument continues, it loses its relevance to modern man. Gradually it passes from the scene, surviving only as vestigial, nostalgic memories and rituals, devoid of meaning and substance.

This conventional view of the impact of modernization fails to account for the explosion of ethnic politics in Third World "modernizing" societies, for its stubborn persistence below the surface of state repression in the Leninist polities of Eastern Europe and the Soviet Union, and especially for its unexpected reappearance during the 1960s in Western Europe and North America, which had experienced modernization for

---

[18]Deutsch, *Nationalism and Social Communication*. For a contrary and more accurate perspective on the effects of modernization, see Robert Melson, and Harold Wolpe, "Modernization and the Politics of Communalism, a Theoretical Perspective," *American Political Science Review* 64 (1970), 112–30.

more than a century.[19] The more plausible explanation argues that modernization generates intense competition for material opportunities and advantages while mass communications, urbanization, and expanded education foster political participation. In an environment of rising expectations, ethnic solidarity proves to be the most useful and available strategy by which people can position themselves to compete for access and shares of scarce political and cultural as well as material values. Instead of disintegrating into atomized individuals, ethnic solidarities themselves become modernized, endowed with new, vital functions in a highly competitive environment. Where, for example, members of one ethnic community, through luck or aggressiveness or unequal historical opportunity, have achieved disproportionate control of political power or material resources or cultural prestige, how can their dominance be effectively challenged except by organized activity? And if differential treatment can be imputed to ethnic preferences or exclusions enforced by formal rules or informal practices, then the challenge must logically come from ethnically organized competitors whose members are collectively disadvantaged by the prevailing rules and practices that distribute power, wealth, and status.

Thus modernization has reinvigorated ethnic solidarities. But the salience of ethnic conflict can best be assessed in the context of its institutional framework—the modern state.[20] During the past two centuries the territorial state, while facilitating the processes of social and economic modernization, has become the universal unit of macropolitics. The world is divided into territorially bounded states whose claims to sovereignty over all the peoples within their borders are recognized as legitimate by international law and practice. Thus the territorial state has everywhere become the arena in which competing ethnic group claims are asserted, contested, and regulated.

With the universalization of the territorial state has come the dramatic expansion of its activities. The minimum, night-watchman state is a nineteenth-century memory, the lingering fantasy of neoclassical economists. All modern states aspire to penetrate their societies with police and ju-

[19]Milton J. Esman, ed., *Ethnic Conflict in the Western World* (Ithaca: Cornell University Press, 1977); E. A. Teryakian and Ronald Rogowski, eds., *New Nationalism of the Developed West* (Boston: Allen and Unwin, 1985); Joshua Fishman, *The Rise and Fall of the Ethnic Revival: Perspectives on Language and Ethnicity* (Amsterdam: Mouton, 1985).

[20]Brass, "Ethnic Groups and the State"; Donald Rothschild, ed., *The State and Ethnic Claims: African Policy Dilemmas* (Boulder, Colo.: Westview Press, 1983); Milton J. Esman and Itamar Rabinovitch, eds., *Ethnicity, Pluralism, and the State in the Middle East* (Ithaca: Cornell University Press, 1988).

dicial controls, to raise taxes that finance numerous services from education and transportation to public health and agricultural extension, and to regulate many aspects of economic and social behavior. Through regulation, promotion, and distribution the state has become an important, often the most important, allocator of resources to society. These allocations, however intended, produce differential consequences among regions, classes, and ethnic constituencies. The benefits and costs of the state's expanded activities and interventions are seldom shared or perceived to be shared equitably by all elements of society. Disgruntled factions soon learn that unless they mobilize to make credible claims, others will certainly preempt them. This applies to ethnic communities as well.

Rules established and enforced by the state determine the goals that ethnic communities may legitimately pursue and the strategies and tactics they may employ. State policies regulate access to and enjoyment of such material values as education, government and private employment, government contracts, business licenses and institutional credit, land and capital assets. They stipulate the terms of participation in government and politics—voting, representation, and office holding, both civil and military. They govern the use and status of languages in schools and universities, in public administration, and in official communication.

Given the high stakes, any collectivity that purports to defend and promote the interests and life chances of its members must mobilize to impress its preferences and concerns on the agenda of the state. In some cases the policies and programs of the state actually invite ethnic mobilization, converting latent ethnic sentiments into activist organizations, as when educational or employment opportunities are distributed according to ethnic criteria. But even without specific incentives, the competition for "fair shares" in states that contain multiple ethnic communities virtually compels political activation. Passivity earns few rewards, whereas powerful incentives exist for ethnic communities to respond to collective grievances, threats, or opportunities by mobilization. The expanded activities of the modern state have not created ethnic identity and solidarity, but they have provided compelling incentives for their activation. These, in turn, have precipitated the recent volume and intensity of ethnic politics.

The state, then, is a party to most contemporary ethnic conflicts. Where the state enjoys some autonomy from ethnic contestants, as in Canada, its elites can attempt to function as neutral umpire or arbitrator, negotiating rights, statuses, and resources and employing sanctions in

ways that are reasonably acceptable to the contestants and that enable
the polity to survive. Where, on the other hand, the state is controlled
by one of the contending communities, as in Malaysia and Israel, it is
invariably perceived as partisan. Its actions in the incompatible roles of
partisan and umpire tend to exacerbate tensions, forcing the regime to
rely on sanctions as the principal means of conflict management. In either case the state participates in the conflict.

Two factors complicate the structural dimensions of ethnic conflict.
First, are divisions, factions, or cleavages within ethnic communities.
Internal divisions based on class, occupation, ideology, kinship-lineage,
and competition for leadership are common, perhaps inevitable, in all
ethnic communities. Factions compete for control of the community's
resources and for the right to represent the community in its relations
with outsiders. Although all factions are usually committed to bottom-
line goals, competitive politics are a continuing reality within all ethnic
communities. Even under conditions of acute stress they are seldom
monolithic, and this internal pluralism affects their capacity to mount
collective strategies and to pursue common goals.

Although they are likely to be more unified and cohesive than ethnic
communities, states too seldom respond monolithically to ethnic conflict.
They may contain hard-line and soft-line factions, some more inclined
to repression, others to accommodation. Representatives of the state apparatus may share common positions where the integrity of the state is
at issue, but elsewhere their divergent perspectives on ethnic claims may
intersect with internal divisions in ethnic communities, creating complex
coalitions between elements of the state apparatus and factions within
ethnic communities. Thus internal divisions may affect the state's capacities to act, much as they constrain the capacities of the ethnic communities. The implications of internal divisions, especially within ethnic
communities, have not been examined sufficiently or systematically in
the literature on ethnic politics.

A second structural variable is the analytical distinction between stratification and segmentation. Where the relationship between competing parties is primarily stratificational, the dominant ethnic community controls
the bulk of power, wealth, and prestige and allocates them to their collective advantage, relegating others to subordinate positions.[21] The contrast-

---

[21]Some scholars working with models of domination-subordination equate ethnic with
subordinate and treat the study of ethnic conflict, particularly race, as essentially an ex-

ing relationship is segmental, where each of the competing parties contains a full range of class actors—owners, managers, professionals, as well as workers and peasants—maintains parallel sets of institutions, and participates in the operations of the economy and the polity on equitable terms. Because few real life situations are completely stratificational or completely segmental, these relationships are variable. They tend, however, to conform more or less to one pattern or the other: stratificational for South African Blacks, segmental for Malaysian Chinese. The distinction is crucial, for the configurations of conflict depend significantly on the initial distribution of resources, status, and power among the ethnic communities.

Levels and Issues

When ethnicity becomes politicized it affects society at all levels. Its effects on the individual personality, including marginalization of the targets of discrimination and the associated pathology of self-hatred, have been closely analyzed by psychologists and psychoanalysts, as have the needs of insecure and downwardly mobile individuals to dominate, scapegoat, and victimize members of weak and unpopular minorities. The psychodynamics of ethnic, including racial and religious, group contacts remain rich and rewarding subjects of research for scholars concerned primarily with understanding individual behavior and interpersonal relations.[22]

At the community level, the academic domain of anthropology and sociology, a large body of literature has treated interethnic group encounters, group prejudice and discrimination, and processes of accommodation and confrontation, in rural as well as urban societies.[23] Especially prominent during the past two decades have been analyses of ethnic encounters and conflicts in labor markets, the social consequences of labor migrations, and the emergence and fate of "middleman minor-

---

pression of victimology; this topic is addressed briefly by Schermerhorn, *Comparative Ethnic Relations*, 8–9. Ethnicity and class may coincide, but frequently they do not; ethnic communities may contain a range of classes, some of them antagonistic.

[22]Vamik D. Volkan, "Psychoanalytic Aspects of Ethnic Conflicts," in Joseph Montville, ed., *Conflict and Peacemaking in Multiethnic Societies* (Lexington, Mass.: Lexington Books, 1990), 81–90.

[23]Robin Williams, *Strangers Next Door: Ethnic Relations in American Communities* (Englewood Cliffs, N.J.: Prentice Hall, 1964); and Milton Gordon, *Assimilation in American Life* (New York: Oxford University Press, 1964.)

ities." For many years analysis at the community level, where the state is a remote or passive presence, dominated the study of "intergroup relations." Even now, along with attention to the evolution and practices of individual ethnic communities, such analysis continues to generate the bulk of academic writing on the ethnic phenomenon, especially in the United States.

Political scientists and political sociologists focus on government and the state. This institutional level of society is engaged when ethnic relations produce tensions that cannot be managed by the parties themselves or by local authorities, that disrupt the social order, or that threaten the survival of the polity. When ethnic conflicts challenge the social order, the state must intervene with regulation, programs of action, or policies addressed explicitly to the claims of organized ethnic contestants. Alternatively, ethnic issues may be placed on the agenda of the state as a consequence of measures taken by the regime to promote or defend its own priorities. When interethnic relations claim a major share of the attention and energies of senior politicians, they become by definition issues of macropolitical concern. This is the level of analysis on which we concentrate in this book. Ethnic relations at the level of the individual, the neighborhood, and the workplace are important and interesting. To students of government, however, they become consequential when they command the attention and resources of the state.

States, however, cannot be treated as closed systems, even when regimes attempt to control outside influences. In the late twentieth century, rulers can no longer insulate their societies from external forces. Cross-border movements of money, goods, people, weapons, and especially ideas subject ethnic politics everywhere to transnational influences. Domestic ethnic tensions spill over state borders, while external events and pressures impinge on the course of domestic ethnic politics, affecting the behavior and the tactics of ethnic contestants and governments alike. In international politics ethnic pluralism is a source of vulnerability for some states and a potential advantage for others. Ethnic communities normally attempt to recruit diplomatic and material support from sympathizers outside the borders of their state. Governments may exert their influence in ethnic disputes beyond their borders in response to domestic political pressures or strategic interests. International organizations may intervene to protect human rights, relieve suffering, or terminate violent conflict. Transnational factors complicate both the analysis and the management of ethnic struggles, thus requiring a fourth level of analysis, transnational factors and their effects on domestic ethnic conflicts (see Chapter 9).

Just as ethnic solidarity is a free-standing reality—neither a pale platonic shadow of the deeper reality of class, nor a constructed myth concealing the purely individualistic pursuit of material self-interest— equally real are the values over which ethnic communities compete. These values include, above all, relative political power, control over territory, access to and participation in the decision-making institutions of the state, or, alternatively, autonomy within the polity or complete separation. They include terms of access to education and employment, especially higher education, professional careers, and business opportunities. They also include the status of minority cultures, especially the use of minority languages in education and official transactions, and the symbolic issues of recognition and respect for a community and its culture.

The competing goals of mobilized ethnic communities may not be incompatible; many are successfully compromised and adjusted. The conflicts over apportionment of scarce values, however, are unmistakably real—not illusory, as some scholars imply, not misperceptions by the parties of underlying, higher-order, positive sum common interests of which the parties had been unaware but which can emerge through creative mediation.[24] Because the stakes that divide ethnic communities are real, they are likely to generate civic or violent conflict and to be regulated either by repression or by accommodation and compromise. Once regulated, conflicts can resurface as circumstances change and fresh discontents emerge. Civil war in Sudan between the regime in Khartoum controlled by Muslim Arab speakers in the North and Black Christiananamist peoples in the South appeared to be resolved by mediation in 1972, but broke out in brutal violence a decade later. Although some conflicts are definitively settled, the great majority rise, subside, and recur. Some ethnic communities may gradually disappear but most persist, redefining their goals, reacting to fresh events, pursuing their collective and conflictual interests. Of particular interest is the salience of economic factors and of economic policy measures in precipitating, exacerbating, mitigating, and managing ethnic-based conflicts (see Chapter 8).

[24]For examples from the school of conflict resolution concerned with ethnic conflict, see John Burton, *Conflict and Communication: The Use of Controlled Communication in International Relations* (New York: Free Press, 1969); and his *Resolving Deep-Rooted Conflict: A Handbook* (Lanham, Md.: University Press of America, 1987).

Major Concepts and Sources of Data

Two concepts are critical to understanding the dynamics of ethnic politics, the first of which is *ethnic mobilization*. What precipitates organized political action by ethnic communities, why and how are they drawn into political activity, and how do they sustain their efforts? What motivates potential political entrepreneurs, leaders, and activists to invest their energies in the risky venture of mobilizing a constituency whose commitments may be ambiguous and fleeting? How are goals defined, strategies designed and implemented, tactics selected and revised, and commitment maintained in the face of external opposition and internal division? Once drawn into combat, how do the leaders of ethnically defined communities attract and manage the material, human, organizational, and spiritual resources necessary to sustain effective action? How do leaders adapt to unexpected threats and opportunities, how do they maintain control over the forces they have unleashed, and how do they prevent demobilization? Surprisingly, the process of mobilization, a necessary condition for ethnic politics, has not been addressed systematically by students of this subject.[25]

The second crucial concept, *conflict management,* shifts the focus from mobilized communities making demands to those responsible for containing and channeling these demands and maintaining the polity. Under contemporary conditions, those in political control, the governing elites of the modern state, are primarily responsible for managing conflicts, including those based on ethnic grievances, that reach the state's agenda. This is the case even where the capabilities of government are limited and their own policies may have precipitated or aggravated the conflict. What can state elites do to regulate the demands of organized ethnic communities? Why do they choose accommodation in one situation and repression in another? What are the likely consequences of alternative choices? How do sequences of challenges by mobilized ethnic communities and responses by the state mitigate or exacerbate the intensity of conflict?[26]

---

[25] A notable exception is Maurice Pinard. See his "Motivational Dimensions in the Quebec Independence Movement: A Test of a New Model," in Louis Kriesberg, ed., *Research in Social Movements, Conflict, and Change,* vol. 9 (1989), 225–80; and Sarah Belanger and Maurice Pinard, "Ethnic Movements and the Competitive Model: Some Missing Links," *American Sociology Review* 56 (1991): 446–57. Mobilization has been a concern of students of social protest movements, few of whom have focused on ethnic movements. A number of concepts in Chapter 2 are drawn from their work. See reference in note 11, above.

[26] Leading examples of the extended treatment of this subject are Horowitz, *Ethnic*

Chapter 2 specifies and elaborates the main variables within the basic themes of ethnic mobilization and conflict management and provides a conceptual framework for the empirical chapters and the comparative analysis that follow. As sources of data I draw on four separate homelands experiences from different regions of the world, subjects of my study for nearly two decades: Malaysia, Israel-Palestine, South Africa, and Canada. In the next four chapters I review and analyze each of these well-documented cases during the period since World War II. Chapter 7, by contrast, focuses on the politics engendered by recent labor diasporas in North America, Europe, and Japan. I also incorporate data from other countries, including the former Yugoslavia, Sri Lanka, Russia, and Britain, to further illustrate and elaborate points covered in my selection of cases.[27]

Two contextual factors may also significantly affect the generation, evolution, and outcomes of ethnic conflict. Accordingly, Chapter 8 analyzes the values at stake when ethnic groups collide, including the effects of macroeconomic performance, economic expansion, and economic stagnation. To what extent is economic growth a solvent for ethnic conflicts? Chapter 9 reviews and evaluates the effects of external, transnational forces on the intensity and direction of domestic ethnic politics, draws summary insights from the empirical chapters, and proposes general statements, including some with policy implications, about the origins, dynamics, and outcomes of the global phenomenon of ethnic politics. These conclusions may be consequential for action as well as for understanding. They help us address a phenomenon that, with the ending of the Cold War, has become today's most pervasive and dangerous expression of organized conflict.

Groups in Conflict; Lijphart, *Democracy in Plural Societies*; and Montville, *Conflict and Peacemaking*, 449–542.

[27]There is no a priori theoretical reason for the selection of these cases. All, however, are consequential, well documented, geographically dispersed, and accessible for extended visits and personal interviews.

2

A Common Conceptual
Framework

In this inquiry I examine the processes of ethnic mobilization and conflict management in four different homelands settings and in several contemporary labor diasporas. To facilitate comparative analysis and to contribute to the development of theory, a research enterprise such as this must be guided and disciplined by a common conceptual framework. Fortunately we are not venturing into terra incognita. There has emerged an abundant literature, academic and polemical, that describes, analyzes, and evaluates many of the ethnic conflicts that have occurred during this century. The well-documented cases we examine in this book are in that respect representative. In their attempt to understand ethnic politics as a general phenomenon, observers and analysts have formulated concepts and attempted to substantiate and defend general propositions. Some writers have elaborated policy prescriptions intended to mitigate or even resolve ethnic conflicts. This considerable fund of ideas, including debates among scholars, provides the starting point for the concepts that are set forth in this chapter and will be subjected to empirical testing in the chapters that follow.

Definitions

In Chapter 1 I set forth a working definition of the concept of *ethnic community*: a group of people united by inherited culture, racial features, belief systems (religions), or national sentiments. Membership in an ethnic community is normally an ascriptive phenomenon, a relationship into which the individual is born.

Ethnic identity is the set of meanings that individuals impute to their membership in an ethnic community, including those attributes that bind them to that collectivity and that distinguish it from others in their relevant environment. A psychological construct that can evoke powerful emotional responses, ethnic identity normally conveys strong elements of continuity, but its properties can shift to accommodate changing threats and opportunities.

Ethnic solidarity denotes obligations and responsibilities of individuals to their community. Solidarity is established and maintained by socialization processes reenforced by social controls, economic incentives, and external pressures. The constituency bases for the solidarity that is necessary to ethnic political organization are the ethnic communities whose cohesion and sense of continuity reflect their perceptions of common peoplehood, collective interests, and destiny. Solidarity implies commitment to defending these interests and maintaining boundaries—though the definition both of boundaries and of interests may shift over time—in relationship to significant others in their environment. The greater the solidarity, the more likely the emergence of ethnic political movements.

An *ethnic political movement* represents the conversion of an ethnic community into a political competitor that seeks to combat ethnic antagonists or to impress ethnically defined interests on the agenda of the state. An ethnic political movement purports to reflect the collective consciousness and aspirations of the entire community, though in fact the latter may be split into several tendencies or concrete organizations, each competing for the allegiance of the community and for the right to be its exclusive representative. Our unit of analysis is the ethnic political movement. In analyzing such movements, however, we often focus on concrete organizations that are, at least temporarily, the main protagonists and weapons of an activated ethnic community—for example, the United Malays' National Organization (Malaysia) and the African National Congress (South Africa)—but we do not overlook significant factions and competitive organizations within the same ethnic political movement.

An *ethnic nation* is a politicized ethnic community whose spokesmen demand control over what they define as their territorial homeland, either in the form of substantial autonomy or complete independence. Most claimants to the status of nation—Swedes, Japanese, Malays, Québecois, Turks—are ethnic communities as we define that concept. Some nations—the United States, Australia, Brazil, Ivory Coast—are multiethnic; in these cases, nationality and national sentiments reflect common citizenship, commitment to a common way of life, or allegiance to a set of civic values and institutions. And some states are not nations at all, but multinational polities containing two or more nations; for example, the United Kingdom, India, the former Soviet Union, and Nigeria. Nationhood is usually, but not always, the expression of a single ethnic community. Therefore we use the term *ethnic nation* to designate a people which demands or actively exercises the right to self-determination— political control within their homeland.

Nationalism is the ideology that proclaims the distinctiveness of a particular people and their right to self-rule in their homeland. As an expression of ethnic solidarity, nationalism tends to glorify a people's history, accomplishments, and aspirations; to preach the obligation of loyalty to the community, its institutions, and symbols; and to warn against external threats.

Having defined these key concepts, we can now address the two related processes of ethnic mobilization and conflict management that are critical to understanding and explaining ethnic politics.

Ethnic Mobilization

Mobilization is the process by which an ethnic community becomes politicized on behalf of its collective interests and aspirations. This process requires an awareness, usually promoted by ethnic entrepreneurs, that political action is necessary to promote or defend the community's vital collective interests. This awareness results in the recruitment of individuals into the movement or into specific organizations that purport to speak for the movement. Likewise, financial and other material resources required for political action are drawn to the movement. We examine the proportion of the ethnic constituency recruited into the movement, and the roles they assume as leaders, activists, ordinary members, or sympathizers, for the implications of these proportions for the effectiveness of the movement is an important focus of our inquiry. We also examine the commitment of individual members and supporters, the incentives that attract, maintain, and reenforce their identification with and attachment to the movement and its objectives, and their willingness to contribute their resources—loyalty, service, money, and even their lives.

Since mobilization may involve considerable effort and often great risks, we must ask why ethnic communities mobilize. What circumstances, conditions, or events precipitate mobilization? The literature on social movements offers the most useful and rigorous treatment of the processes of collective mobilization.[1] Most of this literature deals with protest movements—of women, environmentalists, students, labor, peasants, homosexuals—whose purpose is not to capture the state but to impress their values on public policy.[2] Though ethnic movements seldom figure in this literature, its perspectives provide a useful point of departure for research on what precipitates the conversion of disadvantaged, discontented, or threatened groups into active communities struggling for their collective interests.[3] Scholars generally agree that the existence of collective grievances is not sufficient, in itself, to precipitate mobilization, for throughout recorded history many aggrieved and disadvantaged communities have borne their lot passively. The main theoretical dispute is between those who emphasize such negative factors as grievances, threats, and relative deprivation and those who focus on the positive incentives and expectations that lead to mobilization.

The concept of relative deprivation refers to the gap between a group's current status and prospects and what appear to be reasonable and legitimate expectations, or to a gap between what comparable groups are believed to enjoy and what is available in material, cultural, and political

---

[1] Examples of this literature include *American Behavioral Sciences*, 1983, special issue on social movements, 26 February; W. A. Gamson, *The Strategy of Social Protest* (Homewood, Ill.: Dorsey Press, 1975); A. Oberschall, *Social Conflict and Social Movements* (Englewood Cliffs, N.J.: Prentice Hall, 1973); Sidney Tarrow, *Struggling to Reform: Social Movements and Policy Changes during Cycles of Protest*, Western Societies Paper no. 15, Cornell University (Ithaca, N.Y., 1983). See also the sources cited in Chapter 1, note 11.

[2] Some ethnic movements limit their goals to influencing state policy on their behalf. Unlike most protest movements, however, many ethnic movements aspire to capture an existing polity or to dominate and operate a new state.

[3] Why have students of social movements neglected ethnic phenomena? My hunch is that most of these writers are located on the left of the political spectrum and find ethnic phenomena illegitimate or uninteresting. Maurice Pinard is one scholar in the social movements tradition who deals explicitly with ethnic movements. See Pinard and Sarah Belanger, "Ethnic Movements and the Competitive Model: Some Missing Links," *American Sociology Review* 56 (1991): 446–57; and Maurice Pinard, "The Quebec Independence Movement: A Dramatic Reemergence," McGill University, Department of Sociology, Working Papers in Social Behavior, Spring 1992. I am indebted to Pinard for a number of concepts and insights that appear in this chapter.

satisfactions to the collectivity and its members. Mobilization may be prompted by a shift in the group's collective expectations or in the "reference group," the significant other, with which they compare their own situation. Mobilization may be the result of events that seriously threaten the community or, alternatively, present opportunities too promising or attractive to resist. Some events may present, simultaneously, potential threats and unexpected opportunities. Periods of political transition such as the dissolution of multinational states or rapid decolonization accelerate ethnic mobilization, because resultant uncertainties about security or the distribution of power often generate perceptions both of threats and of fresh opportunities.

I hypothesize that "defensive" mobilization in response to a clear and present threat to a group's established position will produce more rapid and aggressive collective action than "offensive" mobilization to exploit opportunities for uncertain future benefits. For this reason ethnic entrepreneurs choose to highlight real or imagined threats to the community's status, security, and well-being. Mobilization is a dynamic process that varies in intensity at different times; therefore, the conditions that trigger, invigorate, and maintain mobilizing efforts are a major concern in this book.

Ethnic mobilization on a significant scale is likely to be the consequence of mixed motives and incentives. In real life, behavior can seldom be attributed to a single motive. Specifically, I hypothesize that (1) mobilization for macropolitical objectives is unlikely in the absence either of a strong sense of collective deprivation or of a perceived threat to the community's established position, interests, or values; (2) although necessary, grievances and threats may not be sufficient incentive to mobilize without a reasonable expectation that the effort will yield practical benefits. Positive incentives, the promise of greater power, security, dignity, or material benefits are also needed to motivate participation. These positive incentives may be collective or selective, the latter promising special rewards to the more active participants; (3) some people may be motivated by a sense of solidarity or of individual moral obligation to their ethnic community; they expect little or nothing in personal rewards to repay their efforts or to compensate for their risks. We expect that relative deprivation or threats as well as positive incentives account for mobilization and, further, that different individuals will be motivated by different sets of incentives, not all of them self-serving.

Once ethnic mobilization is under way, however, the ensuing conflicts may develop a momentum that is difficult to control. Where ethnic divisions have been politicized, ethnic partisans may seize upon apparently routine problems as grievances insulting or threatening their community and requiring enhanced mobilization and activism. Overheated rhetoric and slogans implying violence may be employed as a mobilizing technique. Disputed census figures, alleged discrimination by law enforcement authorities, and controversies over land, employment, or commercial transactions can produce ugly rumors that inflame community activists and precipitate uncontrolled interethnic violence. In 1967 some Chinese in the state of Penang protested as discriminatory what the Government of Malaysia considered a routine currency exchange measure, precipitating three days of bloody rioting between gangs of Malays and Chinese. Mobilization seldom occurs spontaneously; once under way, however, it may activate and radicalize impatient, violence-prone, even criminal elements whose actions cannot be controled or disciplined by the leaders of the community or of its factions and for whom violence may become a form of self-justifying behavior, even a way of life. Ethnic mobilization may set in motion collective behavior that cannot be manipulated by the mobilizers, but triggers violence that exacerbates interethnic hostility or antagonisms between an ethnic movement and the state.

What sustains and advances ethnic movements once mobilization is under way? I identify seven critical factors:

POLITICAL OPPORTUNITY STRUCTURE

The political opportunity structure establishes the context in which ethnic movements shape their strategies and tactics, and perhaps their ideologies and goals as well.[4] It furnishes incentives, limitations, permissible boundaries, potentials, and risks that inform the behavior of ethnic entrepreneurs and activists and influence the expectations of their constituents. It enables and facilitates certain actions, constrains and proscribes others. Leaders may choose to comply with the terms of the opportunity structure or to defy them, but as rational actors they must take the political context explicitly into account.

There are two dimensions to opportunity structure: (a) the rules and practices that enable or limit the ability of the ethnic movement and its component organizations to mobilize, to propagandize, and to assert claims for access, participation, redress, or benefits; and (b) the propen-

---

[4]This useful concept has been developed and elaborated by Sidney Tarrow. See his "National Politics and Collective Action: Recent Theory and Research in Western Europe and the United States," *Annual Review of Sociology* 14 (1988): 421–40.

sity of the political establishment to consider such claims as legitimate and subject to possible accommodation. In general, the more open and accommodative the political environment, the more ethnic movements will be inclined to employ legal strategies; the more closed and repressive the opportunity structure, the more they will resort to extralegal and violent methods. As both (a) and (b) are positive in Canada, French-Canadian nationalists have relied almost entirely on methods sanctioned by Canada's constitution. As (a) and (b) in apartheid South Africa were entirely negative, the African National Congress had no option but to adopt, albeit with considerable reluctance, revolutionary strategies and violent tactics. In Northern Ireland, (a) prevailed—mobilization, propaganda, and electoral participation were available to the Catholic minority, but (b) was entirely closed—Catholic grievances and demands were systematically disregarded. In that more complex situation the movement was cross-pressured, some factions choosing violence as the only way out of the impasse, other factions persevering with legal activities combined with nonviolent protest, despite their apparent futility, in preference to further repression and bloodshed.

The choices of strategies and tactics for an ethnic movement are affected by the nature of the political environment it encounters and the opportunities available to promote its claims. Whereas the foregoing examples refer to ethnic movements asserting demands for redress of grievances or improvement in their status, opportunity structures also affect the strategies of ethnic organizations committed to resisting or reversing changes and defending the status quo. The incentives and constraints provided by the opportunity structure may even determine which collective identity, ethnic or other, best serves the needs of individuals. Political opportunity structure, then, is a crucial explanatory variable in this study; what is required are more subtle and nuanced descriptions and analyses of how variations in the political environment influence the behavior of ethnic movements.

LEADERSHIP

Every social movement offers four roles: leaders, activists, members, and sympathizers. Those participants with the greatest investment in the movement are likely to occupy leadership positions or to compete for these roles.[5] At early stages of mobilization these are likely to be ethnic

---

[5] For a systematic treatment of the leadership factor, see Anthony D. Smith, *The Ethnic Revival in the Modern World* (Cambridge: Cambridge University Press, 1981).

entrepreneurs—Arafat, Herzl, Mandela—whose vision, energy, and persuasiveness inspire and shape the original direction of the movement. Leaders symbolize the movement and bear major responsibility for guiding it, for articulating its values, for defining collective interests, for setting strategies, for managing relations with outsiders, and for resolving internal conflicts within the membership and among factions within the movement. I am interested here in identifying the societal and educational strata of the ethnic community from which leaders emerge and the incentives that motivate them to accept these roles. Does leadership in ethnic communities normally arise, as some authors argue, from the ranks of intellectuals, including journalists, teachers, lawyers, clergymen, whose education, propensity for critical thought, detachment from conventional economic responsibilities, dissatisfaction with their marginal status in society, and verbal skills predispose them to assume the risks and burdens of leadership? Or do leaders emerge also from other strata of their community? What determines the sectors of the community from which leaders are likely to originate?

Of great importance is the relative cohesiveness and competition within the ranks of leaders and aspirants to leadership roles. Leaders of ethnic movements must divide their attention between enemies and prospective allies on the outside and opponents within their own ranks. I hypothesize that some competition for leadership in fact strengthens ethnic movements, raising new issues and attracting hitherto unmobilized elements from their constituency. There is, however, a threshold beyond which competition can become destructive, consuming energy and resources in internecine disputes and impairing the capacity of the movement to cope with external threats or capitalize on opportunities. Leadership succession is another significant factor that affects the viability of ethnic movements. Must, for example, the original entrepreneurial and charismatic leaders eventually yield to managerial successors? State elites may also function as ethnic entrepreneurs, activating followers by inventing or exploiting threats from ethnic enemies in order to buttress support for themselves and their regime.

Activists invest all or a significant share of their energies in the movement, performing the numerous essential tasks of recruitment, organizational maintenance, propaganda, fund-raising, demonstrations and other public events, and even physical combat. Because their activity keeps the movement functioning, and because of their links to the community, activist cadres are an important resource and support base for the leadership; their interests and preferences must therefore be taken

into account in formulating policy. We examine what sustains and rewards the commitment of ethnic activists, how their needs and preferences influence the directions of the movement and of concrete
organizations, and how the activists relate to rank and file members. An
important audience for leaders and aspirants to leadership, activists are
nevertheless followers, they do not function as decision makers.

Rank-and-file members contribute funds and services, turn out for
public demonstrations, work in election campaigns, provide moral support, shield activists from hostile authorities, and may even do their
share of fighting. Sympathizers are members of the ethnic community
who have not joined the movement or any of its organizations but are
known to share its aspirations and may be available for future recruitment, financial contributions, or other services.

IDEOLOGY

Ethnic mobilization is facilitated by and indeed usually requires an ideology,[6] a coherent set of articulated beliefs which (1) define the collective
identity and the criteria for membership, emphasize their common endowments, entitlements, grievances, and aspirations, and identify the
outsiders who challenge or thwart their legitimate aspirations; (2) explain and justify the need for the movement, the struggles it undertakes,
and the costs of participation; and (3) visualize the ultimate successes,
the goals that make the mobilization and the struggle worthwhile. Ideology helps to shape and define the content and the contours of ethnic
identity, to endow the collectivity with moral sanction for their struggle,
and to arm the movement with meaning and purpose that transcend the
routines of everyday existence. The intellectuals who construct a movement's ideology may choose selectively from an often fictional history
to celebrate ancient heroes that should be emulated, to identify historical
enemies that may reappear in different guises, and to reveal golden ages
in the past that the present generation should endeavor to recreate and
redeem for future generations. As the framework of meaning and the
worldview that justifies particular goals and strategies, ideology is especially important for homeland peoples, vindicating their right to self-
determination on ancestral soil.

6On the implications of ideology for social action, see Howard Williams, *Concepts of
Ideology* (New York: St. Martin's Press, 1988); Jorge Lorain, *The Concept of Ideology*
(Athens: University of Georgia Press, 1979); and Karl Mannheim's classic, *Ideology and
Utopia* (New York: Harcourt Brace and World, 1936).

Malay intellectuals have created the powerful myth that Malay Muslims as the indigenous people/native sons/bumiputera are ipso facto entitled to a special position in the governance and the culture of their country for which immigrant peoples (Chinese) cannot qualify. The Chinese counter with the emotionally less powerful ideology of a Malaysian Malaysia, claiming equal status because of common citizenship, local birth, and economic performance. As we see in Chapter 3, both ideologies facilitate mobilization within their communities but fall on deaf ears among their adversaries. In contrast, the French-Canadian ideology that Québécois constitute a "distinct society", that Quebec is not a mere province like the others, that its government has a special obligation to preserve and promote its cultural distinctiveness, appears to have been accepted by Canada's English-speaking political class, though less so by its rank and file.

Ideologies of ethnic movements normally emphasize the common interests of all members of the community and thus the need for unity. Differences in wealth, region, kinship, or occupation pale in the face of the common threats and common destiny that all members of the community necessarily share. Misguided or self-serving individuals or factions that tolerate or cooperate with the oppressors and thus undermine unity must be convinced of the error of their ways or neutralized. Historically, nationalism has been the enemy of Marxism because it rejects class conflict even as it glorifies national unity and solidarity. An ethnic ideology may define its community as a subordinated and oppressed people, but the oppressor is the state controlled by an ethnic enemy, not a class fragment of their own people. All members of the community are victims because of their ascribed ethnic status, and all therefore are obligated to mobilize, resist, and overcome the injustices that afflict them all. Thus ethnic and ethnonational ideologies begin by positing unity as an obligation of every individual and as a necessity dictated by common fate.

Whatever its specific content, ideology has a dual purpose: to reassure, inspire, and sustain the participation of activists, members, and sympathizers within the ethnic community; and to project and legitimate to outsiders, including the authorities, a desired image of the movement and its demands. In the current era of instantaneous global communication and mass media, foreign audiences may become an important target of ideological messages from competing ethnic communities. Themes and content may be modified for different audiences, inside and outside the community, and in response to changing circumstances. Similarly, factions within the movement may emphasize different themes, intensifying internal tensions and competition for the allegiance of the constituency.

ORGANIZATION

Efficient organization is essential to any social movement that engages in sustained political combat, civil or violent.[7] Formal organizations alone allow for the aggregation of material and human resources, prepare for their purposeful deployment, provide for the division of labor, maintain infrastructures for communication, and facilitate the socialization of individuals into the movement. They are the indispensible weapon for political struggle. Therefore, ethnic leaders necessarily invest substantial energies in building, strengthening, and maintaining organizations.

Most ethnic movements are composed of a plurality of organizations with distinctive leadership orientations, ideologies, and fund-raising sources, as well as links with different sectors and strata within and even beyond the ethnic community. Whereas, for example, the Palestine Liberation Organization (PLO) serves as the symbolic expression of the Palestinian national movement, it is actually a loose federation of competitive organizations, each claiming to represent the authentic version of Palestinian nationalism and the correct path to its fulfillment. We examine the implications of organizational pluralism for the effectiveness of ethnic movements. Our hypothesis, once again, is that organizational pluralism facilitates mobilization by multiplying links into the community and enhancing opportunities for leadership and participation, while simultaneously inhibiting solidarity and complicating the tasks of combat with ethnic antagonists and state authorities.

Social movements are strengthened by and may depend upon preexistent organizational and communications networks. These networks constitute resources that enable collective action, in the absence of which all the organizational elements essential to collective action would have to be constructed anew. Thus the U.S. civil rights movement in the 1960s drew much of its leadership, activist cadres, mass support, funds, and

---

[7]The vast literature on formal organizations is summarized by Bertram Gross in *The Managing of Organizations*, 2 vols. (Glencoe, Ill.: Free Press, 1964). On organizations for social action, see the classic by Philip Selznick, *The Organizational Weapon* (New York: Arno Press, 1977).

meeting places from established networks of Black churches, just as Irish nationalism in previous generations had capitalized on the infrastructure of Catholic parishes. Similar religious, cultural, and economic networks can be found in most ethnic communities; like labor unions in Quebec and South Africa, they can be coopted into the political struggle. How networks promote or inhibit ethnic political movements remains to be examined. Although they may permit recruitment en bloc, they may also attempt to impress their own goals on the movement, exacting a price for their participation, alienating other potential supporters, and limiting freedom of action for the leaders of the organizations with which they affiliate.

GOALS

What accounts for the collective goals that ethnic movements espouse, the end-state, the intended outcomes that justify the costs and the risks of mobilization? Assume that these ultimate goals are variations of *hegemony*, maintaining or taking control of the state; *autonomy*, secession from the state leading to revisions of interstate borders or territorial or institutional self-management within the framework of the state; or *equitable inclusion* within the polity, society, and economy on nondiscriminatory or more favorable terms. How clear are these goals and how united are the various components of the movement in their pursuit? How might the goals of homelands movements differ from those of immigrant diasporas? How do conflicts over goals reflect organizational cleavages within the movement? For example, though the ultimate goal of the Palestinian national movement is Palestinian statehood, its component organizations, like those of its Zionist enemy, are divided along many dimensions, including those who favor a secular and those who insist on a religious polity.

Are there meaningful distinctions between ultimate and proximate goals? Do energies consumed in pursuit of the latter have the effect of displacing or indefinitely postponing the former? Though the ultimate goals of ethnic movements generally remain constant, they can be modified by external events, by generational succession, or by internal organizational learning. How do circumstances outside the movement, for example, the unexpected dissolution of the Soviet state, precipitate changes in the goals of recently repressed national movements? Generally, what factors explain changes in goals and what effects will such changes have on the intensity of ethnic mobilization?

RESOURCES

The strategies adopted by ethnic political movements must bear some relationship to the resources available for mobilization within the community and from external sources. Potential resources include population numbers as a proportion of the total within the boundaries of the territorial state, the relative geographic concentration or dispersion of the community, and the wealth that can be mobilized for the collective struggle, as well as the movement's organizational and communications skills. Other resources include status and access to political elites, relative cohesion or fragmentation by economic interests, ideology, or kinship structures, and ability to tap moral, diplomatic, and material support, including weapons, from fellow ethnics or sympathizers beyond their borders. Each of these demographic, material, and political resources facilitates or constrains ethnic movements, endowing them with potential strengths and imposing realistic limitations on their aspirations and strategies. We examine how an ethnic movement's initial fund of resources may affect its goals as well as its strategies, how mobilization may accumulate resources that enable more ambitious strategies, and how performance, in turn, influences the future availability of resources.

Many ethnic movements, for instance, the Québécois, rely primarily on the domestic resources they can mobilize for their struggle. Some movements have access to and rely heavily on outside support, but such resources may have strings attached, constraining as well as abetting their strategies. Thus various organizations that comprise the Palestinian national movement are supported by more or less sympathetic Arab governments; the autonomy and consequently the choices of strategy for these Palestinian organizations are limited, therefore, by the expectations and requirements of their external patrons.

STRATEGIES AND TACTICS

The strategies and tactics of ethnic movements and of their component units reflect the uses they make of the resources they command. They may be directed as much to maintaining internal mobilization as to coping with threats from outsiders or capitalizing on opportunities to advance their program. Collective action may encompass such civil methods as working within the rules of the polity through propaganda, interest group pressures, elections, legislative processes, judicial litigation; it may also involve the deliberate flouting of these rules, from civil disobedience and nonviolent disruptions to terrorism and insurrectionary violence. Ethnic movements may assert maximal claims in a strident or threatening style, or they may moderate demands by conciliatory methods. They may, at different times, bargain, compromise, petition, demonstrate, or resort to confrontational or violent methods. They may enter into open or tacit coalitional arrangements with other actors in the polity, including factions within the authority structure. Specific actions may arise from compromises over differences within ethnic organizations. They normally reflect deliberate calculations among leaders, but these plans can be undermined when the leadership is unable to exercise control over dissident factions or undisciplined elements, as when the Zionist leadership was incapable of preventing terrorist acts by factions under future prime ministers Begin and Shamir.

We shall be asking what explains the different strategies adopted by ethnic movements and their changes over time. To what extent are they the consequences of ideological commitments or of pragmatic assessments? I also identify the responses of movement leaders to critical events and unanticipated opportunities to enhance their position even when these opportunities require changes in established strategies, such as Chairman Arafat's opportunity during the late 1980s to gain U.S. recognition in return for his own recognition of Israel as a legitimate state. This maneuver demanded fundamental and wrenching change in his movement's ideology and goals, the prospect of which precipitated intense internal dissension that compromised the credibility of his response to the U.S. initiative. How then do ethnic movements accommodate their strategies and tactics to changing circumstances and cope with the internal rigidities and vested interests that inhibit their ability to adjust?

The framework of analysis laid out here constitutes a political perspective on ethnic movements. For analytical purposes, I have divided the process of mobilization into seven variables: opportunity structure, leadership, ideology, organization, resources, goals, and strategies/tactics. Ethnic movements mobilize to attack the prevailing distribution of power, wealth, and status and the rules of access to these values; or they countermobilize to defend themselves against threats launched by ethnic movements to their acquired positions. The leaders of ethnic movements must cope simultaneously with internal competitors—endemic to all ethnic movements—and with external adversaries. Adversaries may be hostile ethnic communities or the regime in control of the state. Unless the goal is secession, control of the state apparatus or at least significant influence, access, and participation in government signals the likely success of ethnic movements. Therefore ethnic movements are necessarily concerned with their impact on the state and with how the authorities respond to their challenges.

Conflict Management

Our second principal concern is how state authorities respond to the challenges launched by mobilized ethnic communities and how they attempt to regulate or manage ethnic conflicts.[8] In most cases the challenge to the status quo in ethnic group relations originates in an ethnic movement's demands for official recognition of their claims or specific measures to redress their grievances. The burden of conflict management normally falls on the elites who operate the state apparatus, since the policies and practices of government are the principal targets of mobilized ethnic movements. Willful or incompetent actions by government may actually generate ethnic conflict, provoke protests or challenges from aggrieved ethnic communities, and place the state in the incompatible roles of both precipitating and managing ethnic conflicts.

The normal inclination of political authorities is to defend existing structures of ethnic relations at minimum cost to the regime and to the dominant ethnic community, yielding only marginal concessions that do not fundamentally modify the status quo. There may be two exceptions to this general expectation (1) When the government does not represent and is not controlled by a dominant ethnic community. The government of Canada enjoys some autonomy from competing ethnic communities and can afford to consider and even promote policy changes that offer prospects for solving immediate disputes and for mitigating intergroup tensions. (2) When the challenger to the status quo is the government itself. That government may represent an ethnic community that has recently gained control of the state apparatus and set out to implement an agenda that calls for consolidating the hegemony of the community it represents. The behavior of the Afrikaner regime that took control of South Africa in 1948, with the objective of implementing apartheid, exemplifies this situation. Here the government is both challenger to the status quo and the instrument for conflict management. In order to con-

[8] Good summaries of recent concepts of conflict management applied to ethnic disputes appear in Donald L. Horowitz, *Ethnic Groups in Conflict* (Berkeley, University of California Press, 1985), 563–684; and Joseph Montville, ed., *Conflict and Peacemaking in Multiethnic Societies* (Lexington, Mass.: Lexington Books, 1990), 1–130 and 447–544.

solidate domestic support and enhance their precarious legitimacy, state elites may decide to play the ethnic card, usually at the expense of a vulnerable minority. Examples are Idi Amin's summary expulsion of Uganda's Asians and Slobodan Milosovič's revoking the long-standing autonomy of Serbia's Albanian minority. Such self-serving, cynical resort to ethnic politics by state elites is often coercive, inflicting gratuitous damage and pain on ethnic minorities.

There are three categories of long-term goals that governments pursue in the management of ethnic conflicts: 1) to depluralize their society so that it becomes increasingly homogeneous; 2) to legitimate, maintain, and even foster existing patterns of pluralism; and 3) to reduce the political salience of ethnic solidarity while accepting social pluralism as a continuing reality.

The goal of depluralization can be implemented by such draconian measures as genocide, physically eliminating ethnic minorities, or expelling them from the country (ethnic cleansing), or combinations of these two methods. Organized exchanges of populations across international borders constitute a somewhat more humane version of expulsion. State elites seldom agree to reduce ethnic pluralism by yielding territory populated by ethnic minorities; the sacred quality ascribed to ancestral territory renders it inalienable. Revisions in international borders are usually the consequence of military defeat or the collapse of multiethnic polities, rarely of peaceful or consensual adjustments to reduce ethnic pluralism. Conversely, the world offers plentiful instances of the time-tested employment of harsh processes aimed at depluralization. The Arab-Muslim regime in Sudan has been employing a combination of massacres, starvation, and expulsions to clear the southern third of their territory of troublesome and rebellious non-Muslims or to impose on them an Islamic regime. By turning their weapons on civilians and by forced evacuation of tens of thousands of Croats and Muslims from regions of Croatia and Bosnia, the Serbs have been clearing non-Serbs from territories they claim to be inhabited mainly by Serbs with the intention of uniting these areas into a "Greater Serbia"; at the same time they adamantly resist any suggestion that Kosovo, an area they claim to be historically Serbian but which contains a 90 percent Albanian majority, should be granted autonomy, not to mention the right to secede from Serbia.

The more civilized method of promoting depluralization is to foster and reward the gradual assimilation of individuals from minority ethnic communities, immigrants as well as homeland people, into the dominant society. The techniques employed to promote assimilation include incentives, sanctions, or both, such as induced acculturation through education, government services, mass media, and economic opportunities in the language and lifestyles of the dominant community; cooptation of ambitious and upwardly mobile members of minority communities; encouragement of intermarriage; and nondiscriminatory access to educational and economic opportunities.

The message conveyed by such measures is that those who wish to succeed must first acculturate, then assimilate by affiliating with the national mainstream. Policies of assimilation may be implemented by less benign means, such as requiring minority individuals to change their names; proscribing education, mass media, even religious services in the minority language; refusing to provide public services, including judicial processes, in any but the official language; and harassing voluntary associations serving ethnic minorities. The expectation is that such measures will convince ethnic minorities of the futility of maintaining separate collective identity and solidarity, and thus facilitate assimilation. The risk, of course, is that such coercive measures will backfire, generating resentment and inducing minorities openly or by stealth to resist the loss of their distinctive collective identity, institutions, and culture.

The main alternative to the goal of depluralization is official acceptance of ethnic pluralism as a legitimate and continuing reality. Again, there are both consensual and coercive expressions of this strategy. Its harsher form is institutionalized discrimination, in which members of an ethnic community experience systematic deprivation and subordination in the political, cultural, and, usually, economic realms. The state elites do not expect that societal pluralism can or should be eliminated; they do, however, insist that the superordinate position of the dominant ethnic community be preserved. Examples of ethnic communities subordinated by these common practices include Kurds in Iraq, Blacks in South Africa, Catholics in Northern Ireland, Tamils in Sri Lanka, Gypsies in Romania, and Arabs in Israel. In the latter case Arabs enjoy formal status as citizens of the Jewish state, and their religious and cultural autonomy are guaranteed, but they are effectively excluded from participation in political decision making, they are suspected by many Jewish fellow citizens of disloyalty to the state, and they encounter discrimination in employment, economic opportunities, and public services.

The more benign strategies of institutionalized pluralism concede formal equality to recognized ethnic communities. The most common structural expressions of this approach are federalism and consociationalism, which may occur separately or in combination. Federal and federallike arrangements confer territorial autonomy and a degree of self-rule on ethnic communities, prominent examples being the major ethnic communities—Bengali, Tamil, Marathi—in India, French-speaking Québécois in Canada, and German speakers in Italy's South Tyrol. For statecraft, the principal risk associated with federalism is that territorial devolution may be the prelude to demands for complete separation. Territorial autonomy is often combined with assurances of equitable participation in the activities of the central government and fair shares of the benefits available through the state. The latter is a dimension of consociationalism which confers on all recognized ethnic communities the right to participate in decision making, to protect their distinctive interests, to manage their own institutions, and to share in government employment and economic benefits in rough proportion to their numbers. There are many versions of consociational power sharing, all of which reject majoritarian politics in favor of respecting and protecting the rights, security, and status of minorities.[9]

Standard consociational practices are vulnerable to charges that they are elitist and undemocratic, since decision making is largely a matter of negotiation and compromise among established leaders of the various communities. They are also vulnerable to collapse, as necessary compromises worked out by moderate leaders may be denounced as betrayals of the true interests of their communities by more militant or extremist politicians attempting to "outbid" the moderates for support of their ethnic constituencies. The defining features of federal and consociational processes in their many concrete forms is their recognition of the permanence and the legitimacy of politicized societal pluralism. They attempt to shape a political culture of mutual respect for the concerns and aspirations of each community. They search for consensual means to compromise disputes that inevitably arise to insure the security and accommodate the needs of all recognized ethnic communities within the framework of a single state.

A less common approach to conflict management is the effort by state elites to reduce and eventually eliminate the political salience of ethnic pluralism that is nevertheless expected to continue as a social fact. The military rulers of Nigeria, in shaping the constitution of its second re-

[9]The standard work on consociational politics is by Arend Lijphart, *Democracy in Plural Societies* (New Haven: Yale University Press, 1977); for a critique of the consociational paradigm, see Alvin Rabushka and Kenneth A. Shepsle, *Politics in Plural Societies* (Columbus, Ohio: Merrill, 1972).

public, proscribed any political party or organization that employed ethnic names, symbols, or slogans. Political parties were required to have branches in at least two thirds of the states, a winning presidential candidate was repaired gain at least 25 percent of the vote in at least two thirds of the states, and each state was guaranteed at least one representative in the federal cabinet. The original three large regions of that country, each dominated by a single ethnic community, have been broken up into twelve, then nineteen, and finally thirty states to diffuse the hostile ethnic blocks. A related measure aimed at depoliticizing ethnic solidarity is to foster crosscutting affiliations, associations based on collective identities and common interests and loyalties—ideological, economic, occupational, generational, gender, recreational—that can neutralize and override appeals to ethnic solidarity. This approach is encouraged by many governments in the hope that political choices and political behavior will be governed increasingly by cross-ethnic economic and other common interests at the expense of ethnic solidarity.

The more authoritarian the state, the more closed its political opportunity structure, the more inclined it is to employ repressive measures to control ethnic minorities. It may exclude them from citizenship, political participation, and office holding, civil and especially military; it may limit their access to education or the right to use their language in schools or in government. It may deny them the right to own land or engage in the more productive and respectable economic activities. It may subject them to discriminatory exactions such as special taxes. It may even resort to physical intimidation including pogroms where mobs are unleashed by the authorities to intimidate, murder, and plunder unarmed members of ethnic minorities. Some regimes are content to employ a limited range of repressive methods sufficient to insure the subordinate status of an ethnic minority. Others, like the apartheid regime in South Africa, choose to institutionalize a comprehensive repertory of repressive tactics.

Critics of democracy assert that open competitive politics favors the politicization of ethnic communities and the consequent danger of interethnic extremism and violent destabilization of the political order. They maintain that authoritarian methods and a strong state are needed to restrain ethnic politics in divided and conflict-prone societies. This notion is a frequent justification for military rule and for one-party regimes in ethnically plural societies, including Tito's rule in Yugoslavia, the KANU dictatorship in Kenya, and the Suharto–New Order government in Indonesia.

For democratic regimes the preferred methods are accommodative attempts to appease ethnic grievances or to yield to demands by symbolic or real concessions, thereby avoiding violence. When real concessions are deemed necesary in the political, economic, or cultural realms, the state must exercise caution to forestall the emergence of backlash among elements in society which might oppose the concessions or feel threatened by them. Accommodation is often more a matter of style than of substance, the willingness of government to accord respect and recognition to ethnic minorities, to entertain their complaints and claims, and to attempt to broker consensual compromises. A regime may be prepared to consider and accommodate certain demands while proscribing others. The Malaysian government entertains complaints from Chinese sources about discrimination in higher education, but it bans as seditious any challenge to the constitutionally defined special position of Malays, though this embodies precisely the main grievances of the non-Malay half of the population. Some ethnic communities may be officially recognized as political actors, others denied. Thus the Malaysian regime recognizes Indians as a political constituency, but not Ceylonese or Eurasians.

Election results also matter. Had the Labor Party won the 1992 general election in Britain, the government would probably have attempted to accommodate Scottish demands for autonomy (devolution); the victory of the unionist Conservatives effectively foreclosed that prospect. The 1992 electoral victory of Labor in Israel opened more opportunities for the accommodation of Palestinian demands than had been available from the previous Likud administration.

Challenge and Response: Processes and Outcomes

A government's goals and how it implements them are affected by factors akin to those that facilitate or constrain the very ethnic movements that challenge them. These factors may include the political opportunity structure, that is, the constitutionally sanctioned rules of access to political and economic resources that governments must live with, though to be sure governments may attempt formally or by interpretation to alter them to their advantage. These goals are often determined or influenced by individual or factional judgments, producing cleavages within the dominant ethnic community and in the government that speaks for them. Internal cohesion is a variable for political regimes. Divisions may allow ethnic movements to penetrate and influence government policies in their favor and even promote expedient de facto coalitions between factions in government and factions within the ethnic movement. These patterns of dynamic interaction affect the methods and sometimes even the goals of mobilization and conflict management.

Interactions between ethnic movements and governments are a challenge-response process. Normally the challenge to the status quo originates in ethnic movements, while government must attempt to manage the conflicts precipitated by these demands in ways that maintain the existing order at minimal cost. At times, however, measures taken or proposed by government actually precipitate the challenge. Each round of challenges and responses sets the stage for subsequent rounds in a sequence that may eventually modify the strategies or goals of both parties. Such conflicts are seldom resolved or finally settled. Therefore I find the abundant literature on "conflict resolution" of little value in analyzing or understanding ethnic conflict at the macropolitical level. Since the parties are likely to survive as long-term actors within the same political system, we can expect continuing challenges from mobilized but discontented or threatened ethnic communities and the continuing need for authorities to respond to the ensuing conflicts. We would expect each party to the continuing conflict to experience organizational learning, to benefit from dynamic feedback from previous encounters, including fresh appreciation of their own capabilities, resources, strategies and those of their opponents, and to modify accordingly their own tactics and even their goals.

The paradigm of ethnic politics outlined here emphasizes processes over outcomes, because few such conflicts yield final outcomes. A few of the depluralizing goals of mobilization and conflict management, such as genocide, expulsion, and secession, may succeed in "settling" conflicts; assimilation may have that effect but only in the long run. Changes in international borders resulting from successful insurrections or the collapse of multinational states may resolve some conflicts, but most successor states will themselves contain ethnic minorities, thus renewing the cycle. In most cases, the results of individual episodes merely set the stage for subsequent episodes. The intensity of mobilization and of conflict may rise and fall, recede or revive, but seldom disappears. The parties remain to engage one another in subsequent rounds. Because ethnic conflicts are so seldom definitively settled, we focus not on predicting, explaining, or advocating final outcomes, but on examining how the results of particular encounters affect the resource position and the strategies of ethnic movements in challenging the status quo, and the goals and methods employed by the state in its efforts at conflict management.

Normative Dimensions of Ethnic Politics

The master hypothesis that informs this study is that ethnic collective identity and politicized solidarity are free-standing societal phenomena. They are not myths, fantasies, or surrogates for deeper realities such as class, nor are they perverse expressions of personal ambition, elite manipulation, or psychological malaise. The boundaries they draw, the loyalties they embody, and the meanings they reflect influence the daily routines of community life in quiet times and may move group members to heroic deeds in times of stress. Ethnic sentiments cannot be isolated from economic, political, and cultural incentives or constraints, for the specific issues at stake are often influenced by such factors. Ethnic solidarities, including national, religious, and racial sentiments, can be manipulated and exploited by self-serving politicians, often with tragic human consequences; they can also enhance the lives of their members and be moderated and regulated by competent and responsible statesmanship. Instead of attempting futilely to define ethnic solidarity out of existence as myth, false consciousness, or "constructed" fabrications, social scientists ought to recognize it as a powerful, pervasive, and enduring reality whose dynamics require careful investigation in order to be better understood.

Many observers deplore ethnic solidarity and ethnic politics as inherently atavistic ("tribalistic"), reactionary, and subversive of individual dignity and reponsibility. They equate politicized ethnicity with fanaticism, irrationality, and needless human suffering.[10] The doctrine of national self-determination is condemned as mischievous and absurd, encouraging and legitimating the demands of small, nonviable minorities for sovereignty, threatening to destabilize international borders and provoke armed conflict. Such parochial allegiances are believed to have no place in a world in the process of global economic integration. Such observers have no patience with ethnic solidarity; they want it to go

---

[10]A random selection of titles expressing these views yields Orville Patterson, *Ethnic Chauvinism: The Reactionary Impulse* (Cambridge: Harvard University Press, 1977); Stephen Steinberg, *The Ethnic Myth* (New York: Atheneum, 1981); Benedict Anderson, *Imagined Communities: Reflections on the Origins and Spread of Nationalism*, rev. ed. (London: Verso Press, 1991).

away and soon, to be supplanted by proletarian solidarity or, more likely, by the vindication of individual human rights in a democratic framework. Such negative normative judgments overlook palpable realities that confront contemporary statecraft, including basic human needs for security, community, meaning, and welfare to which ethnic solidarities respond and the enhanced dignity and improved quality of life that ethnic movements may yield. How could they retain the loyalty and participation of their members if their appeal was based primarily on irrational fears and hatred?

Attacks on the moral legitimacy of collective ethnic identity and solidarity may preface intellectual currents and patterns of societal organization that will eventually deemphasize or supplant them. For the foreseeable future, however, they constitute societal realities that are better confronted than exorcised. This study recognizes but does not concentrate on normative issues. Far more interesting and useful than judgments about the moral legitimacy of ethnic solidarity are efforts to understand the dynamics of ethnic politics as realities underlying widespread societal conflict in the modern world and to explore various means by which such potentially destructive conflicts can be mitigated and regulated. I neither deplore nor celebrate the phenomenon of ethnic solidarity. In the spirit of scientific inquiry, I accept it as a pervasive, persistent, and consequential reality. To be sure, moral judgments between the claims and the behavior of parties to specific ethnic conflicts—Serbs/Croats, Sinhalese/Tamils, Afrikaners/Blacks—are certainly indicated, but they should be neither overhasty nor simplistic. As the cases in this volume demonstrate, the moral equities between parties to ethnic conflicts are often hard to untangle or reduce to categorical judgments: is the moral high ground held by Malays or Chinese? Rather than denigrating or proscribing ethnic solidarities as illegitimate, I find it more productive to explore and analyze ongoing processes of mobilization and conflict management, especially those that promise to mitigate tensions, reduce their intensity, and foster patterns of consensual coexistence.

Malaysia:
Native Sons and Immigrants

Before consolidation of British rule in the mid-nineteenth century, peninsular Malaya was an underpopulated riverine civilization in which insecure royal families and disputations chieftains contended for control over a society devoted primarily to subsistence farming and fishing. Despite intraethnic differences based primarily on the provenance of ruling houses, many from Indonesia, Malayan society was culturally united by language, customs, and especially allegiance to a single faith, Sunni Islam. Small numbers of Muslims from the Middle East and from India and immigrants from Indonesia readily assimilated into Malay society.

What created today's pluralism was the imposition of internal peace and order. The British imperial presence opened opportunities for economic development and demands for labor to which the indigenous Malay peoples did not respond. For three-quarters of a century, until the great depression of the 1930s, hundreds of thousands of hard-working pioneers from the impoverished provinces of South China migrated, entirely on their own, to seek their economic fortunes in this turbulent and underdeveloped frontier territory. Their labor and enterprise developed the lucrative tin industry in the Kinta and Klang valleys and much of the commercial agriculture, including pineapples in Johore and vegetables in the Cameron Highlands. From these beginnings they spread into retail and wholesale trade, small industry, construction, and finance—into the numerous profitable niches between large-scale European enterprises and Malay peasant society. They became a typical immigrant middleman diaspora. When the construction and maintenance of roads and railways, and later the tapping of trees on the vast and lucrative European-owned rubber plantations, failed to attract either Malay or Chinese workers, the British imported contract labor in large numbers from south India. By the 1930s immigrants outnumbered native Malays by nearly three to two, especially in the economically more productive and prosperous states on the west coast of the peninsula.

The British chose to govern Malaya by indirect rule. The status and security of the traditional Malay rulers were confirmed and reenforced by British protection and subsidies, eliminating the omnipresent threat from fractious, insubordinate chieftains. Although the rulers, in return, were required to accept the "advice" of British residents, principally on questions of security and economic development, the sultans and rajas retained firm control of all matters involving the Muslim religion and Malay customs—in effect, most of what touched the daily lives of their Malay subjects. The British evolved the doctrine of trusteeship: They would protect the "special position" of the indigenous Malay people; they would as far as possible respect their rights and customs, not interfering with their traditional social structures and way of life. Modern education, for example, would not be thrust on Malays, except for a small group from royal households who would attend the local equivalent of a British public school, where they would be trained in the English language for positions as junior government administrators. Malays would be protected from the competitive pressures of modern economic development for which they were considered culturally and even biologically unsuited; these roles would be left to the eager immigrants.

Thus, in the decades before World War II, there developed in Malaya a pronounced ethnic division of labor. Government was entirely in British hands, with Malays occupying junior administrative roles. Plantations and large-scale industrial, commercial, and financial houses were European owned and managed, but Chinese and Indians held skilled labor, middle management, and clerical positions. Education in the English language, the passport to subordinate employment in government and in European enterprises, was available mainly in the cities, where few Malays lived, and often under Christian sponsorship, which Malays shunned. Small industry, wholesale and retail trade and money lending, the processing of agricultural crops, and technical and skilled labor of all kinds were predominantly Chinese. Though Malay intellectuals had begun to express some misgivings, most Malays appeared to acquiesce in this ethnic division of labor; they were not disposed to work with the discipline and competitive intensity of the Chinese. Firm British rule and the support of the Malay ruling houses produced a pattern of peaceful coexistence in this plural society.

The British authorities and their Malay clients chose to regard immigrants as temporary sojourners, birds of passage or guest workers who had come to Malaya to earn money but had no long-term interest in or loyalty to Malaya and intended to return to their country of origin. Malaya, they firmly believed, was the Malay homeland, belonging as a matter of right to its original inhabitants. Their special position required protection from the economically aggressive immigrants, for example by reserving large tracts of land for exclusive Malay ownership. Many non-Malays did indeed return to China and India, but many more chose to remain. They had accumulated assets and developed a way of life that they could not hope to duplicate in the land of their ancestors, which their Malaya-born children had never even seen. They retained strong sentimental attachments to their former homeland and to its language and culture, which they hoped to maintain and transmit to their children, but they had made the break. A settled diaspora, they and their offspring had come to stay.

By the outset of World War II, a plural society had emerged in Malaya, with entirely separate and parallel religious and social institutions, separate residential patterns, and a rigid division of labor. As well as maintaining peace and order, British rule legitimated the existing structures, especially among Malays, by excluding from the public agenda the suggestion of any possible political role for the immigrant communities. The latter refrained from challenging this understanding and focused their political energies on the problems of their ancestral countries.

The Mobilization of Malay Nationalism

The era of unmobilized peaceful coexistence ended abruptly with the speedy and humiliating defeat of the British by the Japanese early in 1942, which exploded forever the myth of European invulnerability and superiority. During their three and a half year occupation, the Japanese patronized the Malay ruling establishment as prospective partners in a Japanese-led Greater East Asia Co-Prosperity Sphere; they even tolerated Pan-Malayan sentiments inspired by Indonesian nationalism. The Japanese also sponsored Indian nationalism, including the organization in Singapore and Malaya of an Indian National Army that would cooperate with the Japanese in liberating India from British imperial rule. Chinese, however, were treated with unremitting hostility and brutality as enemy aliens. An estimated five thousand Chinese were tortured and executed by the Japanese authorities. Chinese merchants were abused and squeezed unmercifully for "voluntary" contributions to the Japanese war effort. Thousands of young Chinese were conscripted for labor and transported out of the country.

In response, elements of the underground Malayan Communist Party (MCP) organized a Malayan Peoples Anti-Japanese Army (MPAJA) that undertook guerrilla harassment of the Japanese military; the British furnished some weapons and technical assistance. The anti-Japanese resistance was led and manned almost entirely by leftist-oriented Chinese youth, who suffered severe hardships and incurred numerous casualties.

After the Japanese surrendered in August 1945, the MCP-MPAJA fighters began to settle scores with Malays, especially with Malay policemen, whom they regarded as collaborators with the Japanese in their persecution of Chinese. These bloody reprisals set off a sequence of counter-reprisals, which resulted in heavy loss of life and property on both sides and indicated the potential for communal violence in this plural society once an external colonial presence was removed. Order was gradually restored after British forces returned, but sporadic violence continued. Although Chinese guerillas turned in some of their weapons in return for small cash payments, by no means did they disarm entirely, nor did the MCP abandon its underground organization.

The postwar British authorities felt little obligation to the Malay establishment, which had collaborated with the Japanese, but they accorded considerable respect to the Chinese who had led the domestic resistance. For the new structure of government, they designed and began to implement a "Malayan Union," which substituted a centralized colonial regime for the previous pattern of indirect rule through Malay sultans, relegating the latter to purely symbolic and religious roles. Citizenship and political participation would be available to all persons who were born in Malaya or could demonstrate that they regarded it as their permanent home. The implications were unambiguous: Malaya would become a multiethnic polity with equal political rights and opportunities for all its permanent residents regardless of race or background. While enfranchising resident Chinese and Indians, the union would end the special position of Malays to which the prewar British regime had been committed. The British extracted the "consent" of the individual sultans to this new dispensation by offering them no choice.

The Malay response was as rapid and decisive as it was unexpected from a people reputed to be politically passive. The threat that ignited Malay society was the prospect that the immigrant Chinese and Indians, equal in numbers but more advanced educationally and more aggressive economically, would soon dominate political life as well. The protection previously afforded by the status of the Malay rulers and the special position of the Malays as the indigenous people would be stripped away. In their own country, Malays faced the dismal prospect of total subordination to an immigrant people; they would be reduced to the pathetic position, as some Malays phrased it, of the "red Indians in North America."

From this unexpected threat grew Malay nationalism as a modern political movement. Before World War II, Malay nationalism, unlike the Chinese, Indian, and Indonesian national movements, had barely taken root and was politically insignificant. Its first expression after World War I came from students returning from the Middle East, especially from the Al Azhar University in Cairo, who sought Islamic purification and renewal. The second stage, secular in tone, appeared in the 1930s when young men trained as Malay schoolteachers espoused anti-imperialism, pan-Malayanism linked to Sukarno's Greater Indonesia, and antifeudal social reform. The Malay political and religious establishment, supported by the British, easily controlled and encapsulated these early manifestations of Malay nationalist protest.

The Malayan Union, however, posed a clear and present challenge to the status and prerogatives of the aristocratic establishment. From this dominant class emerged the leadership that mobilized Malay society into a political movement determined to protest, challenge, and defeat the Malayan Union scheme. So impressive was this unexpected Malay mobilization, so effective was the supportive lobby in London of ex-Malayan colonial administrators, and so feeble was the countermobilization of Indians and Chinese in favor of the proposal, that the British government soon backtracked and capitulated. The Federation of Malaya which replaced Malayan Union in 1948 restored the prerogatives of the Malay rulers and greatly limited citizenship opportunities for non-Malays. It was a spectacular victory for the United Malays' National Organization (UMNO), the new vehicle of Malay nationalism.

Though UMNO's leadership was aristocratic, it was able to mobilize mass support and enthusiasm because of the participation of Malay schoolteachers who became the principal grass-roots activists, because of the deferential character of a poorly educated peasant society, and because of pervasive fear, derived from recent wartime and postwar experience, that the Chinese had designs on their country, religion, and way of life. UMNO quickly built a structure that penetrated every Malay village. UMNO included functional sections for youth and for women, and because of its standing in aristocratic circles it was able to incorporate the bureaucracies of most Malay states. An elaborate system of internal governance and communication evolved, including representative organs, but during the first two decades UMNO was in fact a top-down structure dominated by high status personalities, particularly its president and Malaya's founding prime minister, Tunku Abdul Rahman.

UMNO's ideology has not varied since its creation. Malays are the indigenous people of Malaya, the native sons, the "bumiputera." This status confers on them a special position vis-à-vis the "immigrant" communities, including the right to establish and maintain a Malay-style polity and to ensure the primacy of Malay culture and Malay institutions. Immigrants are entitled to fair and generous treatment, but only within a framework that respects the special position of the Malays and accommodates their political and cultural hegemony. UMNO's ideology promoted social modernization and economic development so that Malays could aspire to higher material standards of living. Government, it held, must help Malays overcome their educational and economic disadvantages resulting from colonial neglect. So crucial is the bumiputera idea that much of Malay-inspired historiography has been devoted to demonstrating that Malays were indeed a settled society, the masters of Malaya prior to European colonialism and long before the arrival of Chinese and Indian immigrants—counteracting the charge from non-Malay sources that most Malays are, in fact, recent migrants from Indonesia.

UMNO succeeded in uniting and mobilizing into a broad national movement the elites and the masses of Malay society and in sustaining that cross-class alliance over an extended period. The Malay aristocracy was defending the right of the various royal families to govern Malay society; they were also protecting their own monopoly of administrative posts in government and the prospect that they would rule the country when the British departed. To the Malay masses the issue was clear: Would their country belong to and be run by their own people or by infidel immigrants? Would Islam and the Malay language prevail in their land, or would the godless Chinese? Whatever the failings of their own ruling class, their position was legitimate in Malay society, a legitimacy vindicated by their defense of all Malays against displacement and subordination by aliens. In support of these fundamental rights, UMNO mobilized Malays of all classes and from all regions of the country into a national movement. Because of the depth and intensity of this mobilization, UMNO never lacked the resources needed to maintain its organization, pay its numerous functionaries, and conduct election campaigns. Much of UMNO's day-to-day grass-roots work was contributed by village-based school teachers and other volunteers. In 1955, when UMNO became the party of government, with access to official patronage on a large scale, the availability of resources became much less a problem than how to distribute them among numerous claimants within UMNO's political machine.

The original goal of UMNO—to defeat the Malayan Union—succeeded completely, demonstrating to Malays the clout that a united people could exert even under a colonial regime. With the outbreak in 1948 of the MCP-led insurrection—dubbed "the emergency" by the British— UMNO confronted an even graver threat to Malay interests, the domination of their country by a Chinese-led, infidel, communist movement that would subvert the existing social structure, undermine the status of Islam, eliminate the special position of the Malays, and, they feared, transform Malaya into a de facto province of China. UMNO cooperated fully with the British in suppressing the insurrection and made common cause with conservative elements among non-Malays who were prepared to respect the prevailing social stuctures. As the issue of independence loomed, UMNO leaders took a cautious position: since the British were perceived as essentially friendly to Malay aspirations, their hasty departure was less important than ensuring the final defeat of the Chinese-communist insurgency, the willingness of non-Malays to accept a future in which Malay rights would be politically and culturally secure, and greater confidence in UMNO's ability to operate a modern state.

In the early 1950s, when UMNO leaders became convinced that these conditions were imminent, they cautiously embraced the goal of independence. As their objectives became less defensive and more positive, they began to emphasize the importance of uplifting the socioeconomic position of Malays, to enable them to to compete with the immigrant peoples in a modern economy. This new emphasis implied abandonment of the long-standing British policy of protecting Malays from exposure to modernization and economic competition. Instead, government must be prepared to intervene actively to make educational and economic opportunities available, on a preferential basis if necessary, to the Malay masses.

UMNO pursued a course consistent with its posture as a nonrevolutionary national movement working under a sympathetic and supportive colonial authority. Leaders cooperated closely with the British and their tactics were entirely nonviolent. They also found it expedient to cooperate with moderate non-Malay groups, since the British indicated that independence would be possible only if the successor regime could draw significant support from all the major ethnic communities. This stipulation led to the formation of the multiethnic Alliance Party.

Despite the remarkable mobilization achieved and maintained by UMNO, Malay society proved no more successful than others in avoiding internal political cleavages, beginning with factions within UMNO itself. Aside from inevitable conflicting personal ambitions and the shifting alignments they yield, the main split has been between "ultras," who insist on the militant promotion of Malay cultural and economic interests regardless of the views of non-Malays, and moderates willing to take into account the interests of accommodative non-Malays who since 1955 have been their partners in government. Tensions between ultras and moderates have divided UMNO since the beginning and have generated intense conflict.

Of the two minority strains of Malay political thought outside UMNO, the more consequential is incorporated in the Islamic Party (PAS), UMNO's main rival for the support of its core Malay constituency. PAS is the political expression of Islamic activism and fundamentalism in Malay society. It demands that Malaysia become an Islamic state governed in conformity with *sharia* law. In the East Coast State of Kelantan, the PAS government has incorporated *sharia* into the state's penal code. PAS accuses UMNO of insufficient, merely symbolic concern for Islam, of neglecting the impoverished and deprived Malay rural masses, and of serving the interests only of the morally corrupt Malay privileged classes and their infidel Chinese associates. Thus it combines social and economic populism with Islamic fundamentalism and hostility to non-Muslims, especially the Chinese, accusing UMNO both of hedonistic secularism and of sacrificing the birthright of the Malay-Muslim masses. PAS has attracted dissident Malay intellectuals, but its cadres come mainly from the ranks of Islamic religious functionaries, especially in the northern and East Coast areas where Malays have benefitted least from modern education and economic development. PAS has provided a continuing challenge to UMNO's dominance over its ethnic constituency and its claim to be the sole authentic voice of the Malay people. It has compelled UMNO's secular leadership to undertake large-scale programs of mosque building, promotion of pilgrimages to Mecca, and similar conspicuous measures to demonstrate its devotion to Islam. But the more UMNO and its government identify with Islam, the more non-Malays feel threatened, excluded, and alienated.

The left-wing Malay parties present a less serious problem. They have propounded the need for radical social change within Malay society, the elimination of "feudal" attitudes and structures, the implementation of land reform (which would threaten rural elites who tend to be affiliated with UMNO), and the removal of exploitative rural middlemen and moneylenders (who tend to be affiliated with UMNO's political allies, the Malayan Chinese Association). They advocate multiracial social democracy and oppose the development of a bumiputera capitalist class. Some of these parties have a pan-Malayan orientation, implying some form of association with Indonesia, which threatens both the UMNO leadership and their Chinese allies. Without sacrificing the special position of the Malays, they advocate class, rather than ethnic, solidarity and have, unsuccessfully, attempted cooperation with left-oriented non-Malay parties.

The Malay parties that attempt to mobilize along class lines have never been able to reach more than a small circle of intellectuals and students. UMNO has condemned them as communists or fellow travelers and government has harassed them and arrested and detained their leaders. Social and economic protest in Malay society tends to be channeled along legal populist and religious lines, rather than along social-structural lines that challenge the prevailing social order but do not appeal to the Malay masses.

Defensive Mobilization of Non-Malays

During the British colonial period prior to the Japanese occupation, immigrant Chinese and Indians were expected to be apolitical; for the most part they willingly complied. The British and Malays regarded them as "sojourners" or guest workers who would eventually return to their homeland. Successive Chinese regimes collaborated with this policy, since they adhered to the doctrine of *jus sanguinis,* according to which all ethnic Chinese, wherever they resided, remained forever subjects of the Chinese state. Immigrants, especially Chinese—Indians being already British subjects—were free to pursue their economic interests but were expected to behave themselves politically and take care of their own community needs. Chief among the latter was education. The economy-minded British colonial authorities made no provision for the children of immigrants. Therefore Chinese organizations arranged to import teachers from China to instruct their children, usually in the Mandarin tongue, using Chinese mainland textbooks and following mainland curricula that had no relevance to conditions in the Malayan diaspora. In this way Chinese parents hoped to maintain their culture, especially their language, and prepare their children who might opt to return one day to the homeland.

These teachers brought Chinese nationalism to Malaya. Like most young Chinese intellectuals after the turn of the century, they were inspired by the republican teachings and writings of Dr. Sun Yat-sen. The nationalist revolution of 1911 was supported financially and enthusiastically welcomed by large numbers of Chinese in Singapore and Malaya. The nationalist organization, the Kuomintang (KMT), provided teachers, journalists, and other intellectual leaders of the Malayan Chinese communities. After the communists became active in China in the 1920s, Marxist-trained cadres began to arrive in Malaya to compete with the nationalists, attracting adherents in the trade unions and among secondary school students. Their message of anti-imperalism and social revolution, though focused primarily on China and India, disturbed the British colonial authorities, who closely monitored their activities, deported several activists, and finally outlawed the movement in 1936.

The Japanese invasion of mainland China in the mid-1930s united Malayan Chinese of all political persuasions in fund-raising, demonstrations, and well-organized boycotts of Japanese goods. The British attempted to limit these activities as part of their appeasement posture during the Chamberlain era. Though China was the focus, these organizational efforts represented the first step in the politicization of the Malayan Chinese diaspora.

The second stage was the three-and-a-half-year Japanese occupation that began with the defeat and surrender of British forces in February 1942. In response to a systematic and unremitting campaign of persecution by the Japanese, the underground Malayan Communist Party (MCP), Chinese in leadership and membership, launched an anti-Japanese guerrilla campaign that won widespread sympathy and respect among Chinese. Subsequently it provided the organizational nucleus of the major insurgency, the "emergency," that challenged British rule for nearly a decade after 1948 and persisted for nearly four decades as an underground outlaw movement headquartered in the jungles of southern Thailand. The inability of moderate, noncommunist Chinese—and of their Indian counterparts—to exert any influence in favor of the Malayan Union scheme contrasted with the impressive performance of the Malays who mobilized behind UMNO. This failure highlighted the need for an organization that could claim to represent the majority of law-abiding Chinese and promote and defend their collective interests in an increasingly politicized environment.

From the beginning of large-scale immigration Chinese society in Malaya had been divided among Hokkienese, Hakka, Cantonese, Hainanese, and Teocheu, all of whom brought their cultural and linguistic differences with them from their provinces of origin in South China. There were also "Baba" Chinese, prosperous merchants who were British subjects with long residence in Penang and Malacca and little residual knowledge of any Chinese dialect. Residence in Malaya had produced the inevitable class differences among a dynamic people, between propertied capitalists, merchants, and guildsmen on one hand, and, on the other, impoverished unskilled workers, miners, and peasants, many of the latter cultivating small plots illegally. Cleavages also existed between the unschooled and the educated, and, further, between those educated in Chinese and in English. As the need for political mobilization became evident, these social, cultural, and economic divisions produced the three antagonistic political groupings that have continued to characterize Malayan Chinese society.

The first was the MCP. Its leaders were ideologically committed intellectuals, but its rank and file were poor, Chinese-educated youth who saw no future for themselves in a state dominated by Malay politicians and collaborating Chinese capitalists. In such a polity their culture and language would be denigrated, they would have no economic prospects, and they would be politically marginalized and powerless. They advocated an anti-imperialist, revolutionary struggle that would bring about a socialist society with equal rights, opportunities, and status for all Malayans regardless of race, and equal recognition and respect for the languages and cultures of all resident Asians. Their courage in combat and their exemplary defense of Chinese interests earned them widespread sympathy from the Chinese masses—whom they championed and intimidated at the same time—even among many who did not share their ideology or their socialist goals. To the British and their Malay associates, however, they were a ruthless revolutionary force, subversive of the established political, economic, and ethnic structures of Malayan society and, after 1949, a dangerous local outcropping of the People's Republic of China.

The traditional leadership of the Malayan Chinese communities had been provided by its successful businessmen who had the time, money, and skills to devote to community management and representation. They dominated the dense networks of voluntary associations, chambers of commerce, dialect associations, and occupational guilds through which the Chinese communities managed their common concerns in the absence of any support from the colonial authorities. In 1948 several combined factors produced the Malayan Chinese Association (MCA): the need to demonstrate to the British and the Malays that the most Chinese were indeed loyal and willing to cooperate both in the suppression of the insurrection and in political progress toward eventual self-government; the need to provide practical assistance to the many rural Chinese who had been exploited for contributions by the MCP cadres and then relocated "for their protection" behind barbed wire in "New Villages" by the British in order to interdict assistance to the insurgents; and the imperative need for a political voice to assert and protect Chinese cultural, economic, and political interests so that lost opportunities like the Malayan Union scheme would not be repeated.

The establishment of the MCA was the symbolic if belated acknowledgment by mainline Chinese opinion in the Malayan diaspora that, sentimental factors aside, their future and that of their children lay in their land of residence, not in their ancestral homeland. The threat of Malay political dominance and the exclusion of legitimate non-Malay interests forced them to choose which status would be appropriate for them in a postcolonial Malayan state: that of temporary Chinese residents, or that of full-fledged Malayan citizens of Chinese background. Fence-sitting was no longer an option. Only citizenship would enable them to claim the status and rights required to resist the threat of institutional subordination in a country that was destined soon to achieve independence.

As businessmen their goals and their politics would be pragmatic: to maximize freedom of enterprise, maintain their culture, and achieve citizenship on an equal basis for all Chinese who regarded themselves as Malayans. The founders of MCA had long experience dealing with Malays of all classes and felt fully competent to negotiate practical arrangements with their leaders; as minority businessmen they were expert in the art of give and take. They were willing to accommodate Malay claims for political and cultural hegemony as well as symbolic acknowledgment of the special position of Malays as long as these could be reconciled with their own minimum goals. Following UMNO's example, MCA soon had chapters in all Chinese settlements throughout the peninsula and ample funds to finance organizational activities and political campaigns. Their first priority was to establish credibility within their own constituency by providing practical assistance to needy Chinese in the New Villages.

A third group of Chinese, small at the outset, but soon to become a major factor in Chinese politics, was the English-educated middle class, born in and fully committed to Malaya. They rejected both communism and Chinese cultural chauvinism in favor of a nonracial democracy in which all Malayans as individuals would enjoy equal rights, opportunities, and responsibilities on a meritocratic, nonpreferential, nondiscriminatory basis. In refusing to acquiesce in second-class status for themselves they in effect rejected the bumiputera myth, the special position and entitlements of Malays, since Malaya belonged to all its people, not to a single race. They reserved special contempt for the MCA elites, whom they labeled tools of the Malay establishment, sacrificing the interests of the majority of Chinese and other non-Malays to feather their own capitalist nests.

During the brief period 1963–65, when Singapore was incorporated into the new Malaysian entity, these English-educated Chinese became enthusiastic followers of Singapore's prime minister, Lee Kuan-yew, who preached in favor of a "Malaysian Malaysia" in which all Malaysians would enjoy full equality in all respects, while state-sponsored preferences would be available to the "have-nots" of all races. After Singapore was expelled in 1965, the Malaysian Chinese middle class transferred their support to the Democratic Action Party (DAP), noncommunal in principle, but actually the political vehicle of non-Malays who insisted on complete equality in the country they regarded as their homeland. The DAP became the main parliamentary opposition to the dominant Alliance and its successor, the National Front, polling a majority of the non-Malay vote.

Emergence of the Alliance

The great political invention of the Malayan elites was the Alliance, an electorally dominant political party that incorporated three ethnic movements, each responsible for mobilizing, representing, and disciplining its constituency. The conservative leaders of the three Malayan ethnic communities blundered into a consociational arrangement that explicitly recognized and institutionalized the primacy of ethnic solidarity in Malayan politics. Under the rules of the Alliance the leaders of the three ethnic movements were to bargain out quietly in camera the competing claims of their communities, and thus avoid inflaming the public on sensitive, emotionally charged, violence-producing issues. Political participation in a Westminister-type polity would thus be restricted in the interest of public order and peaceful intercommunal coexistence.

As the reality of independence loomed, all the ethnic elites showed marked hesitation. Malays had few quarrels with British rule that protected their special position and entitlements, and they were not sure they were ready to take over a modern state containing a large, economically aggressive Chinese minority. Non-Malays, too, found British colonial rule bearable, for it protected their lives and property while safeguarding their cultural and economic freedom. Independence would replace this security with Malay hegemony. Envious of Chinese educational superiority and economic success, Malays might be tempted to use their political power to abridge the rights and opportunities of non-Malays. Independence was not exactly thrust on Malayans, but neither did they struggle and sacrifice for it, nor did they welcome it with great emotion. It seemed an inevitable historical development to which they must adjust.

Once the MCP-led insurrection was under control, the British indicated that independence would depend on an interethnic political arrangement that satisfied the basic needs and aspirations of all the communities. The first hesitant step toward the Alliance occurred when a joint UMNO-MCA slate won twenty-six of twenty-seven seats in the 1952 Kuala Lumpur municipal elections. This expedient blossomed into a full-fledged partnership that won fifty-one of fifty-two seats in the 1955 federal parliamentary elections, setting up the Alliance government that piloted Malaya toward independence in August 1957 and that survives in modified form to this day.

The 1957 constitution was forged by the conservative elites of the three ethnic movements, with helpful intermediation by the departing British, who had their own security and economic interests to protect. Under the terms of this consociational bargain, Malays would control the government, but non-Malays would acquire citizenship by birth or naturalization and could freely vote and hold public office, including ministerial portfolios. The conferral of citizenship, an important milestone for Chinese in Southeast Asia, was regarded by Malays as a major concession. The symbols of the state would be entirely Malay, including the monarchy, which would rotate every five years among the Malay sultans; Islam would be the state religion, but freedom of worship would be guaranteed; Malay would be the national language and, after sharing equal status with English for ten years, would become the official language as well. The special position of the Malays was explicitly recognized. Government could provide special compensatory preferences without any time limit for Malays in higher education, government employment, and certain occupations. Non-Malays were assured freedom of economic enterprise, but government could intervene to uplift the economic position of the bumiputera. This set of intercommunal compromises and accommodations comprised the charter that would be administered along consociational lines by the ethnically inclusive but Malay-dominated Alliance Party.

The Malayan publics were not directly consulted on the terms of this constitutional bargain. It was not acceptable to Malays who favored an Islamic polity or to "ultras" who opposed the conferral of citizenship in their country on alien Chinese. Nor was the agreement acceptable to non-Malays who were committed to individual equality regardless of ethnic origin and therefore rejected the special position of Malays and the implied second-class status for non-Malays. Herein lay the seeds of future conflict, but in the optimistic environment of *Merdeka* (independence) the bargain struck by the leaders of the Alliance seemed to command widespread support. Immediately before independence and thereafter, politics in Malaya (known as Malaysia after 1963, when it incorporated the ex-British colonies in northern Borneo and, for two years, Singapore as well) have followed ethnic lines. This phenomenon is partly explained by societal and psychological structures that encapsulate members of the three main communities in ethnically exclusive institutions. These societal patterns are reenforced by government, which classifies the public as bumiputera or nonbumiputera and provides differential treatment and access to public services accordingly. Except for the explicitly communal Malayan Chinese Association (MCA) and the Malayan Indian Congress (MIC), non-Malay partners in the National Front—the post-1971 successor to the Alliance—have attempted to be noncommunal in their membership and their platforms. Perforce they have been non-Malay, mainly Chinese, because they have been unable to attract significant Malay participation. Malays see no reason to support any party that refuses to recognize their special position in the Land of the Malays (the official name for Malaya in the Malay language) and the entitlements that this entails.

Probably the majority of non-Malays would prefer a noncommunal pattern of politics that would symbolize equal status for them and allocate educational, employment, and economic oportunities according to individualistic, meritocratic, market-based criteria. Under present conditions these criteria would yield them a substantial competitive advantage. As a practical matter they would accept for a limited time special government preferences to help deserving Malays, as long as these did not enroach seriously on oportunities for non-Malays. Malays, almost to a man, insist on preserving their bumiputera rights. The main function of UMNO has been to administer policies and programs that implement these entitlements. Because UMNO needs non-Malay associates to legitimate their rule over a society that is nearly 50 percent non-Malay, non-Malay political movements participate as junior partners in the Alliance. There they articulate certain non-Malay interests, within limits set by their UMNO senior partners, and share in government patronage.

Conflict Management

Before World War II, the management of ethnic conflict presented few challenges to the British colonial authorities. Each of the communities functioned in its separate institutional enclaves, little overt competition arose among them, and none was mobilized for political action. European supremacy and British colonial rule were not seriously contested. The friendly Malay establishment was patronized and protected, and its control of Malay society was secure; the separate, apolitical economic and cultural activities of the Chinese and Indians were tolerated. Indeed, the British took measures against Chinese secret societies more for their criminal extortions of Chinese businessmen than for their occasional expressions of support for Chinese nationalism. The British also harassed and subsequently outlawed communist organizations, mostly Chinese in origin and membership. With no major indigenous nationalist movement to cope with, with rigid institutional pluralism and a well-recognized ethnic division of labor, conflict management before World War II presented few difficulties for the colonial authorities.

When the British returned in late 1945 the situation was transformed. A major fraction of the Chinese community had mobilized under the MCP. The ill-fated Malayan Union scheme precipitated the political mo-

bilization of Malay nationalism and, shortly thereafter, the reactive mobilization of Indians and moderate Chinese. Indigenous political energies
had crystallized along ethnic lines. European colonialism in Asia was
fading and British statesmen searched for a formula that would at once
protect western security interests against militant communist expansion
from China and simultaneously preserve Britain's substantial economic
investments in an independent Malayan polity. Insuring the consensual
inclusion and participation of all the ethnic communities under conservative, western-oriented leadership, the multiethnic Alliance structure
was ideally suited to British objectives. In the brief transition from self-
government to full independence, the British nurtured the Alliance arrangement and the constitutional bargain that it produced as a formula
that could insure interethnic harmony, stable government, and economic
development along capitalist lines in a sovereign, postcolonial Malayan
state.

The consociational Alliance regime lasted fourteen years, until May
1969. It built on the premise that Malaya would remain indefinitely a
plural society with a respected position for all its ethnic communities.
Individual citizens would be included in politics and make claims on
government only through ethnically exclusive organizations federated in
a single umbrella party, the Alliance, whose leaders would operate the
government and broker differences according to the general formulas
and understandings that underlay the 1957 constitution. This consociational arrangement required good will and mutual trust among the leaders of all the ethnic blocs, a consensus on the goals of the polity and the
rules of the game, and the ability of each ethnic elite to enforce its joint
decisions on its constituents. The arrangement did not promise to diminish pluralism but only to realize viable and tolerable coexistence. Nor
did it promise to banish conflict, but only to manage with mutual respect
and hard bargaining the controversies that would inevitably arise.

Given an institutionally plural society and a polity structured explicitly
along ethnic lines of cleavage, communally defined issues must soon
command the political agenda. Virtually every problem that government
encountered, even those that on the surface appeared ethnically neutral,
proved to have competitive ethnic implications. Elements in each community presented insistent demands that government do more to promote and defend their interests, declaring meanwhile that their own
representatives in the Alliance were insufficiently militant in advancing
their community's concerns and too accommodative to the selfish, un-
reasonable demands of their ethnic partners. Outside the Alliance, in

both the Malay and the Chinese communities, lurked ambitious political competitors eager to outbid the current leadership, to champion the maximal ethnic claims of communal activists, and to pounce on the Alliance elites for selling out to their ethnic opponents.

From Malay circles arose the charge that UMNO leaders were not doing enough to promote the national (Malay) language and were allowing the Chinese to avoid learning and using Malay by tolerating the continuing dominance of English in education and government. Malays insisted, especially in their biennial Bumiputera Economic Congresses, that government do much more to raise the depressed economic status of Malays, who had virtually no stake in the modern economy—industry, finance, plantations, commerce—who were virtually unrepresented in the professions and skilled trades, and whose mean income was less than half the Chinese average and not improving in relative terms. When, at the behest of their Chinese partners, the Alliance government blocked the efforts of its Malay minister of agriculture to reduce the role of Chinese merchants in rice marketing, rural trading, and moneylending, Malay intellectuals bitterly accused UMNO of betraying and abandoning the interests of the average Malay and perpetuating the exploitation of bumiputera peasants by avaricious and unscrupulous Chinese middlemen.

Chinese pressed their MCA representatives on two counts: they were insufficiently represented in Parliament because constituency boundaries had been unfairly drawn. Rural (Malay) districts contained many fewer persons than urban (Chinese) districts. On this issue, however, UMNO was unwilling to compromise, since the overrepresentation of Malays helped to guarantee Malay political dominance, a critical understanding in the original Alliance bargain. In 1959, the inability of MCA to win concessions on this issue split its ranks and undermined its credibility among its constituents. Its failures on language and education were similarly costly. Chinese claims that the maintenance of their culture required at least symbolic official status for the Chinese language and, more important, government financing for Chinese-medium secondary schools were summarily rejected by UMNO as contrary to the national language policy that had been part of the original Alliance bargain. While UMNO argued that Chinese were constantly attempting to alter the terms of the Alliance bargain, opposition parties charged MCA with ineffectiveness in defending Chinese interests. Its leaders were accused of pandering to UMNO and exerting themselves mainly to insure the economic freedom and lucrative patronage of the capitalists who controlled the MCA, with little concern for the economic or cultural needs of the average Chinese. In effect they were maintaining the Malayan version of the normal Southeast Asian symbiosis between indigenous powerholders and wealthy Chinese.

The most destabilizing episode involved the emotionally charged issue of language, always close to the core of identity. Malays insisted in 1967, after a decade in which English was an official language, that the independence bargain be honored and Malay assume its proper status as the sole official language. Chinese demanded that English continue, in fact if not formally, as an alternate language in public administration and in secondary and higher education. Ultras on both sides clashed in noisy and threatening confrontations. The Alliance elites worked out a precarious compromise that eliminated English as an official language but allowed for its "liberal" use in government and education; but far from settling this issue, their efforts exacerbated the bitterness and sense of betrayal in both camps, undermining confidence in the Alliance system. Tensions that continued to beset the consociational Alliance were best relieved by external threats that united the ethnic partners. The first was Sukarno's "confrontation" against the British-inspired formation of Malaysia in 1963, which he attacked as a neocolonial, imperialist plot. The patriotic response to Indonesian bullying resulted in an overwhelming victory for the Alliance in the 1964 election. The "Malaysian Malaysia" campaign by the Singapore leadership also united the Alliance partners: UMNO could not tolerate attacks on the special position of the Malays, and the MCA feared that the Singapore-based People's Action Party would steal their Chinese constituency. Both applauded the expulsion of Singapore in 1965.

The incorporation as East Malaysia of the former British holdings of North Borneo and Sarawak into the new entity of Malaysia expanded the scale of the polity and introduced new elements of ethnic pluralism and complexity. To simplify this presentation, however, I have limited this chapter to peninsular West Malaysia, the former Malaya, which includes 80 percent of Malaysia's population and which dominates its politics.

May 13, 1969, and Its Aftermath

Ethnic tensions surrounding the May 1969 general elections and ensuing events shattered the consociational experiment. During the campaign both Alliance partners were forced on the defensive by militants in their community who questioned their commitment to the needs of their ethnic constituents and perceived their solicitude for their partners to be excessive. In the name of a Malaysian Malaysia, Chinese opposition parties rejected second-class citizenship, in effect challenging the special position of Malays, to which they argued they had never assented. They condemned MCA for sacrificing Chinese cultural and language rights. Malays, including many in the ranks of UMNO, attacked the established UMNO leadership of Tunku Abdul Rahman for not promoting Malay economic interests and for excessive compromising on the national language issue. Raw ethnic charges and violent incidents dominated the election campaign. The result was a setback for the Alliance, which won less than half the votes and emerged with a much reduced majority in Parliament. The MCA lost more than half its seats to Chinese opposition parties. In the Kuala Lumpur area, the victorious Chinese dissidents celebrated in the streets by taunting Malays with provocative racial epithets. Malays were alarmed that they had lost control of the government of the state of Selangor, which surrounds the capital city. Riots erupted on the night of May 13, with heavy losses of life and property, especially among Chinese. An estimated eight hundred were killed in the Kuala Lumpur area and six thousand lost their homes before order was reestablished. Under emergency regulations, a Malay-dominated National Operations Council suspended Parliament, ruled by decree, and terminated the consociational era. Prime Minister Tunku Abdul Rahman, who symbolized consociational politics, resigned and was replaced by his more militant deputy, Tun Abdul Razak.

UMNO leadership attributed the breakdown of public order to two factors: Malays' fears that their special position guaranteed by the constitution was being threatened by agitation for a Malaysian Malaysia and government's failure to redress the economic inferiority and deprivation of Malays. Unless these two sources of anxiety could be allayed, peaceful ethnic coexistence would be impossible. UMNO leaders therefore drafted a constitutional amendment designed to "entrench" the special position of the Malays and make it a punishable offense to question publicly or even in Parliament the status of the Malay language, the sovereignty of the Malay rulers, the special position of Malays, or the citizenship rights of the immigrant communities. Public advocacy of a Malaysian Malaysia would henceforth be punishable as subversive. This permanent abridgment of democracy was justified as essential to the preservation of public order in Malaysia's conflict-prone environment.

Malays were reassured, but the political opportunity structure for Chinese had become significantly constrained.

Before Parliament reconvened in 1971, when this constitutional amendment was enacted, the government launched its New Economic Policy (NEP) designed mainly to "eliminate the identification of race with economic function" and secondarily to eradicate poverty among all races. Government would intervene aggressively to ensure that over a twenty-year period the Malay share of ownership in the modern corporate sectors of the economy would expand from less than 2 to 30 percent and that Malays would be represented roughly in proportion to their numbers in all lines of employment, especially in managerial and professional positions. This transformation would be achieved not by confiscation of assets or by denying economic opportunities to non-Malays, but by allocating to Malays a disproportionate share of sustained economic growth and of assets purchased from foreigners. There was not, nor has there been subsequently, any suggestion that eliminating the identification of race with economic function implied eventually eliminating the identification of race with political function. Malay control of government and the special position of the Malays are non-negotiable principles.

The government then moved vigorously to enforce the Malay language policy. Malay became the sole official language of government, displacing English. The English language stream was eliminated one year at a time at the elementary and secondary levels and gradually in the universities as well. Mandarin and Tamil-medium schooling were retained at the elementary level only. No concessions were made for government financing of Chinese language high schools. Though non-Malays grumbled at being forced to use a language in which they would be handicapped and for which they had little respect, they adapted rather smoothly to the Malay language requirements. University admissions, however, were another matter. In the expanded university system, Malay enrollments rapidly rose from less than a third to three-quarters of the total, far higher than their proportion of the population, by an openly preferential system of admissions that overrode the generally superior performance of non-Malay applicants on qualifying examinations. Among middle-class Chinese higher education had been an important channel to upward occupational mobility. No policy of the postconsociational era has been so bitterly resented by non-Malays as this form of affirmative action, which they regard as blatant discrimination against their children. This policy has forced many non-Malays to send their offsprings abroad at high cost for a university education. The assurance by senior government officials that the ratios would gradually be adjusted to reflect ethnic proportions in Malaysian society has been received with skepticism by non-Malays.

Non-Malays were not consulted in these policy changes; they retained neither a blocking nor a veto power. The government was transformed into a hegemonic Malay regime in which non-Malay parties that agree to accept the new dispensation may participate, but in a clearly subordinate status. In the post-1969 Alliance, which was subsequently converted into a more inclusive National Front, MCA and MIC continued to be represented and their senior personalities continued to hold office but no longer retained senior ministerial portfolios. Despite its access to government patronage and the lucrative economic oportunities it could offer its chief supporters, MCA lost its capacity to deliver the Chinese vote and thereby much of its usefulness to UMNO. Widespread, highly publicized corruption and destructive factionalism further discredited MCA among its increasingly cynical constituents. A substantial number of non-Malay professionals with portable skills emigrated, mostly to Canada and Australia. Leading Chinese capitalists found it expedient to diversify their investments through networks of Chinese multinational enterprises in the Southeast Asian region and beyond—one reason that private sector investment targets in Malaysia's successive five-year plans were underfulfilled.

Most non-Malays have not suffered economically; indeed their mean per capita incomes still substantially exceed the Malay average in a fast-growing economy that has expanded over more than two decades at the annual average rate of 7 percent, more than quadrupling in size. They complain, however, of discrimination in higher education and in employment, especially in government and government-controlled enterprises, and in the awarding of government contracts. They also protest that their economic freedom has been curtailed by governmental preferences for bumiputera enterprises and heavy investment of public funds in government corporations that preempt profitable lines of business in which non-Malays are excluded both from financial and managerial participation. Their politically marginal status makes them feel vulnerable, unable to protect their vital interests, not entirely excluded but not fully included.

The Malay-dominated government controls its ethnic minorities by (1) coopting into prominent and influential positions non-Malay personalities willing to comply with the current rules of the game and with

UMNO-determined policies, in exchange for which they enjoy access to government patronage, including jobs, contracts, and business opportunities at national and state levels; (2) allowing non-Malays considerable freedom of enterprise and of professional and occupational achievement which, despite discrimination in higher education and in some economic roles, enable non-Malays, particularly of the large middle class, to enjoy a substantial stake in the modern economy and a comfortable standard of living that they are disinclined to jeopardize by openly challenging the regime; and (3) repressing opponents who are deemed to be dangerous by restricting their freedom of organization and expression, by intimidating the judiciary, and by detaining and imprisoning suspects without trial, charging offenders either with communism or with provoking ethnic antagonisms. Though some dissident Malays have been targets of these harsh methods, their weight has been felt disproportionately by non-Malays, especially intellectuals. The manifest capacity of this strong state to use repressive methods to enforce its will and defend the ethnic status quo has deterred the use of violent tactics by its non-Malay opponents.

The defeated and demoralized Malayan Communist Party has passed from the scene. The opposition that now encounters repression comes from noncommunists who are guilty less of Chinese chauvinism, though they are often so charged, than of continuing support for the goal espoused by immigrant minorities everywhere, complete ethnic equality. Most of the violence in Malaysia during the 1980s actually stemmed from sporadic outbursts of rural Malay protest, usually traceable to specific economic grievances but fueled by Islamic populist resentment of the UMNO establishment increasingly dominated by bumiputera capitalists who have benefitted from government patronage under the provisions of the NEP. Although economic growth has lifted large numbers of Malays out of poverty, intraethnic distribution of income has worsened and substantial pockets of poverty remain among rural Malays. Islamic activists argue that the Malay-Muslim masses have been neglected and sacrificed, while Chinese exploiters and their privileged allies in the UMNO establishment have prospered because the principles of Islamic justice have been ignored. Fundamentalist Islam, advocating an Islamic state, has developed a militant, devoted following among discontented young intellectuals and rural Malays who have been bypassed by the recent prosperity.

The threat of fundamentalist Islam to UNMO's secular leadership has compelled the latter to highlight Islamic themes on the government-controlled mass media, to champion Muslim causes, such as the Palestinians', and to sponsor and finance such institutions as the Islamic university and the Islamic bank. In its efforts to preempt and neutralize the fundamentalist challenge to its Islamic credentials, UMNO has resorted to ridicule, patronage, and the cooptation of prominent potential leaders of the Islamic movement into UMNO and government positions. These intra-Malay defensive measures, designed to identify the UMNO government with Islam, have further alarmed the non-Malay, non-Muslim communities.

Malaysia is a strong state whose authority is recognized and respected throughout its territory. Though each of its ethnic communities has a potential patron among the great powers of Asia—Indonesia, China, India—they have made no serious efforts to involve outsiders in their domestic conflicts. Except for the moral and propaganda support that the Chinese Communist Party provided to its Malaysian counterpart, the great powers have abstained from intervening in Malaysia's internal ethnic affairs. Ethnic politics in Malaysia have remained mostly free of direct external influences.

The government's principle focus after 1969 has been the restructuring goals of the NEP, involving massive state intervention in the economy to distribute and redistribute corporate assets in favor of Malays and enhance their participation in management. The government uses such policy instruments as preferences, quotas, public corporations, and regulations requiring private businesses, multinational as well as domestically (Chinese) owned, to make shares available to Malays at discounted prices and to train Malays for managerial responsibilities. Evaluation of the NEP after two decades indicated significant progress but not complete success. A large Malay urban middle class has been created along with a small but vigorous and confident corps of Malay capitalists. Individually and through government agencies acting as trustees for the Malay community, Malay interests in 1991 owned more than 20 percent of the assets in a rapidly expanding and well-managed economy but less than the original target of 30 percent. Malays are unprecedentedly active in managerial roles, over-represented in financial institutions closely linked to government, but still underrepresented in the learned professions, retailing, and manufacturing. Under intense pressure from UMNO youth and other organized Malay interests, the government has decided to persevere with its restructuring objectives, converting the NEP to the New Development Policy (NDP), without quantitative targets or a specific time frame, but with a commitment to reevaluate and reconsider the continuing need for that program after ten years, in the year 2000. Malay businessmen, who have displaced school teachers as the principal activists in UMNO, have nevertheless been warned that they cannot depend indefinitely on government support, that they must henceforth become more self-reliant market competitors. Whatever its deficiencies in concept or implementation, the NEP succeeded in shattering the colonial-era division of labor. Malays are now active, prominent, and increasingly self-confident in economic roles from which, prior to the NEP, they had been almost entirely absent.

Non-Malays who regard themselves as victims of the NEP hoped that it would be terminated after twenty years. During that period the non-Malay share in the assets of the corporate sector actually rose to 50 percent, exceeding the original target of 40 percent, while the foreign share fell from 60 to 30 percent. Although they dispute these figures, Chinese concede that they have shared in the general prosperity, their mean incomes remaining substantially above the national average. Economically most Chinese continue to prosper, despite a regime that they believe unjustly circumscribes their educational, occupational, economic, and political opportunities. With the extension of the NEP by another name, they face the spectre of continuing preferences and discrimination that they fear will become permanent, that the government will "keep moving the goalposts back". Their grievances rankle; the political opportunity structure permits them to complain but to exert only marginal influence on policy. Their fate could rest in the hands of Malay ultras and Muslim fundamentalists should the latter succeed in displacing the present relatively moderate regime. Their vision of a Malaysian Malaysia, of full equality, has receded into the indefinite future.

Malay opinion remains united that only radical, government-directed social engineering could have enabled them to break out of an inherently unjust division of labor that victimized them individually and as a community and to participate in the modern economy of their own country. Even the severe and bitter factional struggle that split the UNMO during the late 1980s into two hostile organized blocs had no effect on their common bottom-line commitment to this strategy. Meritocratic, market-based, individual competition would, they believe, have condemned the Malay people to permanent inferiority; those who started out ahead would have stayed ahead, consolidated their lead, and widened the gap. It remains necessary to uplift Malays as a community, they argue, even if that imposes some temporary pain on individual non-Malays. But, Malays ask, have non-Malays, individually or as communities, really been hurt by the NEP? Consider such indicators as their share of ownership, their per capita incomes, their participation in professional and skilled labor employment.

Since the crisis of 1969, communal coexistence in a polity that by mutual consent is destined to remain ethnically plural has been mostly peaceful, providing the stability essential to rapid and sustained economic expansion. As a result Malaysia has achieved the international status of a middle income, newly industrializing country that aspires to be a fully developed modern, competitive economy by the year 2020. Without NEP and its economic restructuring, would the politically dominant Malays have been willing to tolerate the consolidation of Chinese economic and professional hegemony without resorting to violence that would have been far more costly to non-Malays than the regime of moderate discrimination that was actually implemented? All policy evaluation must confront realistic alternatives such as these.

According to the Malay perspective, the consociational regime broke down in 1969 because non-Malays (1) challenged Malay political hegemony, which was part of the original Alliance bargain, and (2) would not accept the radical measures needed to pursue equity for the economically subordinated Malays. Malay elites, in turn, were unwilling to tolerate threats to their political security or to acquiesce in the permanent economic and occupational subordination of their people, the indigenous inhabitants of their land. Has the government's restructuring program of economic growth with ethnic redistribution, they ask, not been effective and roughly to the advantage of all? Has it not protected the legitimate rights of non-Malay citizens, maintained the peace, and distributed prosperity and opportunity to all ethnic communities? In response, skeptical Indians and Chinese now ask if once the goals of economic equity have been substantially achieved, at their expense, will Malays then be ready to dismantle the prevailing discriminatory economic regime? In the interest of national unity, will they then be willing to concede political equity and equality of political opportunity—to accept the deferred right of non-Malays to first-class citizenship?

4

South Africa: Multiple Cleavages

The Republic of South Africa, 471,000 square miles at the southern tip of the African continent, is a highly pluralistic, multiracial, multiethnic society. Of its rapidly growing population, estimated in 1993 at 39 million, 75 percent are Africans or Blacks divided among several ethnic peoples of whom Zulu, Xhosa, Tswana, and Soto together comprise more than 90 percent. Half of South Africa's Blacks live in urban centers, half in rural areas. Crosscutting these ethnic communities are mobilized, competitive ideological movements that add complexity to Black politics. Mixed-race people (Coloureds) comprise 9 percent of the population; Indians, half Hindu and half Muslim, make up 3 percent. Whites number 4.9 million, their proportion of the total having declined since 1950 from 20 to 12 percent. Afrikaners make up 60 percent of Whites, 40 percent are of other European backgrounds, mainly British. Until 1991 racial and ethnic classifications were rigorously applied to every South African; official patterns of segregation and discrimination determined the status and the differential life chances of every individual.

The main line of cleavage has been the confrontation between Whites and Blacks arising from the determined and hitherto successful efforts of the White minority to subjugate and control the political, economic, and cultural status and opportunities of the non-White peoples through coercive instruments of racist policy and practice identified since 1948 as apartheid. Ethnic and ideological divisions among non-Whites have been and remain significant in themselves and have been exploited by the South African government to divide potential enemies and consolidate its rule. Within the dominant White society conflict and accommodation among Afrikaners and Anglos have significantly patterned intergroup relations. Each of these interrelated dimensions of cleavage must be analyzed if we wish to explain the complex dynamics of ethnic and racial politics in this country. Their very complexity may provide opportunities for cross-ethnic and cross-racial coalitions in the post-apartheid transition that is emerging even as I write.

Boers and British

Since Europeans first established a tiny but permanent presence on the Cape Peninsula in 1652, they have considered themselves the "civilized" people, morally as well as technologically superior to the dark-skinned natives they encountered. The first century and a half of White settlement reflected the tight rule of the Dutch East Indies Company, concerned not with colonizing the area, but only with maintaining a watering, fueling, and refreshment station for its ships plying the lucrative spice trade between Europe and the East Indies. The original settlers were Dutch Calvinists, reinforced by French Huguenots and German Protestants who quickly assimilated into the Dutch community. Their language was Dutch, their faith Dutch Reformed Protestantism. The community grew very slowly during the eighteenth century, reaching about twenty thousand Whites and twice that number of slaves and natives. Gradually it expanded its economic base from trading into settled agriculture in the southern Cape area and nomadic cattle raising on the vast semiarid frontier. Indigenous societies, notably the pastoralist Khoi-khoi (Hottentots) were subdued and became servants of the Whites; slaves were introduced from Indonesia and Madagascar. Sexual liaisons between European settlers and natives produced the mixed-race people. Because Dutch notions of racial hierarchy prevented their assimilation into European society, they were relegated to inferior caste status, even though they spoke Dutch and identified with the Dutch Reformed church. The frontier experience, far from their European roots, gradually produced among the White settlers sentiments of distinctive identity, Boer or Afrikaner, speaking the "Afrikaans" dialect of Dutch. By the time the British appeared, first in 1795, then permanently in 1806, displacing Dutch rule, they encountered a people that considered itself native to the area, with its own sense of incipient nationality.

The nineteenth century witnessed a struggle for the survival of Afrikaners as a separate people. British rule established English as the language of government, law, education, and commerce, reducing the Boers and their culture to subordinate status. In 1820, the British brought a large colony of English men and women, the first of several, to settle the eastern region of the Cape Colony. To a significant fraction of the Boers the abolition of slavery in 1834 and the possibility that Blacks might aspire to equality with Whites threatened their security and their way of life. To escape British rule they launched their long march, the Great Trek, into the interior. There at Blood River in December 1838, they gained their celebrated victory over a much larger Zulu force, a victory that in the ideology of Afrikaner nationalism signaled divine intervention on their behalf and confirmed their election as the instrument of God's will in that part of the world.

Deep in the interior, they eventually displaced and subordinated the African peoples and founded two Boer republics, Transvaal and the Orange Free State, based on the explicit principle and practice of White supremacy. Afrikaner identity was consolidated during the last quarter of the nineteenth century, led by Afrikaans-speaking intellectuals and clergymen reacting against the growing hegemony of the English language and the secularization of society under British rule. The material grievances of impoverished Afrikaner peasants enabled these political entrepreneurs to combine economic with cultural themes, although their efforts at mobilization were handicapped by extreme individualism and apathy, as well as antipathy between Afrikaners in the Cape Province and in the Boer Republics. It was the greed and arrogance of the British, at the apogee of their imperial ambitions, that solidified Afrikaner identity and galvanized their political mobilization. The discovery of diamonds on the Kimberly range in 1867 and of enormous gold deposits in the Transvaal in 1886 proved irresistible to the British, who promptly annexed the two Boer republics. In the Boer war, a last ditch effort to resist British encroachment, the Afrikaners in 1899 challenged the might of the British empire. The British finally prevailed in 1902, after a very costly effort.

The scorched earth policy employed by the Boer forces and the atrocities and humiliations of the concentration camps set up by the British military to house displaced Boer women and children produced a legacy of hatred that reinforced Afrikaner nationalism for three generations. Afrikaners emerged from the war defeated, demoralized, and impoverished, their bitterness further aggravated by the aggressive efforts of the victorious British to anglicize South African society by imposing English as the exclusive language of government and education.

The rebellion suppressed and the Boers no longer a threat, the British government moved to apply to South Africa the policy of internal self-government that had been extended to Canada, Australia, and New Zealand, its other dominions settled by Europeans. This required an accommodation and rapprochement with those Boers who were willing to collaborate with local English speakers in governing the country. The deal that was struck with the ex-Boer generals, Botha and Smuts, guaranteed full citizenship rights to members of the Afrikaner majority and equal official status for the English and Afrikaans languages. Abandoning the liberal constitution of the Cape Colony, non-Whites were excluded from the Parliament of the Union of South Africa, but the existing limited franchise for natives and Coloureds in the Cape Province was retained under a compromise that left voting rights for non-Whites to the four provincial governments.

The Union set up what amounted to a "herrenvolk democracy" in a Westminister-style polity that respected political, civil, and judicial rights for Whites, but excluded non-Whites from political participation. Outside government, with its consociational arrangements, there remained two parallel White societies with separate churches, schools, and social institutions and a marked division of labor in which English speakers owned, controlled, and operated the modern sector of the economy as well as most of the professions and skilled occupations in government, mining, industry, and commerce. With some exceptions, mostly among prosperous farmers and professionals in the Cape Province, Afrikaners were an underclass—rural, uneducated, poor, and depressed. The mean per capita income of Afrikaners was estimated at one-third that of English speakers.

Soon after Union, Afrikaner opinion split into two hostile camps. One, led by Botha and Smuts, promoted a policy of reconciliation and partnership with the British, the goal being the evolution of a single South African white nation encompassing two language communities that would rule the country in friendly association with the British empire. Government could take measures to improve the conditions and opportunities of poor Whites, mostly Afrikaners, as long as the capitalist economy remained undamaged, especially the mining sector, on which the material welfare of the country was believed to depend. In the face of protests from the British-owned private sector, unskilled Whites were protected by job reservation from native competition; government employment was expanded mostly for Afrikaner workers; and native agricultural laborers were prevented by masters and servants laws from leaving their employment, guaranteeing White farmers a secure labor supply at subsistence wages. Cooperation with the Empire went as far as active participation on the side of Britain in both world wars.

The opposing camp favored unabashed Afrikaner nationalism. Only by struggle could beleaguered Afrikaners avert the tragedy of cultural extinction by the anglicizing pressure of the expansionist, aggressive British empire and, even worse, the threat of permanent economic subordination to British capitalists and their Jewish associates. So treacherous, they believed, was perfidious Albion that the British would, if it suited their economic and strategic interests, sacrifice White supremacy to appease the demands of the colored races.

According to the ideology of Afrikaner nationalism, the White man is destined by God to dominate and rule over the darker races in South Africa as everywhere. Similar notions about the racial superiority of Europeans, especially northern and Protestant Europeans, were widely held in European intellectual and popular circles in the century before World War II. Europeans were more advanced and "civilized," and this superiority conferred on them the right to rule. They bore the White man's burden, a long-term civilizing mission. Afrikaner intellectuals reinforced the theme of White superiority with a religious sanction drawn from fundamentalist Calvinist interpretations of Old Testament texts that consigned non-Whites to perpetual inferiority and condemned any form of racial mixing as mortal sin, a threat to racial purity that the state was required to outlaw and punish.

The ideology was built on populist and authoritarian principles as well as racial tenets. Afrikaners must liberate themselves from political and economic subjugation through their own efforts. This work would require the monolithic unity of the *volk* of all regions and of all classes, for class conflict within Afrikanerdom would play into the hands of their enemies and be utterly destructive. The struggle for Afrikaner rights and destiny must be a national effort by and for all Afrikaners, sacrificing individual interests where necessary for the solidarity and collective benefit of the nation. Afrikaner masses must overcome their traditional apathy and individualism; they must trust and be guided by the decisions of their leaders.

The goal of Afrikaner nationalism was domination of South Africa within a regime of White supremacy where government power could be employed to raise the social and economic levels of the Afrikaner people. As Afrikaners were the majority among Whites and enjoyed voting rights, the movement took advantage of a favorable opportunity structure, relying on peaceful electoral tactics to pursue their struggle. The challenge was to educate, motivate, and mobilize their majority using the legitimate political means at hand. Recourse to violence by a group of ex–Boer War officers in 1914 and a pro-Nazi underground during World War II were condemned by the mainline nationalist movement.

Leaders came from the ranks of the educated middle class—clergymen, teachers, lawyers, journalists trained at the Afrikaans language universities, especially Stellenbosch and Pretoria. With a strong economic and psychological stake in the preservation and advancement of a distinctive Afrikaner culture, including the Afrikaans language and the Dutch Reformed church, intellectuals became the mainstay of the nationalist movement. A semisecret fraternity, the Broederbond, assembled the political, economic, and academic elites committed to Afrikaner nationalism into an association that deliberated and planned the policies and strategies of the movement; it remained an influential force not only during the struggle for power but during the first three decades of nationalist rule after 1948.

Though Afrikaners were generally a poor people, many became active, dues-paying members of the National Party. The nationalists established an elaborate grass-roots, mass organization that by the 1930s had enrolled nearly half of all Afrikaners into the party and its affiliated youth, women's, sports, and cultural organizations. Constituency organizations played a large role in selecting party candidates and in managing election campaigns. Self-help economic institutions were established, including a large publishing firm, a bank, an insurance company, and a network of agricultural cooperatives. The bank and insurance company became outstanding examples of the party's economic ideology of "people's capitalism," collective self-help, converting the savings of ordinary Afrikaners into investments in Afrikaner-owned and managed businesses; they became large, economically powerful conglomerates serving the Afrikaner people.

The nationalist movement attempted to foster institutional self-segregation among Afrikaners—in religion, education, Christian-national trade unions, and cultural and recreational activities—to resist anglicization, to modernize the Afrikaans language, and to foster pride in the history and culture of the Afrikaner people. To survive, Afrikaners would have to remain a separate people in control of their own destiny. The success of this vigorous cultural mobilization was reflected in the outpouring of mass enthusiasm that commemorated the centenary in

1938 of the Battle of Blood River, a precursor to political victory a decade later.

The strategy of the Botha-Smuts group, which brought essential Afrikaner support to the Union agreement in 1910 and governed until 1924, was to promote the convergence of British and Afrikaner sentiments into a single nationality that would provide a stable basis for White rule. A substantial majority of British voters and a minority of Afrikaners were sufficient to win elections. During the National Party's administration from 1924 to 1932 under the ex-Boer general, Barry Herzog, the state strengthened the cultural and economic position of poor Whites, mainly Afrikaners. Skilled jobs were reserved for White workers and small farmers were granted tariff protection and subsidies. When, to provide stability during the economic depression in 1932, Herzog and Smuts formed the United Party, the nationalist movement split. A "purified" National Party emerged in opposition under the ex-clergyman D. F. Malan, charging that Herzog had sacrificed Afrikaner culture, betrayed the Afrikaner people to British imperialism, and abandoned the ordinary Afrikaner worker and farmer to the mercies of British capitalism. In 1939, after Smuts led South Africa into World War II on the side of the British Empire, the purified nationalists felt vindicated in their insistence that the survival and advancement of the Afrikaner people required exclusive Afrikaner control of the state and the establishment of a republic outside the British Empire. It was this party and this strain of unreconstructed Afrikaner nationalism that won a very close election victory and took power in 1948. The problem of Afrikaner nationalism had been to mobilize its demographic majority into an electoral majority, capitalizing on a favorable opportunity structure. The National Party's conquest of the state was achieved by peaceful and legal means.

That election proved to be a critical turning point in South African history. It brought to power an ideologically driven nationalist movement determined to shape South African society in the image of its doctrine of White supremacy and Afrikaner hegemony. Though most Afrikaners opposed South African participation in World War II, the war brought them substantial material benefits. Prosperity in agriculture benefitted large numbers of Afrikaner farmers and fostered the development of Afrikaner-owned businesses in small towns and rural areas. The rapid expansion of manufacturing industries multiplied job opportunities and precipitated massive migration to the cities. Most Afrikaners were now urbanized, lifted out of the rural poverty that had marked their society since the Boer War. Though experiencing for the first time some of the benefits of modernization, they remained far below the economic and educational level of English speakers. Afrikaner small businesses were still marginal to the British-owned financial and marketing institutions; Afrikaner industrial workers occupied the bottom rungs of the White labor hierarchy, still wary of non-White competition; and middle-class intellectuals were fearful of English cultural hegemony. As a group, Afrikaners felt threatened by hostile forces. The nationalists offered their party as the only reliable instrument to defend Afrikaner culture and the hard-earned economic gains that Afrikaner workers, businessmen, and farmers had realized during the previous decade.

With their victory in 1948, the National Party government set three goals for themselves: to consolidate Afrikaner control of political power, to implement their vision of proper race relations, and to elevate the educational and economic status of their Afrikaner constituents. Their tactics were often flexible, but their goals were steady and uncompromising. For thirty-five years they persuaded the Afrikaner majority that only solid unity behind the National Party and deference to its leaders could ensure these vital goals. In every election until 1984 they increased their parliamentary majority by maintaining this mobilization.

The Nationalists converted the South African state into an Afrikaner polity. With one or two token exceptions all ministers of government were Afrikaners. The expanded civil service and government corporations were so monopolized by Afrikaners that participation in government was no longer a realistic option for English speakers. Politically neutered, English speakers split their votes three ways, among the defeated conservative United Party of the late General Smuts, Liberals and Progressives who rejected apartheid and stood for nonracial liberalism, and the National Party, whose racist views appealed to about a third of English-speaking voters, even though they could not qualify for membership in that exclusively Afrikaner organization. Though many English speakers sincerely rejected the substance as well as the style of the regime's racist policies, and a few paid a very high price for their convictions, the majority came to terms with the regime while enjoying the luxury of blaming the Afrikaner government for its blundering excesses and the embarrassment of foreign criticism. A small but growing minority of educated Afrikaners opposed the racial policies of the National Party, while a much larger proportion of English speakers tacitly supported them.

Prior to 1948 non-Whites were treated as a caste, much like Blacks in the southern United States before the civil rights movement. With minor exceptions, they were excluded from political activity, relegated to subordinate and menial roles in the economy, and consigned to segregated and inferior amenities and public services. The racial order was enforced partly by law, partly by informal custom. Loopholes did exist, however, which allowed Indian merchants to operate in the central business districts of the towns, Coloureds to live near White residential areas, and Africans to own and operate farms outside the native reserves. The Nationalists were convinced that these loose patterns had to be tightened according to strict notions of racial segregation. They therefore enacted a large body of legislation designed to implement their vision of apartheid.

Among its principal provisions were those that (1) formally assigned all South Africans to a racial category—White, Coloured-mixed race, Indian-Asian, and Bantu-African; one's status in society and one's life chances were totally regulated by official registration in a racial category, regardless of the preferences of individuals; (2) proscribed and criminalized any form of interracial marriage or sexual liaison; (3) enforced strict White–non-White segregation in public facilities and amenities; (4) established separate residential areas for each racial category, combined with separate educational and other services; and (5) strengthened the pass laws or influx control, requiring all Africans outside the reservations or "homelands" to carry passes or reference books, the objective being to limit Africans in the urban areas to those whose labor was needed by the White South African economy. Those with passes could live in slum dwelling in overcrowded segregated native "townships" on the periphery of cities; others would be punished for evading the regulations and sent back to their desolate and impoverished homelands, 13 percent of the territory reserved for 75 percent of its people. The underlying principle was that Africans were foreigners in White South Africa; they belonged in their homelands and were acceptable only as guest workers. This mass of regulations required the forced movement and relocation of an estimated 3.5 million people, the imprisonment of even greater numbers of violators, and large Afrikaner-staffed bureaucracies and police agencies to enforce them.

Originally the Nationalists could justify apartheid in the straightforward nineteenth-century language of White supremacy. The Nazi holocaust in Europe, the emphasis on human rights in the Atlantic Charter and in the United Nations (of which South Africa was a founding member), and decolonization and the ensuing emergence of independent

Asian and African states together delegitimated simple racism as a basis for public policy. Hence the doctrine, popularized by the immigrant Dutch intellectual and later prime minister H. F. Verwoerd, of "separate development" emerged in the 1950s. Far from being an oppressive imposition, separate development was promulgated as a liberating and humanizing policy, enabling each ethnic community in South Africa to manage its own affairs and to evolve its own distinctive social and political institutions according to the dictates of its own culture. With benevolent South African assistance, each of the recognized African peoples would enjoy the fruits of national self-determination and of cultural and, eventually, political independence.

In the 1960s, the National Party regime undertook to implement this version of "grand apartheid." By 1980 four tribal homelands had accepted nominal independence under compliant African rulers dependent on Pretoria's patronage for economic and, where necessary, police support. (Other homeland rulers, notably the Zulu, refused to accept "independence.") The homelands became sources of labor and dumping grounds for Africans expelled from South African cities for violations of the pass laws, for illegal occupation of agricultural land, for old age or physical dependency. As the homelands were too small, too poor in land and natural resources, and too underdeveloped to support large populations, they became centers of acute poverty and desperation; young men and women were willing to accept large risks to migrate illegally to the cities in search of employment.

By the mid-1970s half the Africans lived legally or illegally in the urban townships, providing essential labor for the expanding economy. The burgeoning demand for skilled workers and junior managers could no longer be satisfied by the slow-growing White labor pool. Business interests, including the new Afrikaner capitalists, urged the government to invest seriously in education for non-Whites—at that time per capita spending for Blacks students was one-tenth that for Whites—and to improve the quality of their lives so that they could function as members of a stable, productive, and increasingly skilled labor force. Job reservations, already less needed as more Afrikaners moved into the middle class, would have to be abandoned. Vigorous expansion of the economy imposed increasing strains on the administration of apartheid. The government would have to find ways to modernize apartheid in order to adapt to these economic changes.

The third objective of the National Party regime was to elevate the socioeconomic status of their Afrikaner constituents. Here they achieved outstanding success. By expanding the public sector, they provided middle-class employment opportunities for large numbers of Afrikaners; by 1980, 45 percent of the Afrikaner labor force was employed in the government or in state-operated enterprises. Education in the Afrikaans language was expanded at the technical and university levels to prepare young Afrikaners for these new employment opportunities. Preferential government contracting and generous provision of capital and credit ensured that the state-nurtured, Afrikaner-owned and managed enterprises soon comprised an impressive capitalist sector. Though still small in comparison to English-, Jewish-, and foreign-owned firms, it was large enough to effectively influence the National Party, to eliminate the anticapitalist strain in the party's rhetoric, and to align it more directly with capitalist interests.

The Afrikaner state successfully appropriated and reallocated for Afrikaner development much of the economic surplus produced by the exploitation of Black labor. In little more than one generation these measures virtually eliminated poverty among Afrikaners and transformed them into a middle-class society. The British-Afrikaner differential in per capita income, three to one in 1910, two to one in 1948, was virtually eliminated by 1980. Educational and economic gaps were closed without threatening the assets or impairing the educational or economic rights of English speakers. By controlling the state, Afrikaners were able to capture the dividends of sustained and rapid economic growth and to invest them in the Afrikaner community, thus closing the income gap in a remarkably short period of time.

For three and a half decades after their victory in 1948 the National Party government kept a grateful Afrikaner majority solidly and reliably mobilized behind their leadership. There were defections, a few by prominent personalities in principled protest against apartheid, but these isolated events had little effect on Afrikaner unity. The mainstream National Party contained two tendencies: *verligtes,* the enlightened, who advocated the humanization of apartheid by eliminating its more humiliating features, and *verkramptes,* the orthodox, who insisted on its rigid enforcement. The year 1969 witnessed the breakaway of a right-wing verkrampte faction that accused the party leadership of tolerating too many deviations from orthodox principles of White supremacy, such as interracial athletic events.

By the early 1980s, reform had become the order of the day. Prime Minister P. W. Botha, who took office in 1978, instructed Afrikaners that to survive they must adapt. Meanwhile, the business community warned that traditional apartheid was impairing the progress of the South African economy by threatening the availability of skilled labor, limiting the expansion of the domestic consumer market, and impairing the essential flow of foreign investment. Shocked by the Soweto uprising of 1976–77 and concerned about international disapproval, the urbanized, increasingly secularized, better-educated, predominantly middle-class Afrikaner community seemed ready to accept reforms that preserved the essentials of White political power and economic privilege while relaxing the more onerous and demeaning practices of "petty apartheid" and promising more educational and economic opportunities for non-Whites.

One such reform, the 1982 constitution, created two additional chambers of the national parliament, one for Coloureds, one for Asians. This innovation was intended to complete the structure of separate development by providing institutional self-rule for categories of non-Whites that lacked a territorial base. They would legislate and supervise administration of their "own affairs." Although these two chambers could participate in overall government decisions and their leaders could even hold ministerial portfolios in the Government of South Africa, they could be outvoted by the White chamber. No chamber was provided for Africans who, under the doctrine of separate development, were expected to fulfill their political aspirations in their homelands. The great majority of Asians and Coloureds rejected this reform as an extension, rather than a relaxation, of apartheid, but it was approved by two-thirds of white voters in a referendum in 1983.

These limited reforms proved too much for the right-wing. In defiance of the sacred canons of Afrikaner unity, senior members of the National Party broke away to form a Conservative Party committed to the maintenance of orthodox apartheid. Their core supporters were rural and small-town residents and semi-skilled workers whose status and sense of security depended on the maintenance of strict color bars and who felt threatened by non-White economic competition. From their ranks emerged a storm trooper movement, the Afrikaner Resistance League, dedicated to ensuring White supremacy by violence if necessary. Insurrections in the Black urban townships from 1984 to 1987 confirmed conservatives' fears that the National Party's reforms were undermining the foundations of White supremacy and Afrikaner rule. In the parliamentary elections of 1987 the two dissident parties won nearly half the Afrikaner vote, although the National Party retained its comfortable majority by attracting half the English speakers, many of whom deserted the liberal antiapartheid Progressive-Federal Party to support the government's program of moderate reform combined with vigorous repression of the township insurrection.

Afrikaner unity, the keystone of nationalist ideology, had been shattered. The split affected every institution of Afrikaner society, the Dutch Reformed church, the schools and universities, the press, and, of course, the party itself. Beginning in the 1980s the National Party ruled with the indispensable support of a majority of English speakers. Afrikaner-Anglo rapprochement resulting from the embourgeoisement of Afrikaner society and the healing effects of time was reenforced by the radical transformation in South African politics that began in 1990.

Blacks and Whites

For Africans the nineteenth century was catastrophic. They were subjugated militarily by Boers and British, dispossessed of most of their lands, confined to native reserves, and excluded from political power. Denied access to economic power, they were reduced to the status of unskilled laborers driven by hunger and want to work under onerous conditions for subsistence wages in White-owned mines, factories, farms, and households. Only a tiny minority of teachers, clergymen, and medical doctors acquired professional training in segregated institutions.

The Union agreement in 1910 excluded non-Whites from office holding and, with minor exceptions, from voting. The exclusion of Africans from ownership of land in White South Africa was formalized by Land Acts in 1913 and 1936 which delineated the native reserves as scattered patches of the least productive land, amounting to 13 percent of the territory. Africans could participate in the White agricultural economy only in the semi-indentured status enforced by masters and servants laws.

The eight major African nations all had their own social structure and class divisions. This ethnic and social fragmentation delayed political mobilization, which was further hampered by economic dependency, government patronage of traditional chiefs, a dearth of educated leaders, and the coercive vigilance of the White authorities. In 1912, the South African Native National Congress—which nine years later became the African National Congress (ANC)—was founded. Its original members, the majority from Xhosa backgrounds, came from the tiny upper crust of African society—businessmen, professionals, and teachers. They asked that as individual Africans attained educated, "civilized" status and accepted European culture, including Christianity and the English language, they earn the right to full citizenship. They believed that Whites could be persuaded of the reasonableness of their position, which they would urge by exemplary behavior, good works, petitioning, and lobbying entirely within legal channels. Though it gradually gained influence among Africans, ANC's actual membership grew very slowly; as late as 1947, thirty-five years after its founding, paid-up membership totaled less than 5,600.

As Afrikaans speakers and members of the Dutch Reformed Church, Coloureds in the Cape Province continued to hope that they would eventually be accepted and admitted into Afrikaner society. Indians, many of whom were well educated and economically active as merchants and entrepreneurs, felt little solidarity with Africans. As late as 1949, Indians suffered the fate of many middle-man minorities when Zulu mobs pillaged their settlements and businesses in and around Durban, inflicting heavy losses of life and property and chilling any feeling of common interest with Africans. During his twenty years in South Africa Mahatma Gandhi successfully mobilized the Indians, but even he showed little interest in the African majority. Influenced by the Gandhian strategy of nonviolent resistance and civil disobedience, Indians, like ANC members, hoped that the progress of liberal ideas would permit their incorporation into full citizenship.

As the South African economy expanded, so did its need for labor. Growing demand for labor in the cities and desperate poverty in the native reserves generated large movements of labor to urban areas. Extremely low wages—as late as 1980 estimates indicated that Blacks earned one-fifth the rate for Whites performing similar work—and substandard living conditions in overcrowded, segregated townships led to repeated incidents of strikes, boycotts, and other localized protests that were usually suppressed by employers in league with the police. A few trade unions attempted to enroll African workers, but these unions were usually short-lived because of the opposition of Afrikaner workers and the hostility of employers and government. Among the most dedicated and effective organizers in these nonracial unions were White members of the South African Communist Party (CP). After flirting briefly in the early 1920s with White unions committed to job reservations and a racial hierarchy in the labor force, the CP, under instructions from Moscow, decided to concentrate on non-Whites as the genuine proletariat in South Africa. Indeed, communists have played a prominent role in mobilizing South African Blacks, notably in the ANC and its affiliates, such as the Confederation of South African Trade Unions (COSATU).

The National Party victory in 1948 shattered all hope that South Africa might evolve into a state and society that would be open to all individuals and races on a nondiscriminatory basis. As promised, the Nationalists implemented new legislation to convert a loose regime of segregation and subordination into a rigid regime designed to realize apartheid in every dimension of life. It dashed forever the government's wartime promises of expanded and improved education, social amenities, and material opportunities for Blacks, including legalized collective bargaining and security of (segregated) residence in urban areas, possible preludes to more fundamental reforms. Hope died in the hearts of even the most patient and optimistic Blacks, those who had believed that reasoned persuasion and nonviolent struggle might eventually succeed in opening White society and government to non-Whites on a nondiscriminatory basis. The peaceful struggle for inclusive civil rights had been lost.

The threat of permanent subordination and exclusion, combined with the promise of moral and even material assistance from a physically remote but increasingly supportive international community, prompted a fundamental reassessment of Blacks' strategy for liberation. In 1944, there emerged within the ANC a group of educated professionals, encouraged by wartime prospects for reform and dissatisfied with the ineffectiveness of the ANC. Inspired by the successful example of the Indian National Congress and of Afrikaner political mobilization which they had observed at close range, the Congress Youth League, headed by Nelson Mandela, criticized the ANC for its elitism, its remoteness from the concerns of ordinary Africans, and its ineffective tactics. They urged instead that their cause be redefined as a collective national struggle for self-determination within a larger struggle for the independence of all the oppressed peoples of Africa. In taking responsibility for their own national struggle, South Africans must adopt militant and confrontational tactics—demanding, not petitioning—while remaining nonviolent. Following Gandhian precepts, all forms of nonviolent civil disobedience would be employed, including strikes, boycotts, and noncooperation with government; following the Afrikaner example, self-help would be promoted to raise the educational level of Africans and to establish an independent economic base through African-owned and managed businesses and cooperative enterprises.

To implement this conception of their struggle for liberation, the ANC would be transformed into a mass organization that would mobilize and champion the rights of all Africans, regardless of ethnic origin or social class. In 1949, shortly after the National Party's election victory, the ANC adopted a program of action that incorporated the strategy of the Congress Youth League. The ANC would join in the struggle for a non-racial democracy with sympathetic groups from all racial communities, including enlightened Whites and specifically the South African Communist Party. After uniting with Indian and Colored organizations in a massive Defiance Campaign in 1951–52 which protested and challenged the administration of apartheid by, for example, public burning of pass books, and which government repressed by large-scale arrests and bannings, the ANC and its allies in 1955 adopted the Freedom Charter. The Charter, which has remained the ANC's manifesto, calls for nonracial democracy in South Africa, government control of the "commanding heights" of the economy, and equalization of educational and economic opportunities.

Like all ethnic movements, the South African liberation struggle soon divided over ideology and personal ambitions. These splits affected organization and tactics, compounding the demographic cleavages between Asians, Coloureds, and Africans, the latter further fragmented by ethnic structures and loyalties. These differences provided opportunities for the government to coopt compliant elements with selective benefits and privileges. The liberation movement split in the late 1950s into two major ideological streams. The ANC, now in the hands of its Youth League intellectuals and their communist allies, insisted on a racially inclusive ideology and strategy. Whites had a legitimate place in South Africa, entitled to the same—but no greater—rights and responsibilities as other South Africans. Though Africans must take responsibility for their own liberation, they welcomed the participation of all, including Whites, who shared their vision of South Africa as a nonracial democracy. Under Marxist influence, the ANC leadership interpreted their struggle in terms both of race and of class, for oppression had erased the analytical distinction between these categories in the South African context. The revolutionary struggle, they believed, required mass mobilization, the patient building of organizational resources combined with prudent assessment of tactics, for "infantile leftism," or premature, romantic acts of defiance, merely invited the brutal and costly retaliation the South African government unhesitatingly delivered. The ANC, its leaders argued, must organize deeply in African communities both in urban areas and in the homelands, using all available institutional resources, including churches, trade unions, and schools.

A banned, illegal organization after 1960, the ANC was forced to move its headquarters outside South Africa. Its leaders were exiled or jailed for indefinite terms, and the organization was compelled to operate underground; persons prominently identified with the ANC were subject to imprisonment. After the 1960 Sharpeville massacre, in which sixty-seven unarmed Black demonstrators were shot and killed by the police, the ANC leadership concluded that nonviolent tactics were ineffectual against a government that responded to unarmed civil disobedience with unrestrained brutality. Armed struggle would be required; the liberation fighters of the ANC would be known as the "Spear of the Nation," headed by Joe Slovo, a White Commuist Party functionary. Though it would be required to resort to guerrilla violence, the targets would be limited where possible to government installations, thus protecting innocent civilians of all races. With few exceptions this rule held for more than a decade, despite the government's effort to stigmatize the organization as terrorist, until the ANC decided in the late 1970s that White civilians in urban areas should not be spared the costs of this struggle.

The Pan Africanist Congress (PAC) broke away from the ANC in 1959. Their ideology of racially exclusive organization and struggle maintained that Whites cannot be trusted and should not be allowed to participate in the struggle. This suspicion of White motives extended to liberals with their privileged life style and their own agenda and especially to communists, whose class analysis the PAC rejected. Africans, they believed, have a distinctive, superior, and more humanistic culture than Europeans, based on communal cooperation that they identify as African socialism.

Their racial definition of the struggle and their anti-White rhetoric ("one settler, one bullet") evoked a sympathetic response from many Africans, especially students, who found the PAC analysis more consistent with their experience and more persuasive than the more abstract analysis and nonracial program of the ANC. Instead of painstaking organization and prudent strategy, PAC was committed to direct action, convinced that episodes of dramatic defiance and personal heroism could ignite the black masses to spontaneous revolutionary action. PAC set up paramilitary units, Poqo, which attempted a number of violent actions in the early 1960s. Like ANC, PAC was banned in 1960, its leaders imprisoned, its headquarters and training facilities transferred to other countries.

PAC's subsequent history was marked by ideological and personal feuds. Incompetence, romantic strategy, internal feuds, and the ruthlessness of the South African security forces decimated the PAC and minimized its effectiveness. Yet its doctrine continued to exert a strong appeal on young Africans. Not only does the Black-White definition of the struggle make prima facie sense, but so do the militant tactics, the promise of early success though spontaneous mass uprising, and the idealistic millenarian goal of African socialism. These basic ideas were reincarnated in the 1970s Black Consciousness (BC) movement, directly influenced by the Black Power campaign in the United States and its emphasis on Black pride. In the early 1970s, BC swept through the ranks of Black students, who rejected cooperation with Whites but redefined "Black" to include Asians, Africans, and Coloureds as common victims of White oppression. BC also generated enthusiasm in the growing ranks of non-White students and was influential in precipitating the Soweto uprising in 1976–77. Black Consciousness contributed significantly to ideological mobilization; its followers have been responsible for an impressive output in the arts, especially in poetry and drama and in the reinterpretation of South African history from a Black perspective. "Azania" replaced South Africa as the name of their country. The BC movement lacked, however, the discipline, the organizational coherence, and the resilience needed to cope with infiltration, detention, and the unrelenting harassment employed by the South African police. In 1977, the torture and murder of its talented and charismatic leader, Steve Biko, while under police interrogation created yet another martyr to the liberation struggle. Biko's death was a crippling blow to the BC movement.

The emphasis on racial solidarity by PAC, BC, and, more recently, the Azanian Peoples Liberation Organization (AZAPO) continues to tap deep layers of sentiment among Blacks of all ethnic groups who see their daily oppressors as Whites sustained by a totally White power structure. In response to the mobilizing power of this doctrine, the ANC has been compelled to emphasize the national theme in its propaganda and the importance of Black solidarity without, however, sacrificing its long range commitment to nonracialism both in its tactics and its vision of South Africa's future.

A large Black mass organization is the Zulu-led Inkatha Freedom Party dominated by Chief Mangosuthu G. Buthelezi of the Zulu royal house. Inkatha is not a revolutionary organization; it eschews violent methods against the regime and has been allowed to operate freely. It benefits from the considerable patronage available to the Zulu homeland government and the still intact network of Zulu chieftains. Although the Zulu leadership refused to accept independent status for its homeland, it sees continuing value in cultivating indigenous cultures and allegiances and in organizing second tier political units along ethnic lines where this is feasible. Thus Inkatha opposes the main goal of the ANC, which advocates a majoritarian centralized government and insists on the elimination of ethnic categories as a basis for political organization. Inkatha's leadership favors a consociational pattern of government that would incorporate ethnic elements into the structure of a federalized state and grant special protection to minorities, including the White minority. This formula appeals to many Whites, but the ANC regards it as anathema, a ploy to guarantee continued White domination by dividing Blacks along ethnic lines. Inkatha remains a thorn in the side of the ANC and other Black revolutionary organizations.

Buthelezi opposed international sanctions against South Africa as damaging to the economic welfare of Blacks. His contempt for the majority of Black revolutionary politicians—with the significant exception of Nelson Mandela—is reciprocated by Black militants who condemn him as a catspaw of the White establishment. There have been bloody and lethal clashes between members of Inkatha and partisans of ANC in urban townships both in Natal and in the Transvaal. Although many urban-based Zulus reject or are indifferent to Inkatha, many others retain their affiliation either for sentimental or instrumental reasons. Its internal governance is highly authoritarian and has been marked by violence against dissident members of the Zulu nation. Because of its conservatism and its commitment to ethnic structures, Inkhata has been favorably regarded by elements of the government, including the military.

The opportunity structure for Black opposition to the apartheid system was, for four decades after 1948, as unpromising as any in the world. The security forces were lavishly financed, elaborately armed, furnished with the latest in modern transport and communications equipment, efficient and ruthless; they were assisted by an intricate and effective network of informers. Blacks, conversely, were unarmed and economically weak and dependent; their communications media were subject to instant repression; their political organizations were forced to operate underground, while institutions such as churches and labor unions were honeycombed with informers; and their principal leaders were imprisoned or exiled. The homelands were controlled by compliant personalities closely linked to the police; the urban townships on the periphery of White cities could be surrounded and cut off by the security forces. Though the economy depended increasingly on Black labor, Black unions could not sustain long work stoppages because of the sacrifices this would impose on families. Black leaders only recently learned how to use their collective consumer strength to enforce commercial boycotts. Entirely excluded from political participation, the main resources available to the Black struggle were international support and potential labor and consumer power derived from their overwhelming numerical superiority. The challenge was to convert these limited resources into political power sufficient to confront the regime's enormous repressive apparatus.

Both the ANC and PAC worked hard to secure external assistance. With consistent support from African states speaking through the Organization for African Unity and from the Third World majority in the United Nations General Assembly, they attempted, with considerable success, to harrass, stigmatize, and isolate the apartheid regime by excluding it from international forums, promoting arms embargoes, and campaigning for economic sanctions. Several of the "front-line" states in southern Africa hosted exile organizations, provided training facilities for their guerrilla units, and permitted cross-border operations to be staged from their territory, often at heavy cost in military and economic reprisals. The racial struggle in South Africa escalated into the paramount international human rights issue, consuming more time and energy of the United Nations and its affiliates than any other controversy. External assistance, including moral pressure, arms embargos, and, eventually, comprehensive economic sanctions, were crucial, for otherwise the South African government could have treated Black protest as a purely domestic problem, reducing their resistance to impotence.

For a decade or more, until the mid-1970s, the apartheid regime seemed so secure, powerful, and ruthless that it could not be effectively challenged. The prevailing attitude of many Blacks and of White sympathizers was resignation. The only hope lay in gradual reform induced by economic growth that would convince most Whites that strict apartheid was economically unnecessary and even irrational. Some of the more humiliating and oppressive aspects of apartheid could thus be abandoned, as the Afrikaner *verligtes* were proposing, but without seriously compromising the foundations of White supremacy. Internal protests by Blacks were easily contained by the authorities; small-scale guerrilla operations launched by the exile liberation organizations did little damage and had no effect on the stability of the regime. Internal opposition by the minority of mostly English-speaking Whites who demanded reform was brushed aside by the National Party government that firmly controlled all levers of power. It appeared that the government's repressive apparatus would be more than sufficient to contain internal Black protest and resistance for an indefinite period and that international efforts could only embarrass but not damage the regime.

In the mid-1970s circumstances suddenly changed. The Portugese colonies, Angola and Mozambique, which in friendly hands had served as buffers between South Africa and the independent African states, achieved independence under militant Marxist-oriented governments. Rhodesia, another buffer, would soon pass into the hands of a similar African regime. These weak governments could not threaten South Africa militarily, but as front-line states they could provide additional sanctuary and points of access for guerrilla penetration of the heartland. The cost of protecting South Africa's borders suddenly escalated and required more aggressive tactics by the security forces.

During the fifteen years after Sharpeville, a large proportion of the rapidly growing African population had become urbanized. A generation of young people had emerged in the segregated urban slums, better educated than their parents, inspired by the BC slogans of Black pride and Black power and by Maoist notions of the revolutionary mass line. The collapse of neighboring racist regimes, the ongoing insurrection in Rhodesia, and the universal international condemnation of apartheid persuaded these young men and women that White supremacy and domination were not immutable, that apartheid could and must be resisted, and that liberation could be achieved, but only by the initiative of its Black victims. As early as 1968, signaling their more militant mood, Black students broke away from the liberal White antiapartheid student organization, forming their own student association to eliminate their dependence on White paternalism and direct their own struggle for liberation.

The outbreak in Soweto, the sprawling Black slum outside Johannesburg, in June 1976 was precipitated by a decision of the minister of education—a few years later the leader of the breakaway right-wing Conservative Party—to require that Afrikaans be introduced as a compulsory language of instruction in African schools. The police overreaction to the initial student demonstrations led to a number of casualties and further inflamed the students. Police reprisals escalated, but the students refused to be cowed. Mobilized not by a formal organization that could be decapitated by the police, but by a common ideology—indeed, even a government investigation found no evidence of conspiracy or of outside instigation—students took control of the uprising in Soweto and managed it through informal committees. It soon spread to other townships throughout the republic. For several months the students rejected the cautious advice of parents, teachers, religious leaders, and Black township officials, condemning the latter as collaborators. A number of ad hoc organizations sprang up in the townships to provide practical support and assistance to the militant students who risked arrest, torture, and even death. Black deaths associated with the Soweto uprising have been conservatively estimated at more than seven hundred.

Although the students' demands were somewhat vague, shifting from improved educational facilities to the closing of saloons that profited from the despair of Black workers, the Soweto uprising was important as a generalized protest against White domination. In the absence of organizational discipline, a revolutionary movement against an entrenched and determined regime must succeed quickly or it will gradually disintegrate. The Soweto uprising suffered the latter fate. Workers began to resist the students' frequent demands that they stay away from work, resulting in several violent episodes that may have been provoked and abetted by the police. Parents were eventually able to convince their children to take the end of term examinations or risk serious setbacks to their career aspirations. The authorities gradually regained control of the townships and students returned to their classes, although an estimated four thousand slipped over the borders to join the insurgency, mostly in the ranks of the ANC.

Soweto, however, proved a major turning point. Black youth had briefly tasted power; they had even succeeded in carrying their protests to the central areas of several White cities; and for several weeks they had shocked the apartheid establishment, won international acclaim, and held the police at bay. Urban Black youth had been radicalized. Unlike their parents, they would no longer be satisfied with passive alienation. The White regime remained powerful, but not invulnerable. For the first time Coloured and Asian youth demonstrated militant solidarity with Africans, rejecting their parents' aspiration to be one day accepted into the White social order regardless of the fate of the African majority. The rhetoric of the students shifted from attacking apartheid to rejecting the whole system of "racist capitalism."

Soweto indeed shocked the regime. It had, for a time, lost control of the largest Black urban settlement in the republic—and the contagion had spread. To the business community and Afrikaner *verligtes* the message was clear: government must begin to take the needs and aspirations of urban Blacks into account. They could no longer be treated merely as guest workers with no rights in White South Africa. The need for reform, for mitigating or at least humanizing apartheid was apparent. Under the new Prime Minister, P. W. Botha, it would, however, be a managed reform, timed and controlled by the government. Expenditures on Black education were greatly increased, African trade unions were legalized, and job reservations were relaxed and in some cases eliminated. With the cooperation of the White business establishment, measures to improve the "quality of life" of urban Blacks were promoted, allowing more affluent Blacks to build and occupy middle-class housing; elected community councils were set up to provide local self-government in the urban townships; under international pressure, foreign-owned firms were permitted to provide equal pay for equal work, eliminate segregated facilities, and promote Blacks to managerial positions. A President's Council was formed to permit government to consult with Black notables selected by the regime. For the business community that had been urging the moderation of apartheid, these measures would facilitate the development of a better-trained, more stable, productive, and contented labor force; for government the changes would promote the development of a Black middle class that could aspire to and enjoy material abundance and thereby be reconciled to the prevailing social order, depriving the revolutionary forces of potential leadership. The final component of this series of reforms was the 1982 constitution that set up Coloured and Indian chambers in Parliament while continuing to exclude Africans. The government was careful to assure its White constituents that these reforms in no way undercut the mainstays of apartheid and that South Africa would remain securely under the control of Whites and specifically of Afrikaners.

Black trade unions grew rapidly and provided legal mass organizations for urban Blacks; soon they would extend their activities from bread-and-butter issues to active participation in the liberation struggle. Far from expressing gratitude for their improved economic opportunities and quality of life, middle-class Blacks, especially professionals and teachers, became the most articulate advocates for the total elimination of the disabilities imposed on them as individuals and on their people. They refused to be neutralized or coopted by selective material benefits. Reforms that only a few years earlier might have been greeted with approval and even gratitude were dismissed as trivial and irrelevant. Urban Black opinion leaders increasingly accepted the exiled and imprisoned leaders of the banned organizations, especially the ANC, as their spokesmen, even though they could not provide day-to-day direction of the struggle. Only the total elimination of apartheid and the implementation of the Fredom Charter would be acceptable.

The Black struggle was by no means unified ideologically or organizationally, but the center of gravity among urban Blacks had moved decisively to the left. Even the moderates were now demanding the elimination of apartheid and the early transfer of power to the Black majority. Black expectations had changed; substantial income gains achieved by Black workers were taken for granted and concessions by the government to improve quality of life were dismissed as inconsequential; only full equality and participation in government on a nondiscriminatory basis would be acceptable. The gap between the maximum concessions that the National Party regime was prepared to consider and the minimum demands of representative Black spokesmen seemed unbridgeable.

The period 1977–84 was marked by continuing strikes, boycotts, and protests, stepped-up guerrilla operations by the ANC, and demands from the international community for significant reforms. Reform measures enacted and promised by the government only raised Black aspirations; instead of pacifying militancy, they encouraged expressions of impatience. In August 1983, more than three hundred civic, religious, student, labor, and women's organizations from all racial communities formed a United Democratic Front (UDF). By unifying, the groups aimed to sustain the momentum of the struggle and specifically to oppose the new constitutional provisions that perpetuated apartheid. The number of affiliates soon exceeded six hundred. Reflecting the multiracial policy of the ANC, the UDF became, in effect, the legal front for that banned organization.

In late August 1984, the Black townships erupted again, precipitated by the exclusion of Africans from the new constitutional structure and by increases in rents to pay for local services. The uprising began in the townships south of Johannesburg, but soon spread, first to the eastern Cape, then to all the Black townships. Again the leaders were radicalized young people, the "comrades," working without formal organization, though some UDF-ANC influence was evident. This time the student leadership was powerfully reenforced by sympathetic workers emboldened by the successful tactics of their legalized labor unions. A variety of tactics emerged, including a successful two-day general work stoppage in November 1984 and consumer boycotts that disquieted White merchants and extracted some job concessions.

The immediate objective was to make the townships ungovernable by the White regime and its Black employees and collaborators—in effect, to convert the townships into "liberated areas." Black officials were induced to resign their posts; Black policemen who refused to resign or were suspected of being informers were forced to seek the protection of the White authorities or were "necklaced" in rubber tires and incinerated. Rent boycotts were enforced; schools were closed. The young leaders and activists quickly learned how to take advantage of the mass media, demonstrating at the funerals of their fallen comrades before foreign TV crews.

After two years the death toll had exceeded two thousand, mostly Black. Thousands more were imprisoned and detained. Prominent churchmen emerged as leading spokesmen for the Black resistance, notably Nobel Prize winner and Episcopal bishop Desmond Tutu. The UDF demanded the end of apartheid and consultations leading to a nonracial democratic regime. The ANC would have to participate in these discussions; its imprisoned leader, Nelson Mandela, was acclaimed as the symbolic representative of this struggle. Though the majority of Blacks seemed to rally around the ANC, a significant fraction of the township militants insisted on the more revolutionary PAC-AZAPO line. These cleavages led to several violent conflicts between ANC partisans and AZAPO supporters and between both of them and Inkatha forces, whose leadership opposed the township resistance as futile, unproductive violence.

So sustained and intense was resistance in the townships that for more than a year South Africa verged on civil war. The government initially responded with vigorous police action combined with more reforms. The laws against interracial marriage and sexual liaisons were repealed. The government stopped enforcing influx control and the hated pass laws—a major departure from traditional apartheid. In a technical break with orthodox apartheid doctrine and the mythology of separate development, the government formally conceded that urbanized Africans would not automatically lose their South African citizenship when their ethnic homelands accepted nominal independence. Some Africans could now reside permanently in White areas; Black capitalism would be fostered and Blacks would be allowed to operate businesses in the central commercial districts of cities, and to rent land—though they could not own it—for ninety-nine years. Though many Whites viewed those changes as far-reaching concessions, gnawing at the very foundations of apartheid, they fell far short of minimal Black demands and had no effect on the insurrection.

As these reforms failed both to quell the insurrection and to pacify international opinion, in July 1985 the government invoked its emergency powers, then extended the state of emergency for a two-year period in June 1986. It effectively muzzled the domestic press and international news services, suspended judicial protection to persons accused of violating the emergency regulations, gave the police virtually free rein to make arrests, hold prisoners under detention, and use what force was needed to regain control of the townships. By converting the country into a police state under a virtual state of siege, the government finally succeeded in suppressing the insurrection.

By mid-1988 an uneasy peace had been restored, but the alienation of urban Blacks was nearly complete. Though the task of revolutionary mobilization remained to be accomplished, ideological mobilization had been achieved and needed only to be sustained. A sign of the intensity of mobilization was the response to the call by COSATU, the Black trade union federation, for a nationwide work stoppage in June 1988 to commemorate the anniverary of the Soweto uprising; the response was overwhelming, bringing the economy for a day to a total halt. Revolutionary unrest in the townships had become endemic and could be repressed only by naked coercion. The ANC, its allies, and sympathizers could effectively control the townships and even carry the conflict for brief periods into White business and residential areas. The regime and its Black subjects had reached an impasse. The West, including the European Community and even the United States, had imposed comprehensive economic sanctions that were exacting a heavy toll on the weakened South African economy. Morally and economically, the apartheid regime was isolated and bankrupt.

Conflict Management

The task of the National Party regime in managing relations with the English-speaking minority was eased by the heterogeneous composition of that minority. Though the English-speaking establishment is of British origin, a substantial number of White immigrants during the past half-century stem from a variety of European backgrounds, including an influx after 1974 from the ex-Portugese colonies. English speakers are not a cohesive community, and they have not been mobilized into a political movement. Many share the mainline and even the hard right-wing Afrikaner views of race relations. The antiapartheid majority of English speakers expressed their liberal commitments and preferences through the opposition Progressive-Federal Party that functioned entirely through legal and nonviolent channels.

The regime respected the language, culture, and educational interests of the English-speaking minority, who enjoyed the same political rights as Afrikaners. Most important, their economic freedom was protected, assuring them the opportunity to accumulate wealth, practice their professions, and enjoy the world's highest material standard of living. They provided much of the economic dynamism that financed the elaborate Afrikaner state apparatus that maintained White domination and facilitated the embourgeoisement of the Afrikaners. The minority of English speakers and indeed of dissident Afrikaners who were not prepared to accept apartheid were free to oppose the regime through limited legal channels of protest, to emigrate (as many did), or to face the perils and sacrifices of resistance.

White control of the state was enforced by the total exclusion of non-Whites from participation in the polity. Economic subordination was assured by their exclusion from land ownership in White areas and by a White monopoly of financial, mining, industrial, and commercial assets, both private and public. To maintain this system of racial domination and to manage the conflicts it necessarily bred the South African government employed the following methods.

Exploiting divisions within the black majority. The apartheid regime created and institutionalized new ethnic categories and rigidified traditional structures among Africans. The regime's solicitude for the preservation of cultures, the promotion of "separate development" of ethnic communities, and the sponsorship of homelands were transparent attempts to foster and exploit divisions among non-Whites. Coloureds and many urbanized Africans had ethnicity thrust upon them and their descendants, whether they desired it or not. Separate residential areas, separate educational and social institutions, separate structures of administration and governance—all were designed to emphasize separate identity and solidarity, to inhibit common sentiments, organization, and strategy and to stimulate competition and conflict among non-Whites of all categories. In the township revolts, the police instigated, provoked, and abetted interethnic hostility and violence, including the predatory activities of "vigilante" gangs and assassination squads.

Coopting black leadership. Selective benefits were available to Blacks who achieved leadership positions—often with the help and continuing support of South African authorities—and who were willing to cooperate with the regime. Leaders of the ten African homelands administered substantial funds provided by the South African treasury, funds that could be withheld if circumstances required. Homelands leaders controlled substantial patronage with which they and their supporters were expected to keep their subjects quiet. Every homeland supported a battery of departments, each with ministers, senior civil servants and a complement of subaltern technicians and clerks. These officials and their subordinates were guaranteed comfortable living standards and the opportunity to gain wealth through legal and backdoor channels. They controlled licenses, school admissions, and other privileges important in the daily lives of their subjects in the homeland and even in the cities. Similar logic applied to the leadership of the Indian and Coloured houses of Parliament, who managed their "own affairs," and to administrators and officials of the urban townships. Coopted personalities were not expected to be entirely compliant; their credibility was enhanced by occcasional demonstrations of independence. They enjoyed, however, a stake in the existing system— power, material prosperity, even some prestige—all of which depended on the stability and longevity of the regime.

The tactic of promoting improved quality of life for the emergent Black urban middle class, including Black capitalism, home ownership, and local self-government merely extended the strategy of coopting potential Black leadership. The government hoped that material privileges and economic opportunities would lead professional and business leaders, the most dynamic elements in Black society, to separate themselves from the revolutionary struggle and reconcile to the regime. This strategy of conflict management failed because it actually raised expectations for equal treatment, which were then thwarted by the rules and practices of apartheid.

Fostering economic and psychological dependency. The means of production and sources of employment for nearly all Blacks were owned and controlled by Whites, and the physical survival of Black families, especially those in urban areas, depends on regular cash flow from wage employment. Black troublemakers could be discharged from their jobs and, even if they avoided criminal penalties for insubordination, could be exiled to their homelands. In labor disputes involving Blacks, government could be counted on to support employers. Meanwhile, large pools of unemployed Blacks were available to replace discharged strikers. Not surprisingly, the leaders and activists of the Black urban uprisings in 1976–77 and 1984–87 were students and unemployed youth without family responsibilities who had not directly experienced the brutal weight of economic dependency.

The effect of psychological dependency has been insidious and damaging to the Black cause. For many decades, despite courageous episodes
of protest and defiance, many Blacks were convinced that resistance was
futile: White power could not be effectively challenged, and White culture was more powerful than theirs. They internalized some of the self-
serving myths of their oppressors, debased their self-esteem, and resigned
themselves to submission. Education, religion, mass media, and the ubiq-
uity of White power reenforced these sentiments. A major objective of
the Black Consciousness movement in the 1970s was to overcome this
collective self-deprecation and sense of powerlessness by the strident af-
firmation of Black pride and Black power. Black consciousness and the
success of Black insurrections in neighboring states finally overcame this
sense of helplessness among Black youth.

Coercion and repression. The regime fashioned an intricate web of
laws designed to limit freedom of movement, organization, residence,
assembly, and expression for non-Whites. These measures were broadly
interpreted and zealously enforced by large Afrikaner civilian bureaucracies backed by an efficient police force that used physical force unhesitatingly to quell resistance. Their methods included whips, dogs,
beatings, and torture; when deemed necessary, the security forces resorted to state terrorism, including assassination. The police presence
was particularly ubiquitous and intimidating in the townships, where it
was at times reinforced by the military. Both were steadfastly supported
by a government that recognized its security services as the ultimate
defenders of a minority regime that lacked legitimacy among the majority of its subjects.

Organizations opposing the regime were outlawed as treasonous, terrorist, or communist. Individuals could be banned (a form of house arrest), detained indefinitely without trial, or imprisoned. The ability of
the judiciary to protect accused individuals was severely circumscribed,
especially during the state of emergency beginning in 1985. The electronic mass media were owned and operated by the government, the
press was intimidated, and many opposition publications were shut
down. In short, the regime commanded a professionally trained, fully
equipped, efficient and ruthless repressive apparatus that it unleashed
against domestic opponents without hesitation and with deadly effectiveness.

Total strategy. The South African defense establishment under the patronage of former state president P.W. Botha evolved a sophisticated
strategy for defending the regime which combined diplomatic, economic,

propaganda, and domestic reform measures with military and police resources. "Total strategy" involved neutralizing the neighboring "front-
line" African states by air raids and military forays against suspected
ANC training facilities and command centers within their borders, by
arming and supporting guerrilla movements against their weak governments, by interrupting transport routes through South Africa and supplies of electricity on which their fragile economies depend, and by using
South Africa's position as the regional military and economic super-
power to intimidate and neutralize hostile neighbors and reward more
compliant governments, such as Malawi. A scheme was floated to form
an economic association under South African auspices that would include the homelands and the independent southern African states in patterns of mutually beneficial economic cooperation. By building
indigenous arms production facilities, the arms embargo was largely circumvented, and agreements with governments and corporations willing
to trade profitably with a pariah state helped the regime to counteract
economic sanctions.

Under this doctrine of resisting the "total onslaught" by "total strategy," petty apartheid and similar measures were to be dispensed with,
for they were unnecessary to the protection of the regime but needlessly
antagonized and humiliated non-Whites and tarnished South Africa's
reputation internationally. Much of the inspiration for Botha's reforms
beginning in 1979 came not only from international pressure, Black resistance, and the business community, but from a military establishment
that was prepared to go much farther toward modernizing and humanizing racial domination than many Afrikaner politicians. The mainline
National Party leadership converted to the total strategy doctrine and
the domestic reforms that it implied when the military establishment
emerged from the Soweto uprising as the most influential interest group
in the government. But though it rejected doctrinaire ideological apartheid and promoted expedient reforms, total strategy remained unmistakably committed to maintaining White minority rule.

Collapse of Apartheid and Transformation
of South Africa's Politics

On February 2, 1990, the new National Party leader and state president,
F. W. de Klerk, electrified his countrymen with the announcement that

his government intended to unban, to legalize the leading resistance organizations, the ANC, PAC, and the Communist Party, which had been
outlawed since 1960 as terrorist conspiracies. Their leaders, including
Nelson Mandela, who had been imprisoned since 1963, were to be re-
leased, political prisoners freed, and exiles permitted to return. The following day Mandela entered Cape Town to a globally televised hero's
welcome that signalled the impending demise of the apartheid regime.
Fresh reforms had been anticipated to appease international opinion, but
few expected so abrupt a reversal of policy from a National Party government. Why did the elites of the Afrikaner National Party feel compelled to retreat from a regime that their forebears had struggled
mightily to establish and that had conferred such great advantages on
its constituents?

The National Party leadership had reluctantly concluded that the
moral and economic costs of maintaining apartheid were no longer sus-
tainable. The urban insurrection of 1984 had been contained by ruthless
"emergency" measures that had stretched the state's repressive capacities, yet the underlying political and economic grievances could reignite
at any time. During the 1980s the economy had stagnated; now it was
actually shrinking. Economic sanctions by the European Community
and the United States precipitated an economic crisis. Sanctions had shut
off new foreign investment, capital was fleeing the country, trade was
embargoed, and foreign bank loans were unobtainable. As the Cold War
dissolved, the United States and its allies had no further interest in protecting the apartheid regime. Leaders of the business community, Afrikaner as well as Anglo, had been pleading with the government to
initiate reforms that would induce the West to call off the sanctions.
Beginning in 1987, the government under P. W. Botha had been conducting secret negotiations with Mandela, offering to release him from
prison and unban the ANC if ANC would agree to forego armed struggle
and repudiate its links with the Communist Party, conditions which
Mandela rejected. Meanwhile, business leaders and academics had been
meeting outside South Africa with senior officials of the ANC in exile.

Cautious reforms designed to modernize and humanize apartheid
would not suffice. The basic structures would have to be dismantled and
negotiations would have to begin with the ANC to move toward a nonracial polity while protecting the rights, institutions, and property of the
White minority. De Klerk and his associates had been persuaded by
polling data that a majority of the White electorate, including the Afri-

kaner middle class, recognized the inevitability of far-reaching institutional reforms; they would support the government that initiated them
as long as basic White interests were safeguarded. A timely stroke disabled President Botha and brought to the National Party and the state
presidency fresh leadership willing to initiate the necessary if painful
changes. Once the ANC was legalized, negotiations might begin. But
Mandela and his associates refused to negotiate as long as apartheid
prevailed, nor would they suspend armed struggle until negotiations
were underway. Their intransigence paid off.

In February 1991, de Klerk announced in Parliament that key elements of the apartheid structure—the Population Registration Act that
classified all persons compulsorily by race, the Group Areas Act that
segregated residence and public services, and the Lands Acts that restricted Black ownership of land to 13 percent of the total—would be
repealed. The homelands, however, would not be scrapped, nor would
Blacks be enfranchised until a new constitution had been enacted. De
Klerk pledged, however, that his government was committed to universal
adult suffrage in a democratic and unified South Africa. Essential pre-
conditions having been met, negotiations could begin in December 1991.
Nineteen organizations representing all the racial communities sent delegates to the Conference on Democracy in South Africa (CODESA). Extremist groups, including the White Conservative Party and the Black
Pan-Africanist Congress, refused to participate.

The negotiating parties carefully monitored their constituencies. In
March 1992, after the National Party suffered defeats by hard-line conservatives in two by-elections, de Klerk called a referendum among
White voters to endorse the negotiation process; 68 percent, including a
majority of Afrikaners, gave de Klerk the mandate he needed to continue
negotiations. Every decision that might be construed as compromising
the ANC's policies had to be evaluated in terms of its acceptability to the
ANC's militant factions and the possibility that the ANC might be outbidden by extremist Black organizations. The political environment of
the negotiations was contaminated by lethal episodes of violence occur-
ring mainly between Inkatha and ANC supporters. Over a four-year period this violence claimed more than ten thousand lives, the toll in some
months climbing to five hundred. Government security forces were ineffective in containing this mayhem, and Mandela and the ANC accused
government agencies of financing, arming, and provoking Inkatha in
order to undermine the ANC, charges that proved to be true; in December

1992, de Klerk summarily dismissed twenty-three senior military officers for complicity in these offenses. Random killings of Whites by the Azanian Peoples Liberation Army and reprisals by White extremists further inflamed fears on both sides. Economic recession contributed to the climate of uncertainty, distrust, and frustration that threatened large-scale interracial violence.

Nevertheless, behind-the-scenes discussions proceeded, for both wary and suspicious partners, the ANC and the National Party, were eager for an early settlement that would vindicate their decisions to enter into negotiations. The ANC needed the National Party to deliver essential White support; the National Party, which expected to play a prominent role in future governments, needed the ANC because of Mandela's moderate leadership and its command of majority Black support. In preparation for an eventual vote, each party attempted to expand its support base. Having eliminated its traditional color bar, the National Party began aggressively to enroll non-Whites, especially Coloureds and Indians, and to set up offices in the Black townships; the ANC focused on strengthening its organization among Blacks and cultivating leaders in the tribal homelands. The purpose of CODESA was to agree on the main principles to guide an elected constituent assembly that would frame the new nonracial constitution. The vast distance originally separating the National Party from the ANC can be gleaned from the following issues.

(1) The ANC's point of departure was a majoritarian parliamentary system limited only by a bill of rights to protect individuals and minorities. The National Party demanded consociational power sharing that guarantees minority (White) participation in the executive organs of government and a veto in matters that affect their vital interests.

(2) The ANC favored a centralized government that can act decisively and redistribute resources and opportunities to disadvantaged individuals, regions, and communities. The National Party preferred a federalized system with substantial devolution of taxing and spending powers to regional authorities.

(3) The ANC's Freedom Charter advocated the nationalization of mines, banks, and major industries so that government, representing the majority, can control the commanding heights of the economy. It also insisted on far-reaching land reform. As Whites control more than 88 percent of economic assets, the National Party insisted on the protection of property rights and a market-oriented economy.

(4) The National Party advocated continuity in the existing institu-

tions of the state, including the security forces. The ANC demanded the establishment of new institutions to replace the security forces that have acted as instruments of their oppression.

Despite these differences, continuing mutual distrust, inflammatory rhetoric, and extreme sensitivity to the reactions of their constituents, the ANC and the National Party were able to work out important compromises. The National Party abandoned its demand for a second house of Parliament in which overrepresented minorities could block legislation; minority membership in Parliament would instead be assured by proportional representation. ANC conceded a substantial measure of regional autonomy and agreed to the protection of property rights as essential to attracting foreign investment and retaining the capital and skills of the White minority. Land redistribution and equalization of public services for Blacks might be financed in part by raising the South African tax rate from 27 percent of gross domestic product to European levels of about 35 percent, combined with savings from eliminating the bureaucracies that enforced apartheid. The ANC conceded the principle of institutional continuity as long as substantial non-White participation could be assured in the officer ranks of the security services and in senior civil service positions. Both parties agreed to the principle of a judicially enforceable bill of rights to protect personal and property rights.

Final agreement was thwarted, however, and CODESA was forced to suspend its sessions in June 1992, because the National Party insisted that 75 percent of the members of the proposed constituent assembly should be required to ratify a new constitution, while the ANC would not agree to more than 70 percent. This narrow margin reflected the need for both parties to demonstrate that they were tough negotiators and to assure their nervous constituents that their vital interests were being protected. All the political organizations attempted to discredit their opponents within and across the racial divide. Yet negotiations continued, culminating in an agreement that elections based on universal adult suffrage would be held on April 26, 1994, for the national parliament and for regional assemblies based on proportional representation. A multiparty transition executive council with a Black majority was empowered to monitor the government's interim performance and by a 75 percent majority actually override government measures and actions.

As the elites of the ANC and the National Party engage in pragmatic bargaining, their partisans on the streets and in the media indulge in provocative charges and countercharges. Hard-liners among Whites and Blacks mobilize to undermine these fragile agreements. Included in their

"Freedom Alliance" are White extremists who insist that they cannot live in a Black-dominated state; they threaten violence and demand an independent Afrikaner homeland in an unspecified area of the country. Their secessionist demands are echoed in Inkatha circles that demand independence or extensive regional autonomy for Kwa Zulu. The intransigent White cause has been taken up by a group of retired Afrikaner army generals who claim that a majority of Whites now support them, panicking as the prospect of Black rule becomes an imminent possibility. ANC-Inkatha violence continues without letup in the townships. Interracial ambushes, killings, and reprisals occur, in rural as well as urban areas. Anti-White rhetoric is heard not only among PAC and AZAPO supporters, but in the ranks of the ANC as well. The security forces seem unable or unwilling to stem the violence. There is widespread concern that fear, mistrust, accumulated hatreds, and extremism may produce social anarchy, blocking the orderly institutional transition that has been painstakingly negotiated.

Though the shape of the emergent political dispensation in the new South Africa is not clear, it will represent a fundamental transformation in this pluralistic, multiracial, multiethnic polity. No longer sanctioned by law, collective racial and ethnic solidarities will, nevertheless, continue to function as political realities, crosscut, however, by pragmatic interracial and interethnic coalitions. A "grand coalition" between the ANC and the National Party is likely at least during the first five years of the new regime. The continuing hostility between, for example, Zulu and Xhosa and the unwillingness of White and Black extremists to accept a compromise settlement ensure that political violence will persist. The high expectations of Blacks for economic improvements to match their political liberation will certainly be disappointed; even under optimistic assumptions, the economy will not be able to provide employment for the estimated 50 percent of Black youth now without jobs, plus annual increments to the labor force from a rapidly growing population. Whites will be uneasy about their political status, their property rights, and the economic prospects of their children. Many Black former freedom fighters and political cadres will have difficulty finding employment in the security forces and in government. Within a capitalist market economy, group inequalities will continue, Whites and Asians relatively privileged, Blacks relatively deprived. These realities will contribute to political tensions. Moreover, the skilled and enlightened statesmanship of Mandela and de Klerk cannot be guaranteed for the future.

Such uncertainties and elements of conflict threaten the transition to a democratic but Black-led nonracial polity. New rules and processes of conflict management will have to be shaped and implemented for a society that will have to cope for the indefinite future with mobilized ethnic and racial divisions. Whatever the future holds, however, the apartheid regime will be gone and the rules of the game irreversibly transformed.

5

Israelis and Palestinians: Whose Land?

For nearly a century the 10,429 square miles between the Jordan River and the Mediterranean Sea have witnessed the unremitting struggle of two antagonistic national liberation movements for control of the same small territory. Each party has asserted exclusive claims to this territory—Land of Israel/Palestine—and dismissed the legitimacy of the other. The dispute has drawn the intervention of numerous states, regional neighbors, international organizations, and superpowers and has escalated into an issue of global significance. Despite heavy and continuing casualties on both sides, it has eluded all efforts at settlement or even interim accommodation.

The First Half Century, 1897–1948

Zionism, or modern Jewish nationalism, was triggered by the resurgence of European anti-Semitism during the final two decades of the nineteenth century. Not only in autocratic and backward tsarist Russia but even in France, the cradle of the European enlightenment, reactionary authorities could successfully draw on deep layers of popular sentiment to stir up violent expressions of anti-Jewish hatred and rejection. Enthusiastic expectations that enlightenment and progress would insure political and social emancipation seemed to be shattered. The notorious Dreyfus case in France shocked and depressed some of Europe's most assimilated Jews; try as they might, would they always be marginal to European Christian society? Would they forever be physically and psychologically vulnerable? Having rejected the centuries-old ghetto mentality of a sub-ordinated minority condemned to survive by sufferance pending the messianic redemption, these westernized intellectuals began to seek a substitute for the European enlightenment that had failed them.

They found it in secular nationalism, the dominant political ideology of their era. If every nation is entitled by natural law to self-determination, then Jews, one of the world's oldest surviving nations, could not be denied that right. A proper nation must, however, be sovereign over a particular territory. Though other territories were briefly considered, there was never much doubt that that territory would have to be Palestine, the ancient homeland pledged to them by God. Although their ancestors had been exiled nearly two thousand years ago, the Jewish people had never forgotten Palestine in their prayers. Political Zionism, as it evolved, defined the Jewish people as a secular national community, but the movement drew on deep layers of tradition and religious sentiment, the yearning for the return to Zion and for redemption from exile and oppression. According to the dominant social-democratic stream in Zionist thought, Jews could become a proper nation only if they became once again a "normal" people with a normal division of labor, especially in productive activities such as agriculture. Their society would contain a normal share of thieves and prostitutes as well as scholars and priests. But though Jews would once again become a normal people, they would not abandon their calling as the chosen people. They would be obliged to create a new society based on prophetic ideals of justice, both within Jewish society and in relation to their neighbors. The new Jerusalem would indeed be a "light unto the nations," incorporating the most advanced nineteenth century ideals of political and social democracy. As every normal nation is marked by its own language, the vehicle of its distinctive culture, so must the Jewish nation. That national language could not be one of the voices of exile, but only the original and authentic Hebrew. The conversion of liturgical Hebrew, a dead language, to a modern language of daily intercourse became the major, and eventually successful, cultural objective of the Zionist movement.

Despite the formidable diplomatic and communications talents of its senior leaders in the diaspora, including the redoubtable Theodore Herzl and Chaim Weitzmann, and the dedicated commitment of numerous activists, only a small minority of Jews initially rallied to the Zionist cause. Its active opponents included those who continued to regard the Jewish people as a religious rather than a national community. On the one hand were the ultraorthodox who condemned political Zionism as heresy, presuming to preempt the will of God who in his own good time would decide when His anointed Messiah would lead His people back to Jerusalem in glory. On the other hand were reformed Jews whose confidence in the inevitability of enlightened progress remained unimpaired, who aspired to be accepted as full and equal participants in the democratic polities of Europe and North America; they feared that Zionism, by defining Jews as a nation, would expose them to dangerous charges of dual loyalty. Joining them in principled opposition to Zionism were Jewish Marxists, confident that proletarian solidarity and the victory of socialism would eliminate oppression of all kinds. They regarded nationalism as a reactionary sentiment and urged Jews to join the fight for socialism, which alone could insure justice for all classes and all peoples.

Outside these circles the great majority of Jews, though sympathetic to any activity that might enhance the security, pride, and well-being of their people, limited their support to small financial contributions. Millions in Eastern Europe saw their future in the new world and migrated to the United States, the land of freedom and opportunity. The less venturesome determined to make their lives, however unsatisfactory, under familiar conditions in their countries of residence. Few were prepared for the risks of pioneering in a backward, remote, and dangerous country. From 1897 to 1930, a time of few political inhibitions to immigration, the Jewish population in Palestine increased from 25,000 to a mere 180,000, less than 1 percent of world Jewry.

In Palestine as well as in the diaspora, the fledgling Zionist movement was densely organized and sharply divided. The umbrella World Zionist Organization contained three main streams, each with its own organizational networks, publications, educational systems, economic enterprises, and fund-raising activities. The first of these were religious Zionists, convinced that nationalism and the return to Zion were fully consistent with God's will; their main concern was to insure that orthodox religious laws and practices would prevail in the new society. The second stream included the general Zionists, representing the nonideological strain among middle-class elements in the diaspora. They favored free enterprise in a religiously tolerant and democratic political framework. Though dominant in the diaspora, they were subordinate in Palestine to the third stream, the labor Zionists, democratic socialists committed to a pioneering, egalitarian, secular, workers' commonwealth loosely associated with the international socialist movement. Though labor Zionism experienced many internal divisions, some of them bitter and sectarian, including the expulsion of the communists after the Russian Revolution, it became the leading force in the Yishuv (the Zionist community in Palestine) through such institutions as its labor union (Histadrut), its network of agricultural settlements (Kibbutzim and Moshavim), its paramilitary defense units (Haganah and Palmach), and its political wing (Mapai). Under such determined leaders as David ben Gurion, it became the leading force in the struggle for independence and in the formation of the state.

Outside the organizational framework of the Zionist movement was a fourth group, the revisionists, antisocialist, hostile to labor unions, convinced of the unremitting antagonism of all Arabs, and committed to military methods in pursuit of their goal of a Greater Israel on both banks of the Jordan.

Despite these ideological and organizational cleavages and the acrimonious disputes that they continually generated, the ultimate goal of all Zionists was independent statehood in all of Palestine. For tactical reasons, however, this theme was muted in favor of the concept of a "national home," less threatening to Ottoman authorities and local Arabs before 1917 and to the British who took over thereafter under a League of Nations mandate. As long as the number of Jews in absolute terms and in relation to native Arabs remained small, statehood was not a plausible option. In Europe and North America, many Jews and non-Jews who sympathized with the idea of a refuge for the oppressed had grave misgivings about a Jewish state. No purpose would be served by aggravating these fears when the practical possibilities were so limited. But to committed Zionists, including all its leaders, statehood was always the goal. There would be little purpose in creating yet another society where Jews would exist by sufferance as a vulnerable minority.

The most agonizing ideological issue confronted by the Zionists arose from the presence of a large, settled Arab population in the area they intended to reclaim for themselves. No informed Zionist took seriously the vulgar popular slogan "a land without people for a people without a land". Zionist thinkers pondered the unpleasant—and to some the unacceptable—predicament that their national liberation movement might conflict with and even displace or subordinate an established population that bore no responsibility for their oppression.

In grappling with this moral dilemma, Zionists rationalized their activities in various ways. The socialists viewed Arabs as a backward, impoverished proletariat exploited by a selfish and callous ruling class. Zionism would bring great benefits to the Arab masses in the form of higher living standards, health conditions, and educational and cultural advancement. Greatly improved economic conditions and quality of life for the Arab masses would establish foundations for harmonious coexistence. Zionism would benefit everyone in Palestine except the exploitative elites and their hangers-on. Arabs would, of course, enjoy complete religious and cultural freedom; there would be no effort to absorb Arabs, Muslim or Christian, into Jewish society. The Arab masses would be grateful for a much higher material and cultural quality of life; the small minority who would insist on national political expression could be persuaded to move to one of the many Arab countries where they could participate politically as part of the majority. This form of optimistic self-deception based on a putative crossnational working-class solidarity was indulged in, primarily by labor Zionists attempting to reconcile the aspirations of Jewish nationalism with the democratic rights of a local, working-class majority who would somehow be willing to forego their own national aspirations.

Revisionists, by contrast, anticipated that Arabs would be as militant in defending their national rights as any other people confronted by foreign colonizers. They foresaw a long and violent struggle that would have to be decided by resolute military action, by confronting the Arabs with an unyielding "iron wall" to which they must ultimately submit. Like all Zionists, revisionists were convinced that Jews had superior moral and historical claims to all of Palestine, but Arabs could not be expected to acquiesce voluntarily in these claims. Arabs who chose to remain in the Jewish state, in the Land of Israel, would be guaranteed cultural autonomy and generous political rights as individuals, but never as a national minority.

The majority of Zionists fell between these polar extremes and believed that despite unfortunate national antagonisms, common sense would prevail and Arabs would accommodate in practical ways to the benign Jewish presence. Moreover, they had many options in other Arab countries, whereas there was only one small country available for a Jewish homeland. The idea of large population transfers to clear the land of unwanted Arabs was never seriously argued in responsible Zionist circles. The notion of a binational, bicultural, consociational state in which Jews and Arabs would share power was propounded by a faction of labor Zionists and a small group of prestigious Jewish intellectuals, but because it denied the essential aspiration of a Jewish state it gained little support in Zionist circles and could not survive violent expressions of Arab hostility.

The Zionist struggle, first for a national home, then for statehood, was waged simultaneously on two fronts: on the ground in Palestine and in the diplomatic and political arenas of Europe and North America. In the diaspora within Jewish society, Zionists battled for political support, for money to finance immigration, land purchase, and settlements, and for the commitment of individual Jews to move to Palestine. What had once appeared a remote and romantic dream was suddenly transformed into the realm of reality by the Balfour Declaration of November 1917, in which the British government, the leading power of that era, pledged itself to "view with favor the establishment in Palestine of a national home for the Jewish people," but without prejudice to "the civil and religious rights of existing non-Jewish communities." The Balfour Declaration was the product of intense diplomatic pressure by a small group of talented and dedicated Zionist leaders. Britain desperately needed help in its war against Germany, and the British government at that critical time was in the hands of such Zionist sympathizers as Lloyd George, Churchill, and Balfour. The Balfour Declaration was followed by the League of Nations mandate which incorporated its language and provided essential international legitimacy to the Zionist enterprise.

In Palestine, the Ottoman rulers and the Young Turks who had seized power in 1908 were deeply suspicious of the intentions of European settlers and opposed all nationalist movements among their subject peoples. Though they did nothing to facilitate Zionist immigration, they did not prevent it until the outbreak of World War I, which they entered on the side of Germany. In fact, it was less the hostility of the Turkish rulers than the severity of pioneering conditions, the lack of capital and basic amenities, and the disinterest of diaspora Jews that limited the flow of immigrants during the Ottoman period.

During the first two decades of British administration, however, the opportunity structure for Zionist settlement was highly favorable, despite unremitting and frequently violent opposition from Arabs and gradual retreat of the British from the terms of the Balfour Declaration under pressure from Arab governments. In the late 1930s, the British decided to abandon the Balfour Declaration, and under the 1939 White Paper they severely limited immigration and land purchases precisely when the Nazi regime was initiating its Final Solution in Europe. After

1939, legal immigration virtually ceased. Yet the two decades of British protection and the emergence of Nazi rule in Germany enabled the Zionist community in Palestine to increase its strength to five hundred thousand. Less than 3 percent of World Jewry and but a third of the Arab population of Palestine, Jews in Palestine nevertheless constituted a determined, highly mobilized critical mass. With the help of the British, they survived the Arab rebellion of 1936–39. Cooperation with the British in repressing the Arab rebellion and during World War II provided invaluable military experience and skills that prepared the Zionists for the battle for independence in 1948–49.

Resources were meagre, and the costs of immigration, land purchase, housing, settlement, and construction of social and economic infrastructure were high. There was no financial help from any government. A few highly placed European Jews sponsored settlements and provided funds as charitable obligations, but the Zionist movement was chronically impecunious. At times settlement efforts virtually ceased for lack of funds and for lack of immigrants. Since most prosperous Jews in the diaspora had other priorities, most of the money for Zionist enterprises was raised in small amounts from ordinary Jews making voluntary contributions. From 1933, when the Nazis took power, until 1938, Jews who left Germany were allowed to take some of their capital with them. This boosted the Jewish economy in Palestine. By the time American Jews became aroused by the Nazi pogrom of November 1938 and substantial fund-raising became possible, legal immigration and land acquisition had been terminated by the British.

Lack of unity among diaspora Jewry and their disinclination to move to Palestine were severe handicaps mitigated somewhat by Christian sympathizers who provided moral and even political support at critical times. Such support could not have been mobilized without a small group of devoted visionaries who dedicated themselves through many discouraging years to what often seemed a hopeless cause. With few exceptions, Zionist leadership in the diaspora during the first half of the twentieth century came not from the established economic and religious elites of world Jewry, but from a group of maverick intellectuals who had to appeal to Jewish publics over the skeptical and often hostile heads of their established leaders.

The Zionist goal was never in doubt: to build a Jewish homeland and eventually a national state for the Jewish people in all of Palestine. The first phase of the Zionists' dual strategy involved diplomatic initiatives to win support from governments that would permit and protect the colonizing enterprise. This unceasing diplomatic activity included failed efforts to abort the 1939 White Paper and to persuade the Allies during World War II to relax limitations on immigration.

The second element of Zionist strategy involved practical efforts on the ground in Palestine: the reception of immigrants, the acquisition of land, the establishment of settlements, and the construction of economic infrastructure and of social and cultural institutions. They began building from scratch the institutions of a new society. The dominant theme was the pioneering ethos, the reconquest of the land through Jewish labor. The desert would be made to bloom again. Emergent Zionist economic institutions and enterprises, especially those funded and sponsored through the Jewish National Fund, excluded native Arabs, even those displaced by land purchases. Scarce job opportunities had to be reserved for Jewish immigrants who, in order to achieve real independence, would have to learn to master all the skills required in a normal society. In the 1920s the Zionists began to build the network of institutions operating in the Hebrew language—governmental, economic, military, educational—that evolved into the structures of the state in 1948. Thus two parallel, exclusive, and hostile societies, with entirely separate institutions, came to confront one another in this small territory.

The critical event that finally mobilized world Jewry behind the Zionist cause was, paradoxically, the success of German Nazism. Virulent anti-Semitism posed such an imminent threat to Jewish survival, that previously indifferent, non-Zionist and even anti-Zionist Jews in the diaspora became convinced of the desperate need of a haven for their persecuted brethren, first in Germany, then in the vast areas of Europe occupied by the Nazis after 1938. This recognition came too late to rescue the great majority of European Jews, given the closing of Palestine by the 1939 White Paper and the unwillingness of other countries to accept Jewish refugees in substantial numbers. The mobilization of the intact Jewish communities, especially in North America, brought powerful pressure on the international community to open Palestine to the displaced survivors of the Holocaust. It also persuaded international opinion and the governments that formed the new United Nations Organization that these victims must have some place to go and that the only practical possibility was a part, at least, of Palestine, even though the prospect of a Jewish state evoked bitter protest from the Arab world.

The Emergence of Palestinian Nationalism

During four centuries of Ottoman rule, which began in 1517, Palestine was administered from Damascus as two counties of Southern Syria. The lives of its inhabitants were governed by kinship and tribal structures and allegiances, linked to an abstract identification with the "nation" of Islam headed by the Ottoman Sultan who was simultaneously Caliph of Islam. Arab national sentiment as a political aspiration began to emerge only toward the close of the nineteenth century when educated members of the Christian minorities familiar with European nationalist ideas began to promote the secular concept of a distinctive Arab nation. The 1908 victory of the Young Turks dedicated to Turkish nationalism stimulated nationalist sentiments and activity among subject peoples of the rapidly declining empire. Arab nationalism became an important political force during and immediately after World War I, when the Ottoman regime crumbled. Palestinians participated actively in the new Arab nationalist movement, but their dominant leaders and spokesmen favored participation in a Greater Syria under the Hashemite King Faisal.

A distinctive Palestinian national feeling was prompted by circumstances. The toppling of Faisal's short-lived regime in Damascus by the French Army in 1920 and the establishment of British administration on both sides of the Jordan under the League of Nations mandate concentrated the minds of Palestine's Arab elites on this territorially bounded political structure. The British mandate provided a defined arena over which Palestinian Arabs could exert some direct political influence. A further mobilizing factor was the concomitant threat of Zionist encroachment, an expression of European colonialism sponsored and patronized by the British authorities, which could directly affect their lives and well-being. For nearly a half century, however, Palestine's Arabs were cross-pressured by two competing allegiances, Pan-Arabism and Palestinian nationalism, and for most of this period the latter was the dominant influence.

Resistance to the Zionist threat became a mission not only of the Palestinians but of the entire Arab world. Despite bitter antagonisms between competing Arab governments and claimants to Pan-Arab leadership, Arabs united in militant and principled opposition to Zionism. Within Palestine, competitors for political leadership differed in relative emphasis on Palestinian and Pan-Arab themes and strategies, but all recognized that Arab governments, though not always reliable, represented an indispensable asset in their conflicts both with the British and the Zionists.

The Arab position on Zionism was united, categorical, and inflexible: Palestine is and has been Arab and predominantly Muslim for at least thirteen hundred years; it belongs to its native inhabitants. During this long period the Jewish presence in Palestine was negligible. Jews are a religious, not a national community and in any case they have no legitimate moral or historical claim to this land. Arabs are in no way responsible for the oppression of Jews in the Christian world and should not be expected to pay the price for Europe's sins. Zionist immigration and land acquisition should be terminated; the settlers should leave the area and return to their lands of origin. Resistance to this expression of latter-day European colonialism is a sacred obligation of all Arabs and all Muslims. Armed struggle is an appropriate weapon against Zionists as it would be against any foreign invader. While many Zionists agonized over relations with Arabs, seeking to reconcile Jewish and Arab interests, there were no such complications on the Arab side. At the ideological level, Zionism was simple and total anathema.

During the British Mandate the opportunity structure for the propagation of Palestinian nationalism was more favorable than at any time before or after. British authorities encouraged the political mobilization of Palestinian Arabs as long as their tactics remained peaceful. Some British officials sympathized with Palestinians as the native underdogs and considered their mobilization necessary to counterbalance the more aggressive Zionists. Others believed that political participation would favor more moderate and responsible Arabs, facilitating thereby the governance of the territory. Arab nationalism and anti-Zionism could be freely propagated in the press and in educational and religious institutions. The British installed as Mufti of Jerusalem the leading proponent of Palestinian nationalism, Haj Amin el Husseini, and invested him not only with the moral authority of that office but also with control of the substantial patronage and charitable endowments of the Muslim Waqf. Haj Amin's formidable talents were directed at diplomacy, agitation, and finally organized violence that was employed not only against Jews but also against Arabs who were inclined to compromise or proposed coexistence with the Zionists. The Mufti's activities were tolerated by the British until large-scale violence was turned against them in the Arab Revolt of 1936–39. At heavy cost the British security forces finally destroyed the Arab paramilitary infrastructure and Haj Amin was forced to flee the country. The Arab Revolt was successful, however, in that it precipitated the abandonment by the British of the Balfour Declaration.

After the Arabs had categorically rejected the 1937 Peel Commission recommendation for the partitioning of Palestine, the White Paper of 1939 severely curtailed legal Jewish immigration and land purchases. Violence had paid off for the Palestinians.

Leaders of the Palestinian mobilization during the Mandate period came from the patrician families of Jerusalem who combined wealth with education and social prestige. In advocating their cause they enjoyed ready access to the British authorities and to the elites of the Arab states. Through extensive kinship and clientele networks, including leading landowners and merchants, they drew support from a society that was at once the most modernized in the Arab world yet still integrated along patrimonial lines. The Husseini, led by Haj Amin, were the more powerful and militant force; their main competitors, the Nashashibi, with close links to the Hashemite ruler in Transjordan, were more flexible in their tactics and less inclined to violence. Their common goal, however, was the containment and eventual elimination of Zionism, followed by the withdrawal of the British and the emergence of a regime sympathetically linked with the Arab states and the Muslim world.

The Palestinian leadership deployed considerable resources in their struggle against the Zionist threat. Palestinians constituted a large majority of the population—more than two-thirds even after the peak of Zionist immigration in the 1930s—distributed over all areas of the country. Though socially and technologically backward, the Arab population was united in a nascent, cross-class, and inclusive national movement in opposition to Zionism; it provided support and cover for political agitation and paramilitary activities directed by the national leadership. Income and patronage from the Muslim endowments maintained a substantial propaganda network. Other Arab governments, too, were a vital resource in influencing international opinion and finally in turning the British against the Zionist cause. They provided moral, diplomatic, and financial support, as well as weapons and supplies for the Palestinian paramilitary units. As the British withdrew in April and May 1948, the Arab governments moved their armies into Palestine in a coordinated effort to destroy the usurping "Zionist entity" and put an end once and for all to the Zionist threat.

Conflict Management during the British Period

The British who administered Palestine for three decades felt they must reconcile their responsibility to facilitate a Jewish national home with their obligation to protect the civil and religious rights of the Arab majority. In attempting to administer a prototype of the "plural society," they faced what many colonial powers encountered: two hostile peoples, each with a complete set of exclusive institutions, who interacted only in the marketplace and were kept at peace only by the coercive power of the colonial authorities.

British imperial interests complicated the situation. After their victory in World War I the British had little further need for the Zionists. The emergence of Arab states—Syria, Iraq, and Transjordania in the former territories of the Ottoman Empire, the rise of the Saudi kingdom in the Arabian peninsula, and the presence of Egypt on both banks of the Suez meant that Arabs had become a factor in the defense of the imperial lifeline to India and the Far East and in the security of the vital petroleum supply from the Persian Gulf. Thus, though they were committed by international agreement to the Balfour Declaration, the British had to take Arab sentiments increasingly into account.

Their main task was to preserve order and operate essential public services while attempting to balance the often irreconcilable aspirations of the two mobilized national communities. The Arabic and Hebrew languages both received official recognition. Efforts to form a representative assembly with limited legislative powers failed, the Arabs refusing in principle to thus legitimize the Zionist presence, the Zionists declining to accept minority representation in such a body. While maintaining control of all key positions, the British attempted to distribute jobs, contracts, and government services equitably among the communities and their separate institutions, usually by population ratios, to the evident dissatisfaction of both parties.

Since the Palestinians were the more aggrieved party—opposing in principle all Zionist activities—they initiated the violent challenge to the *pax brittanica.* Sporadic deadly attacks on Zionist settlements and on individual Jews were mounted throughout this period, but they only occurred on a large and organized scale with heavy losses of life in 1920–21, 1929, and especially during the Arab Revolt of 1936–39. In every case British security forces succeeded in suppressing these outbreaks, but they led to significant concessions to appease the Arabs. The British tried to protect Zionist lives and property while gradually yielding to Arab demands to circumscribe the Jewish homeland by reducing its area, limiting immigration, and restricting land purchases.

The Palestinians demanded the departure of the British and the formation of a unified independent state controlled by the native majority.

These demands became more pronounced when the British and the French, respectively, yielded their mandates in Iraq in 1932 and Syria in 1936 to Arab regimes. The Zionists, however, needed the British to protect their fledgling community while they expanded their numbers and strengthened their institutions and fighting capacity. Tensions between the Zionists and British were exacerbated by the 1939 White Paper and the subsequent refusal of the British to budge from its terms.

By participating in Britain's war effort after 1939, Zionists gained important military experience. Their economy responded vigorously to opportunities created by the large British military buildup in the Middle East. After World War II, the organized Yishuv and the international Zionist movement sought to break the British blockade on immigration, precipitating violent guerrilla encounters with the British authorities and terrorist tactics by Zionist fringe groups determined to destabilize British rule. Zionists of all persuasions gradually concluded that Britiain had become the main obstacle to the rescue and redemption of the surviving victims of the Holocaust and to further development of the Zionist pro gram. They would be better off if the British left, even though they would have to face the inevitable Arab onslaught on their own.

For opposite reasons Arabs and Jews in the 1940s demanded that the British depart. The expedient of partitioning the territory into Jewish and Arab regions and committing Jerusalem to international trusteeship was accepted by the Zionists, but categorically rejected by the Arabs. Concluding that the moral, political, and economic costs of sustaining the mandate had become intolerable and that these antagonistic national communities had been taken over by extremists and could never be reconciled, the British in 1947 threw in the towel and transferred responsibility to the United Nations Organization. Conflict management to maintain order in this plural society characterized by intense intercommunal hatred between highly mobilized national movements would have required the deployment of an overwhelming preponderance of force. As this was not affordable, Britain decided to withdraw, leaving their former wards to settle their fate.

War of Independence/Palestine War

On November 29, 1947, the United Nations approved the majority report of its Special Committee on Palestine (UNSCOP) that called for the partitioning of Palestine into Jewish and Arab sectors, reserving Jerusalem and the Holy Places for international administration. The boundaries were similar to those proposed by the British Royal Commission a decade earlier. Like the 1937 proposal, this too was denounced by all the Arab states but accepted by the Zionists as international recognition of Jewish statehood, the best they could expect under the circumstances, even though the territory assigned to them was far less than biblical Palestine or than what had been promised by the Balfour Declaration. As the differences between these conflicting national movements seemed irreconcilable, both sides prepared for the inevitable confrontation, which broke out even before Britain's departure.

The ensuing war pitted the Zionist community against the invading armies of six Arab states and Palestinian irregulars (the Liberation Army) under a coordinated command. The Zionists emerged the winner, despite very heavy losses. Before the conclusion of United Nations–negotiated armistice agreements in 1949, Israel's armed forces added territories originally assigned to the Arabs. The Gaza strip was occupied by Egypt; the remainder, including ancient Judea and Samaria on the West Bank of the Jordan, was annexed by Transjordania, which changed its name to Jordan. Jerusalem was split between Israel and Jordan along an armistice line.

Eighty percent of the 750,000 Arab inhabitants of the areas held by Israel fled or were driven out. Many of them were cared for in United Nations–administered refugee camps in lands abutting Israel. Spokesmen for the refugees insisted on their right to return to their former homes; these demands, supported by all Arab governments and many international sympathizers, were rejected by Israel. Unreconciled to exile, despised and rejected as permanent residents by all their host governments except for Jordan, these refugees and their children born in exile became, over the years, the core of a bitter and militantly irredentist Palestinian diaspora.

Humiliation at their unexpected and crushing defeat led to agitation and major political changes in several Arab states. Coordinated by the Arab League, formed under British patronage in 1945, Arab governments steadfastly refused to consider peace negotiations or accord legitimacy to the "Zionist entity." Through diplomatic pressure, economic boycotts, and military-guerilla tactics where possible, they resolved to harass, destabilize, and eventually destroy Israel.

Independent Israel's first act was to proclaim the "law of return," eliminating all barriers to Jewish immigration. In a short time tens of thousands of Europe's destitute Holocaust survivors arrived, creating a difficult but welcome problem of "immigrant absorption." The European wave (Ashkenazim) that emptied the displaced persons camps was soon followed by a large flow of Jews from the Middle East and North Africa (Sephardim), many of them victims of mob harassment and violence abetted and promoted by Arab governments. Most of them arrived in Israel penniless, their property confiscated by the Arab governments they left behind. Zionist spokesmen have characterized this as a population exchange that nullified any moral obligation on their part to readmit or compensate Arab refugees from Israel. Israel's Jewish population escalated from 630,000 in May 1948 to 4 million four decades later.

Deprived of its educated and economic leadership, which had fled, the Arab minority remaining in Israel was traumatized, demoralized, and fearful. Though endowed under Israeli law with citizenship rights and religious and cultural autonomy, they became in fact a subordinated minority in a hostile society that tolerated their presence only reluctantly and treated them as security risks. Those Arabs in refugee camps outside Israel were displaced, dependent, and dispirited by the catastrophe that had overtaken them. Those on the West Bank of the Jordan annexed to the Hashemite kingdom became citizen-subjects of a Bedouin ruler, Arab and Muslim but not Palestinian. Palestinian Arabs, whether under Israeli rule, or refugees, or subjects of Egypt or Jordan, were in no position to fight their battles. Their cause was taken up by Arab governments whose competence and committment to their cause most Palestinians came to distrust. This dependency continued until the time—two decades later—when a new generation would find it possible to recover from their defeat and mobilize on their own behalf.

Second Phase: 1948 to the 1987 Intifada

Their main historic objective once achieved, Zionists shifted their emphasis from the mobilization of their constituency to the consolidation of their precarious state, seeking to defend it against the hostility of their Arab neighbors, to build its frail economy, and to absorb streams of mostly destitute immigrants. Until 1967, the palpable threat to its survival, the fear of a second "final solution," kept Israeli society in a state of continuous alert, despite the activation of internal cleavages between religiously orthodox and secularists and between Ashkenazim and Sephardim. The Arab remnant behind the 1949 armistice borders (the Green Line) was kept under military surveillance as security risks, despite their formal status as citizens. The mobilization of diaspora Jewry had been achieved as a consequence of the Holocaust and of Israel's struggle for Independence. Determined efforts were made to maintain the flow of desperately needed funds, immigrants, and diplomatic support to counteract the relentless efforts of the Arab states, reenforced after the early 1950s by the Soviet bloc, to destabilize and delegitimatize the Zionist state.

The June 1967 Six-Day War was a major turning point for Israel. Their unexpectedly quick and decisive victory over the combined forces of their Arab enemies and the attainment of more secure and defensible borders confirmed their military superiority and eliminated the realistic threat of annihilation by any combination of Arab states. It also brought under Israel's administration nearly a million Palestinians in areas captured from Egypt (Gaza, Sinai), Jordan (Judea and Samaria, East Jerusalem), and Syria (the Golan Heights). All of Biblical Israel, all of the mandate area west of the Jordan, indeed, all the territorial aspirations of modern Zionism were miraculously restored to Israeli rule. Jerusalem was united and annexed to Israel. Almost immediately, sharp new cleavages opened between those Israelis who in principle favored the return to Jordan of at least some of the occupied territories along with their Arab inhabitants and those who insisted, for religious or security reasons, that the territories must be permanently retained.

As the external threat receded, Israelis relaxed their vigilance. With the vigorous expansion of their economy, they began to aspire to the long-delayed satisfactions of a western consumerist society. Nevertheless, more and more of the energies of Israel's leadership were consumed in the management of conflict precipitated by a remobilizing resistance movement that aroused Palestinians in the diaspora communities, in the occupied territories, and eventually in Israel itself.

The events of 1948 had left the Palestinians defeated, dispersed, and demoralized. Those who remained in Israel were a weak, suspect, and dependent minority. Those who found refuge in Gaza under Egyptian control and in Lebanon were denied either political or economic integration; they became wards in United Nations–operated refugee camps, economically destitute, stripped of their dignity, despised by their Arab hosts, and controlled by governments that were willing to champion their cause rhetorically while exploiting their plight for their own political purposes. In Syria those who wished could become citizens, but any autonomous Palestinian political expression was strictly controlled. In Jordan they were incorporated as citizens of the Hashemite kingdom, but again political activity oriented to distinctively Palestinian objectives was rigorously circumscribed by the Bedouin security establishment. Those on the West Bank came to regard themselves, politically and economically, as second-class citizens of Jordan; under Jordanian rule their material standard of living declined. The disaster of 1948 was reenacted by the catastrophe of 1967 when the Palestinians of Gaza, East Jerusalem, and the West Bank—except for those who managed to flee to Jordan—ended up under Zionist control. For the million and a half Palestinians in Israel proper and under Israeli occupation, and for the even larger number of refugees in adjacent Arab countries, the prospect of ever recovering their homeland seemed dismal.

In 1964, three years before the debacle of 1967, a group of exiled Palestinian student-intellectuals founded the Palestine Liberation Organization (PLO). What prompted this initiative was their fear that the consolidation of the Zionist state would deny the core of their homeland forever to the Palestinian people. On the one hand, the collapse of the union of Egypt and Syria (the Nasserite United Arab Republic) and bitter feuds among the Arab states, including a bloody and indecisive war then raging in Yemen, had diminished any realistic possibility that the salvation of the Palestinian people, the recovery of their territory, and the elimination of Israel could be realized by the incompetent and self-serving Arab governments. On the other hand, the success of the Algerian people in freeing themselves from a well-entrenched imperialist settler regime through their own revolutionary efforts seemed exemplary. Borrowing from the Zionists, the Palestinian future would depend on autoemancipation. The calamity of 1967 confirmed this judgment and the strategy it implied. The Arab states might help, the Muslim world might contribute, as might fraternal anti-imperialist forces worldwide, but first the Palestinians must build their own national institutions and take control of their own destiny. After 1967, the territory to be liberated comprised not only Israel proper but the entire land of Palestine, including the areas that the blundering Egyptians, Syrians, and Jordanians had lost to the Zionists in the disastrous June war. The PLO claim to independent statehood directly challenged the Jordanian regime, for both Jordan and the PLO aspired to recover and control the occupied West Bank, including Jerusalem.

The ideology of Palestinian nationalism is expressed in the carefully drafted Palestinian Covenant of 1964, amended in 1968. The relevant collective identity is "Palestinian," fraternally linked to the Arab nation and the Muslim world but enjoying a distinctive national status with rights to self-determination and independence. The goal is the recovery of all of Palestine and the achievement of a "democratic, secular state." As Zionism rejects the claims of Palestinians to any part of the Land of Israel, so Palestinian nationalism rejects categorically the Zionist claim to any of this same territory, their homeland. Palestinian liberation is part of the worldwide struggle against European imperialism and neo-colonialism. The Palestinian nation, successively dominated and victimized by Byzantines, Crusaders, Mamalukes, Turks, British, Jordanians, and Zionists, must now vindicate, through its own revolutionary armed struggle, its inalienable right of self-determination. The Palestinian state would expel all Jews who arrived since 1917 and grant the right of return and the recovery of homes and property to all Palestinian refugees.

The leadership of the Palestinian national movement was of necessity drawn from the diaspora, since those remaining under Israeli rule were in no position to agitate for this cause. The various Arab states were willing to patronize a Palestinian movement as long as it did not challenge or constrain their own goals in the complex interplay of inter-Arab politics. By artful dodging, diaspora-based Palestinian political entrepreneurs were free to articulate Palestinian nationalist goals, to travel freely in the Arab world and beyond, to claim military, economic, diplomatic, and propaganda support, and to preach to Palestinian publics under Israeli control and in the diaspora. The leaders who emerged were mostly educated intellectuals from well-placed Palestinian families. Traditional leadership sources—landowning and merchant families—had forfeited their claims to leadership, had been coopted into the Hashemite establishment, or lacked the skills and the drive to organize and manage a revolutionary struggle. The needed organizational, communications, and diplomatic skills and the motivation to devote themselves to this high-risk enterprise were available in diaspora circles in the ranks of displaced students and intellectuals with dismal career alternatives.

The opportunity structure for organized Palestinian nationalist activity has been complex and variable from country to country. In Israel proper organized PLO activity has been proscribed as subversive to the Zionist state, but sympathy for Palestinian nationalism—in the form of a binational state behind the Green Line and a Palestinian state in the occupied territories—was propagated by the non-Zionist Communist party of Israel. Al-Faj, a daily newspaper in Arabic and English editions, financed by the PLO and expressing PLO views, is published in annexed East Jerusalem where the liberal Israeli press laws apply. In the Occupied

Territories, under military administration, official harassment prevented the formal establishment of Palestinian nationalist organizations, but most Palestinian associations were effectively captured after the mid-1970s by cadres that identify with and accept the discipline of one or more factions of the PLO, displacing the agents of the Jordanian regime. All points in the territories are open to PLO electronic propaganda and PLO money regularly reaches its supporters.

In the diaspora, opportunities for the PLO have varied from country to country. Except for the 1979 defection of Egypt by the Camp David accords, Arab countries adhere in principle to the 1974 Arab League consensus, recognizing and supporting the PLO as the sole representative and voice of the Palestinian people, excluding Jordan from that role. They have persevered in maintaining a formal state of war with Israel. None of them, however, has been willing to permit the PLO to maintain an autonomous political or paramilitary presence, fearing Israeli military retaliation and the diminution of their sovereignty. For such reasons the Fatah wing of the PLO was driven out of Jordan in December 1970 in bloody military engagements. The Fatah relocated in Lebanon, where a weak government was compelled to acquiesce in the formation of an autonomous state within a state, centered in the large Palestinian refugee camps. With weapons and guerrilla-terrorist training generously provided by Soviet bloc countries and funds contributed by the oil-rich Persian Gulf states in exchange for PLO pledges not to destabilize these conservative regimes, the PLO operated for nearly a decade as a government with well-defined specialized units managing its diplomacy, finances, economic enterprises, educational and health services, and military formations that periodically launched operations against targets in Israel and suffered devastating military counterstrikes. This situation continued until 1982, when the Israeli army destroyed the military structure of the PLO, driving them out of Beirut and southern Lebanon. PLO headquarters then moved to Tunis, more than a thousand miles from the homeland it was pledged to recover.

In other Arab countries governments closely monitored PLO activities, severely limiting their freedom of action. Syria's "rejectionist" government has steadfastly opposed any compromise with Israel, which in 1967 occupied and later annexed the Golan Heights. The Syrian regime tolerates only those PLO factions that accept the rejectionist position and holds a veto over their military and terrorist activities. The factionalism that has beset the PLO has been aggravated by the machinations of Arab governments, whose principled support for the Palestinian cause has been constrained by their own calculations of national and regime interest. In 1983, two PLO factions headquartered in Damascus actively assisted the Syrian army in pitched battles that drove Arafat's Fatah units out of northern Lebanon. Jordan has maintained a suspicious, shifting, arms-length relationship with the Fatah wing of the PLO, permitting expedient cooperation in funneling funds to the Occupied Territories while forbidding the location of paramilitary units on Jordanian soil. Complex efforts during the mid-1980s by the moderate Saudi and Egyptian regimes to achieve a joint Jordan-PLO negotiating formula in response to U.S. peace initiatives broke down in 1986 and had to be abandoned.

Like other mobilized ethnic movements, the Palestinians encompass several competitive factions, each with its own ambitious leaders, structures, ideologies, publications, fund-raising channels, paramilitary fighting units, and links with Arab governments and foreign organizations. All are controlled top down by their leaders. They differ by ideology—from economic pragmatists to committed Marxists; by ultimate goals—from the recovery of Palestine to the achievement of social revolution throughout the Arab world; by strategy—from tactical flexibility to rigid rejection; and by the nature of their links with Arab governments—some seeking maximum autonomy, others content to rely on the patronage of a particular Arab government. Ten or more of these factions work within the framework of the PLO; an equal number remain outside, including communists and Islamic activists who maintain separate identities. The Palestine National Council, representing all the PLO factions, meets annually and serves as the movement's legislative assembly. As in all PLO institutions, its various factions are represented by fixed quotas, and delegates are selected by their leaders, not elected by their members.

Fatah, headed by Yasir Arafat, is the largest and wealthiest of these factions and commands the broadest support in the diaspora, the Occupied Territories, and international circles. In the refugee camps that it controls and also in the Territories, Fatah attempts to enroll its constituents into networks of organizations that orient their daily lives to the movement and its mission—specialized units for children, for women, for trade unionists, for agricultural cooperatives, for professionals, for students and intellectuals, and of course for fighters. Fatah succeeded, in its competition with Jordan, in gaining control of most of the existing social and economic institutions in the Territories. It nevertheless preferred to mobilize support locally rather than foster territorywide organizations, fearing that the latter might fall under the control of internal leaders who would pursue their own agenda rather than accept the discipline of the diaspora leadership.

The density and variety of organizations affiliated with and controlled by the various factions of the PLO enhance mobilization, drawing more of the constituency into the movement and providing opportunities for leaders and activists. The resultant factionalism, however, extracts a heavy price, inhibiting coordinated policies and leading to overt and even violent internecine conflict. Before 1988, the more pragmatic Arafat and his allies were unable to accept UN Resolutions 242 and 338, which recognize Israel behind its pre-1967 borders but impose heavy international pressure on Israel to negotiate withdrawal from the Territories, because they knew that several rejectionist factions would withdraw from the PLO and denounce them as traitors. Thus the minority factions, clinging to maximalist claims, influenced and often manipulated by Arab governments, exercised a veto over the movement's policies, operations, and diplomacy.

Unlike most ethnic movements, the PLO, during its first quarter century, did not suffer from serious resource limitations. Except for a diminishing minority in the Territories and in Jordan who continue to prefer King Hussein, most Palestinians considered the PLO their representative, even when they disagreed with some of its policies and tactics. There has been no dearth of displaced young men with few attractive life chances ready to commit themselves as fighters, and there has been an abundant flow of weapons to arm and equip them. The highly educated Palestinian community has produced more than enough people with needed organizational, technical, communications, and diplomatic skills to staff its agencies; Fatah's civilian bureaucracy in the diaspora comprises about five thousand full-time paid functionaries, plus twenty thousand fighters.

Prior to the Gulf War in 1990–91, financial contributions from Palestinians in the diaspora and especially from the governments of Saudi Arabia and the Persian Gulf Emirates provided the various units of the PLO, especially Fatah, with income estimated at more than 500 million U.S. dollars per year, more than enough to maintain their fighters, support a large infrastructure, provide economic, educational, health, and welfare services for Palestinians in exile, and still leave substantial sums for long-term investment, estimated in 1986 at more than 4 billion dollars. The families of prisoners, detainees, and fallen PLO fighters, as well as unemployed university graduates in the Territories, received generous

monthly stipends from the PLO, in the latter case to discourage emigration and insure their dependency on the diaspora leadership. The movement enjoyed unwavering diplomatic support from Arab and Muslim
states, from the Soviet bloc, and from a majority of Third World states,
providing an assured two-thirds vote in the UN General Assembly for
annual resolutions of support for the Palestinian cause, including the
1975 resolution branding Zionism as racism.

The Palestinian movement has been inhibited not by lack of conventional resources, of funds, trained personnel, external support, and competent devoted leadership, but rather by (1) restricted freedom of
operation in Israel, the Territories, and the Arab host states; (2) self-
serving interference by Arab states in the PLO's strategy and activities;
(3) severe, even violent, conflict among the factions that comprise the
movement; (4) the determination of the diaspora leadership to maintain
control of the movement by blocking the emergence of independent leadership and autonomous institutions in the occupied territories; and (5)
tough, determined, and resourceful opposition by Israel and its supporters. The overwhelming majority of Israelis, even those prepared in
principle to exchange territory for peace, have regarded the PLO as a
terrorist organization and a threat to Israel's security and survival.

The PLO leadership has improvised strategies to insure its access to
resources, maintain its structures, and pursue its struggle. It has attempted to maximize its autonomy and freedom of action vis-à-vis the
Arab states, while operating within their borders and insuring their diplomatic and financial assistance. Though the PLO needs the support of
the Arab states, the latter also need the PLO, for in order to fortify their
precarious legitimacy among their own subjects and in regional Arab
circles they must be seen to support the aspirations of the Palestinian
people. The PLO seeks to achieve control of its constituency by intensive
propaganda, the provision of economic and social services, and, where
necessary, coercion. In the Occupied Territories it has struggled to maintain the allegiance of Palestinians against competing Jordanians, communists, and Islamic activists who share their opposition to the Zionist
occupation but do not accept the discipline of the PLO or its component
factions. The communists favor a Palestinian state alongside a non-
Zionist Israel, while the Islamists fuse Palestinian nationalism with Islamic revolutionary military and reject the idea of a secular state.

In their unremitting but unequal struggle against Israel the PLO has
employed simultaneous economic, diplomatic-political, and military tac-

tics. They have encouraged the Arab states and their Islamic and Third World sympathizers to maintain an economic boycott against Israel and against foreign firms that do business with their enemy. They have attempted to gain international recognition as the sole legitimate representative of the Palestinian people, while delegitimatizing Israel especially in United Nations circles as a racist aggressor and an outpost of western imperialism. From the beginning, the PLO has been committed to armed struggle, though a serious military option has never been available. For a nonstate movement, the PLO has been generously equipped, but its forces have mainly engaged in conflicts against hostile sectarian militias in Lebanon supported in many cases by Palestinian splinter groups and by the Syrian army. Never able to challenge the Israeli military, the PLO factions have resorted to limited guerrilla actions and terrorist tactics more often directed against civilian than military objectives. A conspicuous instance was the massacre of Israeli athletes at the 1972 Munich Olympic games. The purpose of these terrorist operations has been as much to sustain the morale of the Palestinian people and keep the Palestinian issue alive among international audiences as to punish and weaken Israeli resolve, reduce immigration, and encourage emigration. Many of the more dramatic acts attributed to the PLO, including aircraft hijackings and attacks against Jewish targets outside Israel, have been perpetrated by minority factions outside the Fatah mainstream. These terrorist attacks have often embarassed the latter, revealing Arafat's limited control over the movement, yet Arafat and his associates have refused to condemn them publicly. Without other military options, the PLO has been limited to minor infiltration cum terrorist operations that confirmed the unwillingness of most Israelis and their sympathizers to consider the PLO a legitimate negotiating partner.

After 1967 the diaspora could challenge the Israeli occupation of the Territories by diplomatic initiatives and terrorist operations, although those in the Territories under Israeli military rule were too stunned to resist until after the 1973 Yom Kippur War, which demonstrated unexpected Israeli vulnerability. Still, they relied primarily on verbal protest and steadfast noncooperation. Most of this had to be symbolic, since the necessities of survival required practical accommodation with the Israeli authorities. Twenty-five percent of the labor force in Gaza and the West Bank traveled daily to jobs in Israel; others worked for Israeli firms in the Territories. Their wages, low by Israeli standards, produced incomes and consumption levels that were unprecedentedly high by West

Bank and Jordanian experience. The 7 percent annual economic growth rates produced relative prosperity but no autonomous sources of economic power for Palestinians. Wage income for Palestinian workers soon undermined the authority of elite families whose power and status had been based on land ownership and trade. The post-1973 period witnessed protests against the expropriation of land, 40 percent of which was taken over by Israel for security reasons or for transfer to Jewish settlements These protests, coordinated by the Palestinian National Front (PNF), an underground umbrella organization led by communists but joined by PLO affiliates, were quelled without difficulty.

Israel's strategy, to favor the traditional and pro-Jordanian clans against the more militant PLO, was slowly but gradually thwarted, especially after the Likud election victory in 1977 which signalled the expansion of Jewish settlements and an entirely unresponsive Israeli government attitude toward Palestinians. The Jordanians had been ineffective, while the PLO, legitimated by the formal consensus of the Arab states, promised a struggle for self-respect and self-determination. The unexpected victory of PNF-PLO—supported candidates in the 1976 local elections demonstrated the ascendancy of the more militant anti-Hashemites in the Territories.

The centers of resistance in the Territories were the four universities that Israel allowed to be established—none had existed before 1967. Among students with very limited employment prospects after graduation, the secular-nationalist PLO competed with communists and, especially in Gaza, with Islamic activists influenced by the Egyptian Muslim Brotherhood. As the occupation dragged on and more and more Jewish settlements were implanted under Likud rule, students became radicalized. Their ever more militant protests resulted in frequent closings of the universities by the Israeli authorities and the imprisonment and deportation of leading student activists. The new generation of Palestinians had no personal experience with the humiliations and the debacles of 1948 or 1967. They were less intimidated by myths of Zionist omnicompetence and the invulnerability of the Israeli military, especially after its defeat in 1983–84 by the Lebanese Shi'ites. They were impatient with the failure of the Arab states and of the PLO itself to rescue them from Israeli rule and, thanks to PLO subsidies, unencumbered by the need to earn a livelihood. Meanwhile, the success of the Afghan resistance against the Soviet army inspired them, and the theme of autoemancipation took hold in their ranks. They could no longer wait for others, Arab states or the diaspora-dominated PLO, to rescue them.

Intifada and Gulf War

The Amman conference of the Arab League in November 1987 concentrated entirely on the Iranian threat to the Gulf states and Iraq. The Palestinian struggle was not even on the agenda; Arafat and the PLO were unceremoniously brushed aside, for their defeats in Lebanon by the Israelis in 1982 and subsequently by the Syrians had severely compromised their standing. Egypt had formally broken ranks and signed a peace treaty with Israel. The Soviets under Gorbachev were losing interest and, along with their satellites, preparing to restore diplomatic relations with Israel. The best that might be expected from U.S. pressure on Israel was some version of a "Jordanian solution," areas heavily populated by Palestinians but of little strategic importance would be returned to Jordan or be united with Jordan in a federated relationship. Jordan would then normalize relations with Israel. More likely, Palestinians in the Territories faced the prospect of "creeping annexation" by Israel, expansion and thickening of Jewish settlements, limited local autonomy, economic deprivation, political subordination, and no chance that any part of their homeland would be redeemed—unless they could take matters into their own hands. Reports of a fat, aging PLO bureaucracy in Tunis enjoying diplomatic games and a luxurious lifestyle remote from the daily humiliations and frustrations of their constituents in the Territories confirmed fears that no effective help could come from the outside. Inaction meant permanent subordination; bold initiatives might duplicate the successes of the Lebanese Shiites and the Afghan rebels.

Thus, with little to lose, the Palestinian youth launched their uprising, the Intifada, in December 1987. Their weapons were both violent and nonviolent: stones, homemade petrol bombs, and limited supplies of small weapons, along with civil disobedience,—strikes, massive demonstrations, the blocking of public services, refusal to pay taxes or cooperate in any way with the occupation authorities, and skillful use of the international mass media. Their objectives were to demonstrate worldwide the harshness and coerciveness of Israeli rule and the steadfast united front of all Palestinians against continuation of the occupation, to restore their struggle to top priority among Arab and Muslim governments, and to make the Territories ungovernable by the Israelis. Hundreds of police and other civil servants were induced to resign their positions rather than continue to enforce the Israeli presence.

The diaspora leadership of the PLO, taken by surprise, was able to offer little practical assistance, except for stepped-up but mostly ineffectual infiltration and terrorist operations. The uprising was sustained and coordinated by a shadowy "unified national leadership of the uprising" comprised of networks of youth and student leaders representing all the PLO factions as well as communists and Islamists. This informal and dispersed leadership could not be decapitated by the occupation authorities. Mass organizations, especially labor unions, women's associations, and student groups, were directly involved. Within Palestinian ranks the uprising achieved impressive solidarity and mass participation with dramatic demonstrations of personal courage and self-sacrifice—and incurred no significant opposition. It extracted a very high price from Israel in internal divisions, international condemnation, and a shattering of the illusion that the occupation could be sustained indefinitely at low cost. But the Palestinians lacked significant logistical support from outside, continued to depend on employment in Israel, and suffered harsh reprisals by the Israeli military, until finally, after a year or so, Israel succeeded in containing the uprising, though episodes of protest and violence continued.

Aside from radicalizing and further mobilizing the Palestinian masses, the Intifada had far-reaching consequences. It sharpened divisions in Israel between moderates willing to yield some territory in return for peace and maximalists who insisted on retaining every inch of the Land of Israel and peopling it with Jewish settlers. The uprising also helped to persuade the PLO's diaspora leadership that their constituents under occupation so urgently needed tangible signs of progress that they must reconsider the maximalist demand to recover all of Palestine. The evident strength of the Israeli state, the withdrawal of Soviet support, the renewal of large-scale immigration from the Soviet Union, and pressure from the United States compelled Arafat, ambiguously and reluctantly in November 1988 at a PNC meeting in Algiers, to accept the 1967 UN Resolutions 242 and 338, recognizing the legitimacy of Israel behind its prewar borders. Arafat committed the PLO to abandon the use of terrorist tactics and limit its demands to a Palestinian state in the Occupied Territories, including Jerusalem. The PLO proclaimed its independence and statehood and assumed the status, in effect, of a government in exile. Most Israelis greeted these gestures with total skepticism. They were denounced as treasonous by rejectionist Arab states and by radical factions in the PLO, but were welcomed by a majority of Palestinians in the Territories. The exception were the growing numbers of young Islamic militants—Hamas in Gaza, Islamic Jihad in the West Bank. Summoning deeper layers of collective identity and capitalizing on the failure of westernization and secular nationalism to redeem them from oppression and humiliation, they condemned Arafat's compromises as a betrayed of their national and their religious obligations.

The Gulf War of 1990–91 proved still another in a long series of miscalculations and disasters for Palestinians. Saddam Hussein's invasion and annexation of Kuwait were enthusiastically endorsed by Arafat and by King Hussein on behalf of the Palestinian majority in Jordan. The immediate result was the withdrawal of vital financial support from Saudi Arabia and the Gulf Emirates, slashing the PLO's annual income by two-thirds and creating a financial crisis for the movement. The conspicuous joy of Palestinians at the flights of Iraqi scud missiles directed at civilian targets in Israel further hardened Israeli hostility and distrust. With Iraq's defeat, the restored government of Kuwait summarily expelled four hundred thousand Palestinians, liquidating the most prosperous and most generous community in the diaspora. As a consequence of this series of setbacks, the Israeli government was able to insist in the U.S.-Russian–sponsored post Gulf War Middle East peace negotiations that began in late 1991 that representatives of the PLO and other non-residents of the Territories be excluded from the Palestinian delegation. The weakened bargaining position of the Palestinians was accentuated by diplomatic recognition of Israel by China, India, and several African states, and the rescinding of the Zionism-racism resolution by the UN General Assembly, signalling the end of Third World solidarity with the Palestinians.

Conflict Management by the Israeli Government

In Israel itself after 1948 and in the Territories after 1967 the government found it necessary to improvise methods to control what the majority of Israelis have regarded as a hostile, potentially disloyal Arab minority. Israel is a Jewish state, and Arabs could hardly be expected to be emotionally attracted to a polity that employs the symbols and expresses the national aspirations of a people with whom they have been engaged in bitter conflict for decades and that necessarily gives priority to Jewish concerns. Moreover, since 1948, Israel has been in a state of uninterrupted war with the Arab world—except for Egypt after 1979—and with organized Palestinians. Safeguarding Israel's security has been its highest priority, and successive governments have felt justified in regarding Arabs under its jurisdiction as a potential fifth column.

It was considered inappropriate for the Jewish state, whose ancestors had suffered severe discrimination as minorities and claimed equality of treatment in lands where they had lived—and where many of their relatives continued to live—to deny equal legal status to its own minorities. Arabs in Israel were therefore endowed from the beginning with Israeli citizenship and with explicit guarantees of religious and cultural freedom; their language was accorded official status. These formal rights of citizenship and entitlements to public services have been respected, but through a series of rather consistent policies the Israeli Arabs, numbering in 1990 eight hundred thousand, or 17 percent of the population, have in fact been treated as a second-class minority. For security reasons they were subjected until 1966 to military rule. Except for the small Druse and Bedouin communities, Arabs have been excluded from military service, a policy that they have not contested, but that nonetheless denies them access to many employment and economic opportunities, for full participation in Israel life requires the fulfillment of military obligations.

In Israel's periodic wars with Arab states in 1956, 1967, 1973, and 1982, the Palestinian minority was passive. This inaction can be explained partly by intensive police surveillance, partly by the fragmentation of Arab communities which is encouraged by Israeli practice, partly by economic dependency on government agencies and on Jewish employers and businessmen, and partly by the cooptation of compliant Arabs into positions of influence. Arabs have been denied the right to develop autonomous economic and intellectual institutions. Even the separate Arab school system is supervised closely by Jewish officials. Those elements in Israel's polity which are relatively sympathetic to the Arab minority—or believe that Israel's long-term interests require a more loyal Arab citizenry—generally take a civil rights approach, advocating freer access by Arabs as individual citizens to educational and employment opportunities. They oppose, however the development of separate minority institutions that might serve as collective vehicles for anti-Zionist or pro-Palestinian national expression. In a formal sense, Israeli citizenship is based on civic criteria: de facto, first-class citizenship is strictly an ethnic entitlement.

Since 1967, the majority of Israel's Arabs have redefined their identity as Palestinians in defiance of Israeli efforts to deny and ridicule the historical basis for distinctive Palestinian peoplehood. Younger, bolder, better-educated leaders have inspired and orchestrated more militant methods of protest, including since 1974 the annual "Land Day" demonstration against Israeli expropriation of Arab-owned land and discriminatory treatment in education, housing, and municipal services. As Israeli Arabs have demonstrated further alienation from Israel and increasing solidarity with their brethren in the Territories, the state's methods of conflict management have not changed significantly. The right-wing Likud-led coalition has no interest in appeasing the Palestinian minority; many of its leaders make little effort to conceal their hostility and their dream that Israel may one day be rid of its Arabs. The Labor Alignment is more inclined to include some Palestinians on its electoral lists, reduce discrimination in the allocation of public services, and decrease barriers to economic and educational opportunity for individuals, but it will not countenance autonomous sources of economic or political power or national status for the Palestinian minority. In Labor circles there is continuing agitation—even among those who oppose Jewish settlements in the Territories—for such measures as Judaizing the Galilee, where Arabs remain a demographic majority, by additional government-sponsored Jewish settlements. Palestinians interpret this as continuing evidence of the intention of Zionists to disregard their interests, threaten their land, and eventually dispossess and displace them. Yet Israeli citizenship does confer definite practical advantages that, given their realistic alternatives, the great majority of Israeli Arabs are not inclined to forego or jeopardize. Their loyalty to Israel is pragmatic and instrumental, and Palestinians are learning to use their voting rights and electoral strength in Israel's highly competitive political system to extract practical benefits from the government. Their influence is exerted within the left-of-center Zionist parties and in Palestinian parties such as the Democratic Front for Peace and Equality, which concede Israel's legitimacy but advocate an independent Palestinian state in the Territories.

Most Palestinians in and around Jerusalem, annexed in 1967 to Israel, have steadfastly rejected Israeli citizenship or even the right to vote in local elections. Such acts might be construed as legitimating Israeli sovereignty in the annexed areas. Unlike Israeli Arabs, few of whom have participated in organized anti-Israeli activities, many Jerusalemites took an active part in the intifada. Prominent PLO-oriented activists and propagandists operate in East Jerusalem, where under Israeli law they are freer to function than under military rule in the Territories.

For more than a quarter century, Israeli rule in the Territories has been governed by a consistent set of policies and practices. The Territories have been under military rule. A Jordanian presence has been tolerated, even encouraged, to relieve the security and financial burden on

Israel and to counteract the appeal of the PLO. West Bankers are considered to be citizens of Jordan. Under an implicit functional compromise, Israel maintains security while Jordan pays most of the civil servants, issues passports for international travel and other kinds of licenses, and maintains active economic links with the Territories through the open bridges. Jordanian law and the Jordanian school curricula apply, as modified by the Israeli military. Until September 1993, the PLO, including all its factions and institutions, was considered a subversive, terrorist organization subject to repression.

Despite agreement on these basic principles, Israelis have been almost evenly divided on strategy and long-term objectives. One group, centered in the Labor Alignment, favors exchanged of territory for peace with the Palestinians and, equally important, with the neighboring Arab states, especially Jordan, Syria, and Saudi Arabia. The preferred negotiating partner has been Jordan, even after King Hussein's symbolic renunciation in 1988 of further responsibility for the Territories. In return for a peace treaty, about 60 pecent of the pre-1967 West Bank, including the main concentrations of Arab population, would revert to Jordan, along with the Gaza strip. Areas required by Israel to insure its security and, of course, all of Jerusalem, would be retained; these would include many but not all of the Jewish settlements. This solution would produce the long-desired peace settlement and normalize relations with the Arab world, and would relieve Israel of the burden of ruling a hostile, indigestible, rapidly multiplying population that, combined with Palestinians in Israel proper, might one day become a majority, threatening either Israel's character as the Jewish state or its democratic structures. A significant minority in the Labor coalition, mostly educated Ashkenazim loosely affiliated with the Peace Now movement, have demanded strong initiatives by Israel to break the long deadlock and begin serious negotiations with the PLO that might result in a demilitarized Palestinian state alongside Israel.

The Likud coalition, secular nationalists and religious activists who ruled Israel from 1977–92, opposes in principle any transfer of territory. They are committed to a "Greater Israel," thus to eventual annexation. Likud supporters believe that Israel has irrefutable historical and legal claims to all of Palestine, that its retention is vital to Israel's security, and that Arab hostility will be mitigated not by territorial or other compromises but only by their recognition of superior Israeli military strength and resolve. A Palestinian state would constitute a lethal irredentist and terrorist threat to Israel's security and survival. Likud's Orthodox partners consider Israeli rule over the Territories a religious obligation, a precurser to the coming Messianic redemption. The annexationists would make any future transfer of territory impossible by implanting Jewish settlements throughout the Territories, including centers of Palestinian population, thereby creating irreversible facts on the ground. In the fifteen years following Likud's victory in the 1977 elections, the Jewish population in the Territories increased from less than 10,000 to more than 120,000. Though some right-wing elements want the Palestinians cleared from the Territories by inducement or coercion, the standard Likud position is that, under Israeli sovereignty, Palestinians would enjoy generous opportunities for local self-government. National status for them, however, cannot be contemplated.

The Likud leadership has been content with the process of "creeping annexation"—progressive integration without formal annexation—while expanding Jewish settlements. This approach avoids the troublesome question of citizenship for the Palestinians. Meanwhile, a plural society has emerged in the Territories: Israeli settlers generously subsidized by the state and governed by Israeli law with full entitlement to Israeli public services, Palestinians governed by a combination of Jordanian and military law with vastly inferior public services. Israelis and Palestinians remain members of rigidly separate and hostile communities, sharing no common institutions.

According to an increasingly influential version of Likud doctrine, Israel has already acquiesced in the establishment of a Palestinian state on the East Bank, which was originally recognized as part of the Jewish homeland under the British Mandate. That state is Jordan with its Palestinian majority; West Bankers who want to live in a Palestinian state might freely betake themselves to Jordan. There is no need to strip Israel of still more of its tiny patrimony to establish a second Palestinian state. Contrary to Labor, which supports King Hussein as a moderate neighbor who might eventually relieve Israel of Arab-inhabited parts of the West Bank, the Likud would prefer that Palestinians destabilize and overthrow the Hashemite regime and establish an explicitly Palestinian state on the East Bank.

The Israeli government has employed several methods to control Palestinians and thereby manage conflict in the Territories. First, they have exploited societal divisions and segmentation among the Palestinians, including Christian-Muslim, pro-Jordanian–pro-PLO, and the traditional *hamula* (kin-based social structures) against national or class associations. Israel has refused to tolerate any Territory-wide Palestinian organizations. Second, they have coopted more compliant and conservative Arab personalities, channeling public services and distributing licenses and permits through organizations under their control. Third, they have enforced economic dependency by ensuring that the economic well-being of large numbers of families and communities depends on employment in Israel, while denying Palestinians control over any significant economic enterprises or institutions. And, finally, they have used military surveillance, including the interdiction of military supplies and weapons; outlawed anti-Israeli and pro-PLO demonstrations; and administered reprisals in the form of curfews, collective punishment, detention and imprisonment, deportation, and the demolition of houses of Palestinians suspected of conducting violent or terrorist operations. The Israeli military has tolerated and even abetted the arming of Jewish settlers, many of them violent, fanatical, and provocative, as vigilantes to intimidate and deter Palestinian opposition. One objective of Israel's frequent retaliations against Palestinian targets outside Israel, and especially of the 1982 campaign in Lebanon, has been to demoralize Palestinians in the Territories so that they would despair of rescue by the Arab states or the PLO and be prepared to acquiesce in some form of limited self-rule.

The more militant the Palestinian challenges, the more draconian the responses, especially the deployment of raw military force in the 1987–90 intifada. Before 1993, no Israeli government was prepared to accommodate any expression of Palestinian nationalism or to tolerate any but very local political activity. The few safety valves allowed, the publication and circulation of pro-PLO newspapers, agitation in the five universities, elections of local officials, were quickly and decisively circumscribed when they overtly expressed solidarity with the PLO or challenged the occupation regime. Israel's strategy of conflict management in the Territories and the highly constrained opportunity structure available to Palestinians delegitimated the Israeli presence and denied it local collaborators. Thus, Palestinians had no effective avenue of political expression short of violent resistance, while Israel, given the unprecedented mobilization during the intifada, had no option but to escalate repression. Where the provocation was deemed sufficient, such as terrorist attacks on Jews, the Israeli government resorted to mass deportations and even to embargos on the flow of Palestinian workers to jobs in Israel.

Like their Palestinian counterparts who favored some practical accommodation and modus vivendi with the Zionists, Israeli moderates were often outbidden by maximalists. Nothing relieved and comforted the

Likud maximalists, the Begins, Shamirs, and Sharons, as much as terrorist acts, expressions of uncompromising antagonism, and reiteration of maximalist claims by Palestinian rejectionists and Islamic militants. The ultras in both camps reinforced one another, strengthening their influence over their constituents.

Peace Negotiations and Back Channels

In November 1991, the United States and Russia sponsored Middle East peace negotiations involving Israel, the Palestinians, and Israel's neighbors, Jordan, Syria, and Lebanon. The external sponsors believed that in the wake of the Gulf War the time was ripe for serious negotiations, due to the PLO's desperate financial predicament and loss of international support, Syria's internal economic crisis and loss of Soviet military backing, Jordan's need to rehabilitate its impaired international standing following its ill-fated support for Saddam Hussein, and the disenchantment of the Saudis and the Kuwaitis with the PLO ingrates who had betrayed them. Under U.S. pressure, Arafat and the PLO had broken ground in 1988 by formally, if obliquely, "recognizing" Israel, though not in writing and by renouncing terrorism. Implicitly Arafat was accepting partition, but on less favorable terms than than those that were rejected by his predecessors in 1937 and 1947. But although the Likud government in Israel was interested in peace settlements with neighboring Arab states, it adamantly opposed yielding any part of the Occupied Territories which they considered inalienable parts of the Land of Israel. It was prepared only to negotiate administrative autonomy for the Palestinians—a Palestinian state being out of the question—and to treat only with non-PLO residents of the Territories, ruling out the "terrorist" PLO, representatives of the diaspora, or residents of Jerusalem. Given the distance between the Likud government and even the most accommodative Palestinians, these negotiations proved to be fruitless.

In June 1992, a Labor-led coalition headed by Itzak Rabin won a narrow electoral victory and assumed office, committed to the principle of exchanging land for peace with Palestinians and expediting the lagging Middle East peace process. A crucial group of low-income Israelis, Sephardim who had long supported the Likud, shifted to Labor, convinced that the Likud regime was ignoring their social and economic needs while lavishing funds on the West Bank settlements. An important faction in the Labor coalition objected in principle to Jewish rule over an-

other people; they considered it inherently wrong, unnecessary, as well
as a threat and a reproach to Israel's democratic values and institutions.
A larger group was convinced by the experience of the intifada that
coercive methods of managing the conflict with the Palestinians were not
working, were exacting unacceptable costs that would not diminish, and
that accommodative methods should at least be explored, even to the
point of negotiating with the detested PLO. As the PLO had taken steps
to recognize Israel, the Labor coalition agreed to negotiate with Palestinian residents of the Territories who accepted the discipline of the PLO,
breaking a long-standing Israeli taboo. With Arab states including Egypt,
Saudi Arabia, and even Syria, both parties shared an interest in containing the expanding influence of violence-prone Islamic militants who reject the legitimacy of Israel and the secular nationalism represented by
the PLO. The Hashemite regime supported these negotiations, as it aspires to a confederation between Jordan and a future Palestinian state.

In deepest secrecy the Labor government and the PLO were induced
to accept an invitation by Norway to hold informal discussions about
the possibilities and terms of an eventual accommodation. These back-
channel negotiations proceeded quietly for more than a year, abetted by
the United States and Egypt. In August 1993, their amazing outcome
was leaked and then announced formally by both parties: a tentative
agreement for mutual formal recognition by the State of Israel and the
PLO. Once the Palestinians formally renounced the language of their
1964 covenant calling for the destruction of Israel, Israeli military and
civilian units would withdraw from the Gaza province and an area of
the West Bank adjacent to the ancient city of Jericho; they would turn
over control of these areas to an elected Palestinian authority that would
administer its public affairs—economic policy, health, education, public
works, and law enforcement. Only foreign affairs and external security
would remain Israel's responsibility. Within two years thereafter, negotiations would be initiated for a permanent settlement based on UN
Resolutions 242 and 338. The transition period would not exceed five
years and the final agreement would address such issues as specific
boundaries, the status of refugees, Jewish settlements, economic cooperation, and the future of Jerusalem, which Palestinians desire as their
capital but whose unity and control by Israel are regarded by the great
majority of Jews as non-negotiable. The agreements do not commit Israel
to a Palestinian state but only to an autonomous authority that might
evolve into statehood, subject to negotiation during the transitional period.

Reaction to this breakthrough was predictable. It was denounced by the Likud and its allies, particularly by the West Bank settlers, as suicidal and a betrayal of a century of Zionist struggle. It was repudiated, in turn, by Islamic militants and rejectionist elements in the PLO, including some in Fatah, as treasonous, abandoning the sacred rights of the Palestinian and Muslim people. Some Israelis regarded the agreement as the opening wedge for Palestinians determined to dismember Israel one step at a time. Some Palestinians excoriated Arafat for accepting demeaning terms that fell far short of their minimal aspirations for statehood in at least part of their homeland. It was praised by most spokespersons for the international community as an act of enlightened statesmanship. The moderate Arab states joined in the chorus of approval and congratulations.

Implementing the initial reconciliation between these old enemies will require a very high order of political skill and unremitting international support, diplomatic and financial. Happily, the elites of the PLO and of the Labor coalition have committed themselves to the success of these negotiations and have a very large stake in their outcome; neither would be likely to survive their failure. The language of the agreements is ambiguous on many details and subject to conflicting interpretations. The practical issues are extremely complex. Though at first the dominant response from both constituencies was favorable, both sides contain skeptics and inveterate opponents. Important organized elements in both societies still assert exclusive rights to control the same territory in its entirety, reject the claims of their counterparts, and remain willing to resort to violence that could impair confidence on both sides. They will seize on any impasse in the negotiations to discredit and undermine them, to outbid their moderate opponents, and to turn their constituents against them. The leadership of the PLO and of the Labor coalition overcame profound suspicions in the face of exigent necessity—recognizing that neither enemy could be destroyed, that the human, moral, and financial burdens of interminable conflict and stalemate had become increasingly intolerable, that international pressures for a settlement were becoming irresistible, and that Islamic extremists had emerged as a dangerous threat to both sides.

In addition to opponents, both the PLO and the Labor government face pressures even from groups that support the peace process. "Insiders" who have carried on the struggle in the Territories insist that the PLO's diaspora leadership share decision making with them, including meaningful participation in the negotiations. They demand that Arafat forego his autocratic and erratic leadership style and accept greater accountability to his constituents. Once the PLO's large bureaucracy is relocated from Tunis to Jericho, "insider" pressures will surely increase. Israeli supporters of the agreements include some who are willing to accept risks for peace, as well as more cautious persons who insist on proceeding slowly and on a narrow interpretation of the agreements. Both tendencies are represented in the government. Burdened by mutual mistrust, Arafat and Rabin have been less successful than Mandela and DeKlerk in helping their partner confront the numerous contradictory pressures they face in their own ranks.

The outcome of this initial breakthrough will be determined by intense negotiations over the next five years, beginning in 1994. There will be many occasions for committed opponents on both sides to derail the talks and to exploit unfulfilled expectations. Arafat's support could be undermined; he might even be assassinated. Islamic-led violence could turn the majority of Israelis against the agreements; the Likud could upset Labor in the next Israeli elections. Whatever the specific outcomes of the peace process, these two talented peoples will continue to share the same small territory that is profoundly meaningful to both of them. Even if Palestine were bisected by formal international borders, a Jewish minority will probably remain in the Palestinian state and a substantial Palestinian minority will persist in Israel; their grievances, claims, and status will concern not only their respective governments, but also kinfolk in neighboring states whose governments or nonofficial factions may be tempted to intervene in the pursuit of domestic or external agendas.

The legacies of a century of hatred and bloodshed may be attenuated, but the achievement and management of the specific, practical terms of a fragile, accommodative coexistence between these two peoples will require extraordinary statesmanship on both sides and continuing participation by supportive foreign governments and international organizations.

6

Canada-Quebec: "Two Nations Warring in the Bosom of a Single State"

There are several dimensions of pluralism in what Canadians call their "ethnic mosaic." Aboriginals—Indians and Inuit (Eskimos)—comprise 4 percent of the population, distributed throughout the ten provinces and two territories, mainly in separate settlements. They have been mobilizing in recent years, with widespread public support, to assert their right to self-government, official recognition of their collective dignity, and control of sufficient resources to maintain and promote their distinctive cultures. Immigrants of non-French and non-British origin, 30 percent of all Canadians, have been acculturating mainly to the English language stream but are assisted by the government's modest "multicultural" programs to preserve, to the extent they desire, elements of their inherited cultures. The principal dimension of pluralism, however, remains the division between English speakers and French speakers. The terms and conditions of coexistence between these two collectivities has for more than two centuries constituted the main *problematique* in Canadian politics. The evolution and management of this cleavage is the focus of this chapter.

There have been two competing versions of the meaning of membership in the Canadian polity. To Pan-Canadian liberals, Canadian citizens as individuals comprise the polity, though they may identify with the English-speaking or the French-speaking cultural and language communities. The main alternative view regards Canada as a "compact" between its two "founding races," the French centered in Quebec, the British in the other provinces. Immigrants of other origins are expected to acculturate and eventually assimilate into one of the two founding nations. The compact theory is promoted by a segment of French-Canadian nationalists, since it implies equal status for their minority community and a privileged position in relation to other ethnic minorities. But neither Pan-Canadian individualism nor the dualistic two nations concept satisfies aboriginal peoples who since the 1980s have demanded official recognition as distinct nations endowed with inalienable rights to self-government within the Canadian state structure.

Origins of the "two solitudes"

In 1759, after a century of colonization, New France was the home of sixty thousand settlers clustered on the banks of the St. Lawrence. In that year a British army defeated the French outside their capital city, Quebec, and in the ensuing treaty, Catholic, French-speaking New France was ceded to the Protestant, English-speaking British crown. As a consequence of the "Conquest and Abandonment," the leaders of the French community—soldiers, administrators, and businessmen—returned to France. The clergy alone remained; to them fell the responsibility of maintaining, if they could, this isolated community under extremely adverse conditions.

Their first success was the reluctant decision of the British Parliament to recognize and tolerate the position of the Catholic church and its educational and welfare institutions at a time when Catholics in Britain were still suspect and disfranchised. The Quebec Act of 1774 also confirmed the feudalistic land tenure system that benefitted the small but influential French rural gentry. The obvious purpose of these concessions was to secure the loyalty or at least the non-belligerence of the elites of what was then a substantial majority of Canada's population and thus prevent their defection to the rebellious colonies to the south. The Church leadership preferred this arrangement to domination by the unruly Protestant and liberal-democratic forces that were soon to become the United States. These preliminary arrangements were fortified in 1791 when the Roman-French legal system was recognized as normative for Lower Canada (Quebec), while Upper Canada (Ontario), recently settled by loyalist refugees from the United States, would be governed by English common law. These measures insured the survival of a Catholic and French-speaking community in North America, albeit under conditions of political and economic subordination within the British empire.

The first significant expression of French-Canadian nationalism emerged in the 1830s when small fragment of that community, led by intellectuals and businessmen, opposed economic measures that they considered discriminatory and protested the refusal of the British authorities to permit representative government. Influenced by anticlerical individualism and Jacksonian ideas of democracy, they precipitated a revolt in 1837 that was easily repressed by the British authorities, who simultaneously quelled an uprising by English speakers in Upper Canada. The British response was to introduce in 1840 a unitary regime that was explicitly designed to encourage assimilation of the French to mainstream British society and culture. The objective was to eliminate the unsatisfactory situation—in Governor-General Lord Durham's celebrated phrase—of "two nations warring in the bosom of a single state" and in the process help the French to cast off the shackles of a reactionary clergy and to participate as individuals in a more modern and enlightened society. This attempt at institutional assimilation proved to be a nonstarter, incurring resistance from French-Catholic society which refused to sacrifice its collective identity. The machinery of representative government that evolved from Lord Durham's report required agreement on all measures by both the English and French components of a single legislature; this proved cumbersome and unworkable. The outcome in 1867, more than a century after the conquest, was the British North America Act (BNA), renamed in 1982 the Constitution Act. The BNA institutionalized a federal system of government for the new Dominion of Canada. "Confederation" was the joint response of the conservative elites of both the English- and French-speaking communities to paralysis of government and the threat of post–Civil War U.S. expansionism.

Confederation and Its Consequences

Under the rules of confederation, French Canadians agreed to remain part of a British dominated but self-governing Canadian state in return for effective political control and cultural autonomy in the province of Quebec. This control included exclusive jurisdiction over civil law, education, local government, and other activities vital to maintaining a French Catholic society. Within Quebec the English-speaking minority of 20 percent would be entitled to use their language in the legislature and the courts—the same rights accorded to French speakers in the Parliament and courts of the central government. Education in Quebec would be organized along confessional lines, so that the Catholic clergy would control the education of French-Canadian children, while Protestant school boards would perform this function for the English-speaking minority. In effect the federal system guaranteed the Quebec-based minority, led by their clergy, effective control over their separate educational, legal, welfare, and cultural institutions.

English and Scottish businessmen in Montreal, the economic capital of Canada until after World War II, owned and operated the major capitalist enterprises—banks, insurance companies, and trading, manufacturing, and transportation firms. They could continue to operate these enterprises in the English language without political interference from the government of Quebec. These arrangements and understandings resulted in a version of what political scientists a century later would recognize as "consociationalism": the elites of each community—the clergy and the small political class of French Canada, and the British business leaders—would manage their own autonomous institutions without interference from the other. Disputes would be negotiated and settled quietly by the elites of the two communities, whose constituents would defer to their judgment. French-Canadian politicians could and did participate, but as a minority of about 30 percent, in the government of Canada located in the new capital, Ottawa. While Parliament and the courts respected French and English bilingualism, the executive agencies of the government of Canada, including their offices in Quebec, functioned entirely in English.

The consequence of the confederation agreements was to guarantee the survival of French-Canadian society in its homeland, Quebec, but at a price. In Quebec, as elsewhere in Canada, French speakers were frozen out of modern economic roles and opportunities except as subordinates. The modern economic institutions were owned and operated by English speakers in the English language. They discriminated against Francophones, who, when admitted to managerial or professional roles, of course worked in the English language and mainly in middle management positions. A pattern of ethnic stratification emerged: French on the factory floor and in subaltern positions, English at professional and senior management levels. Very few French-speaking entrepreneurs were able to raise the capital or develop links in the modern economy that would enable them to move out of the ranks of the petty bourgeoisie. Reenforcing economic subordination was the stagnation of French-Canadian culture under the domination of a reactionary, ultramontane clergy that imposed strict intellectual censorship and resisted modernization as a godless, liberal threat to Christian society.

Quebec epitomized the "two solitudes" that coexisted but seldom intersected. Members of each community lived their lives in segregated enclaves. This situation satisfied Quebec's English speakers, for it confirmed their status as a privileged minority and posed no limitations on their freedom of action. It also satisfied the Catholic clergy, who consolidated their dominant position in French-Canadian society while presiding over the survival of the community for which they felt responsible.

The Strategy of Survivalism (*Survivance*)

The church intellectuals developed an elaborate ideology of conservative nationalism to justify the passivity and economic subordination of their French-Canadian flock. The appropriate goal in life for them was not material affluence, but Christian salvation. God had committed French Canadians in North America to a rural mission, in which the ideal life was that of the yeoman peasant (*habitant*) living in self-contained villages under the moral and spiritual guidance of their priests. Industries and cities that exposed people to the associated evils of liberalism, socialism, materialism, and godlessness should be happily conceded to Protestants and Jews. Beside its seminaries, the church would maintain classical colleges to train the limited number of doctors, lawyers, and other professionals needed to serve the French-Canadian community. The survival of that society would be guaranteed by a high birth rate, which actually succeeded in maintaining French Canadians at 30 percent of Canada's population during the century from 1860 to 1960, despite the incorporation of nearly all immigrants, including those entering Quebec, into the ranks of English speakers.

The church's rural strategy faltered under harsh demographic and economic realities. Rural Quebec could not support its rapidly growing population. From 1890 to 1910 nearly a million impoverished peasants migrated to New England to find employment in textile and other manufacturing industries. An equal number left Quebec for employment elsewhere in Canada. As manufacturing expanded during and after World War I, hundreds of thousands left their farms, moved to Montreal and its suburbs and soon constituted a large urban-industrial proletariat requiring services that the church was ill-equipped to provide. They were vulnerable to secular influences and temptations that their priests had difficulty combatting.

Fundamental to the church's survivalist strategy was its suspicion of government. A strong, active state might be tempted to challenge clerical control over education, health, welfare, and other services which the church considered part of its sacred mission. French-Canadian politicians, educated in institutions operated by the church, generally concurred in this limited conception of the role of the state. English-speaking elites were in substantial agreement, since a weak provincial government insured a low tax regime and noninterference in their affairs. The relative passivity of French Canadians was, however, interrupted by several dramatic instances of protest, first against the summary execution of the French-speaking leader of the prairie-based "Metis" (mixed bloods) in 1885, and more strikingly, against conscription during both world wars. Revulsion against conscription imposed by Canada's Conservative Party government during World War I virtually ensured large Quebec majorities for the Liberal Party in federal elections and contributed to Liberal domination in Ottawa for most of the ensuing 60 years.

French-speaking colonies scattered throughout Canada totaled nearly a million people. They maintained themselves with difficulty, chronically vulnerable to assimilation. There were, however, two exceptions: French Canadians comprised the critical mass necessary to group survival in New Brunswick, where descendants of the Acadians constituted a third of the population, and in Northeast Ontario, adjacent to Quebec. The vital core of French-Canadian society remained in their homeland on the banks of the St. Lawrence.

Prelude to the Quiet Revolution

Quebec emerged from World War II an urbanized, industrialized society whose church-dominated social institutions were losing their struggle to provide essential services. The provincial government under its autocratic, reactionary, and corrupt premier, Maurice Duplessis, had no desire to disturb the status quo. The central government in Ottawa, conversely, had embarked on ambitious programs to regulate the economy through Keynesian policies and to install a Beveridge-inspired welfare state throughout the country. Several federally financed programs were perceived by politicians at the provincial level, especially in Quebec, as dangerous and willful encroachments on the autonomy guaranteed to provinces by the confederal arrangements of 1867. Quebec, particularly, protested and stubbornly resisted many of these measures, refusing, for example, to accept federal grants to support university education.

During the 1950s, economic and ideological forces created significant opposition to the coalition of rural-based politicians, church authorities and their dependent professionals, and small businessmen who continued to dominate French-Canadian society and public affairs. A number of small-scale businessmen faced competition from larger, well-capitalized U.S. and Canadian enterprises that had begun to penetrate the Quebec economy, often with the encouragement of the provincial government. Their pleas for assistance were disregarded. The industrial labor force that had swollen during World War II was confronting the problems of urban life, including housing, health, and welfare, which neither the church nor the provincial government were addressing. The provincial government, moreover, demonstrated its hostility to labor unions by breaking strikes, most notably the protracted and highly publicized action of asbestos workers against foreign-owned corporations in the early 1950s.

The most important challenge to the status quo came from a determined minority of intellectuals, many of whom worked within the highly stressed institutions of the church. Some critics were influenced by the increasingly popular doctrines of post–World War II Catholic humanism, some by social democratic thought, some by anticolonial and neo-Marxist liberationist ideas. All agreed that the economic backwardness, material privation, and cultural stagnation of French-Canadian society could no longer be tolerated and must be reversed. They agreed further that the government of Quebec was an underutilized resource that should be mobilized to promote economic development and cultural renewal. The church should revert to its pastoral role, yielding education, health, welfare, and social services to the state. Quebec required an honest, competent, and progressive government to guide the long-delayed modernization of its society. These intellectuals, ranging from liberals to nationalists, rejected the century-old church doctrine of conservative survival in favor of a positive strategy of state-guided economic growth and cultural liberation. Many of them hoped also that an expanding state apparatus would provide more fulfilling professional careers for members of the French-educated middle class.

The Quiet Revolution

What came to be known as the Quiet Revolution was launched in 1960 with the unexpected victory of the Liberal Party of Quebec. The party's

leadership under Jean Lesage embodied the aspirations of a diffuse coalition of businessmen, trade unionists, and intellectuals. The transformation produced by the Quiet Revolution was remarkable, as its context
reveals. The French-Canadian population, still a distinct people, remained concentrated geographically in the province of Quebec with a
secure majority position of about 80 percent. The federal structure of
Canada enabled this majority to control the government of Quebec,
which in turn wielded wide-ranging powers, considerable—though underutilized—economic resources, and the ability to make convincing demands on the government in Ottawa. Though a minority in Canada,
Quebec's representation in the federal parliament and cabinet guaranteed it a voice in the government of Canada, especially when the Liberal
Party held office.

The Quiet Revolution changed the course of history in Quebec, and
its repercussions still reverberate throughout Canada. Its authors were
committed to the proposition that the survival of a distinctive French-
Canadian society in North America depended critically on its ability to
modernize technologically, economically, and culturally—in short, to
catch up with the English speaking majority. To share the results of
modernization French Canadians must participate fully in the direction
and management of the modern economy. A new identity, "Québécois,"
which proclaimed majority status in their homeland, supplanted the
more passive minority identity of "French-Canadian." The Quiet Revolution turned its back on the conservative, Catholic traditions of its
culture. The society rapidly, even militantly secularized: the explosion of
popular music, drama, poetry, novels—the cultural outpouring of a society that discovered a new dynamic—was self-consciously modern and
secular in its idiom and its messages. During this process of rapid culture
change, an invigorated French language supplanted Catholicism as the
principal marker of the new Québécois collective identity. The French
language, not the Catholic faith, would symbolize that community and
would henceforth require aggressive promotion and protection. The
Québécois now aspired to full participation in a dynamic North American and world economy; henceforth they would control their own destiny in their homeland by capitalizing on the resources of their provincial
government.

The Quiet Revolution regime moved rapidly to expand the the scope
of the government of Quebec. Responsibility for health, welfare, and
especially education were stripped from the church and eagerly assumed
by the provincial government. Education in the French language was

expanded and upgraded, especially at the university level, so that suffi-cient numbers of French speakers would be fully qualified for the pro-fessional, managerial, and scientific positions that would become open to them, first in the expanded government of Quebec and its public corporations and eventually in the private sector. Between 1960 and 1980, the percentage of francophones with post-secondary education increased from 6 to 30 percent, closing the gap with English speakers and putting to rest the canard—dear to many Anglophones—that French Canadians were culturally and perhaps even genetically unqual-ified for high-level roles in a competitive economy. The provincial bu-reaucracy expanded rapidly as government assumed new functions. This growth was paralleled by a network of state corporations designed to stimulate entrepreneurship among Québécois and increase the role of French speakers in the modern economy. During the 1960s, provincial government expenditures grew from 18 percent to 32 percent of GDP. By 1978, 25 percent of economically active Francophones were em-ployed by government or government enterprises. The most celebrated success was the state power monopoly, Hydro-Québec, operating at a high level of efficiency and entirely in the French language. It soon be-came the largest enterprise in Canada. The rapid growth of government and of state enterprises provided middle-class employment and profes-sional and managerial experience for the new graduates of French-language universities, soon the most zealous and committed partisans of Québécois nationalism.

Discarding their conservative predecessors' stubborn attempts to de-fend Quebec's autonomy from encroachment by Ottawa, the Quiet Rev-olution government adopted more aggressive tactics. They demanded that Ottawa return to the province control of a number of social welfare activities, including old age pensions, that were constitutionally assigned to the provinces but had been "usurped" by Ottawa as part of its pro-gram to create a Canada-wide welfare state. To pacify Quebec—and to ensure the future electoral support on which it depended—the Liberal Party government in Ottawa acceded to Quebec's demands to "opt out" of several welfare programs, with financial compensation that would enable the provincial government to operate its own programs and to invest pension funds in activities that would strengthen the French-speaking sectors of the Quebec economy. Quebec's dramatic success in confronting the government of Canada confirmed the confidence that positive action by their provincial state would enable Québécois to be-come, at long last, masters in their own house, *maîtres chez nous*.

The initial successes of the Quiet Revolution generated new problems, new confidence, and new political alignments. The first problem was the sudden realization that, as a consequence of modernization, the Québecois birth rate had tumbled from the highest in North America to the lowest in Canada. This collapse was aggravated by the long-established tendency of immigrants to Quebec to acculturate to the English language. The Francophone proportion of Canada's population was declining and the threat of *minorisation* in Quebec itself, especially in the critically important metropolitan area of Montreal, began to preoccupy Quebec's intellectuals. How could Quebec check this insidious trend and insure that Francophones would retain their majority status in this single French-speaking area of North America?

First, it was argued, future immigrants must be required to educate their children in French-medium schools, eliminating the freedom of choice that had long prevailed for immigrants and French-speaking parents as well. Second, French must become the language of work not only in the state sector but also in the modern sectors of the Quebec economy, including the headquarters of Montreal-based corporations that operated only in English. The private sector too would have to convert to French, so that French would become the language of work throughout Quebec, so that Québécois in the private sector would no longer be required to work in a second language, and so that immigrants would come to regard French as the language of economic opportunity. A bilingual regime that threatened to reduce French to minority status in its homeland could no longer be tolerated. To remain a French-speaking society, Quebec must become a French-speaking economy in a French-speaking ambiance. This change must encompass the private sector of the economy, even if such measures might incidentally inflict some pain on members of the English-speaking minority and violate the liberal notion of individual freedom of choice. The collective needs of the Québécois nation for cultural security in their homeland might have to supersede certain individual rights of Anglophones and Francophones alike.

Like all ethnic political movements, Quebec's Francophones split into several factions, a tendency encouraged by the freedom of expression and organization that prevailed in Canada's open opportunity structure. Traditional nationalism based on the clergy and its networks of rural and small town notables, farmers, merchants, and artisans became a spent force, though the Union Nationale based on this support won its final victory in the 1966 provincial election. Liberal, Pan-Canadian antinationalists, despite the example of that distinguished Quebecer, Canadian Prime Minister Pierre Trudeau, were unable to mobilize a significant following in provincial politics. To Trudeau and his liberal associates, nationalism in all forms is an inherently authoritarian and reactionary doctrine that undermines individual liberty and threatens to condemn French Canadians to permanent cultural and economic backwardness. Yet, while Trudeau carried Quebec decisively in all the federal elections that he contested, the liberal Pan-Canadian views that he espoused mobilized very little support in Quebec's provincial politics.

Neither traditional nationalism nor liberalism commanded significant constituencies in provincial politics after the Quiet Revolution. The main contestants were in their different ways both secular nationalists. Federalists, with their base in the growing French-Canadian business community and with reliable electoral support from the English-speaking minority, advocated a "profitable federalism" that would use Quebec's weight in the federal system to gain increased autonomy and otherwise unavailable economic resources. The provincial government would advance the cultural and economic interests of the Francophone majority. The Liberal Party of Quebec became the political vehicle of those secular nationalists who, on instrumental grounds, could accept a federalist Canada that provided firm assurance of effective provincial autonomy. They could reconcile two loyalties, two collective identities, Québécois and Canadian.

Their main opponents demanded political independence for a sovereign Quebec. During the 1950s, several small independence-oriented groups emerged, espousing diverse economic and social objectives and varying tactics for achieving them. The intellectual environment of the Quiet Revolution provided fertile ground for the articulation of radical goals, including political separation and independence. These groups were brought together in 1968 by the popular radio journalist, René Lévesque, in a new Parti Québécois (PQ) that soon became the main alternative to the federalist Liberals. The PQ included socialists, advocates of a mixed economy, supporters of immediate independence, and proponents of independence by stages. Lévesque was able to impose on this heterogeneous movement the goal of "sovereignty-association," political independence combined with economic union with English-speaking Canada, a formula that would minimize the economic risks of political independence. While promising the extension of the welfare state, intended to reassure their important labor constituency, Lévesque's dominant faction in the PQ also emphasized their willingness to respect and work with private capital, Francophone and Anglophone, Canadian and foreign. Their approach to independence would be deliberate but gradual and would fully respect democratic procedures. Socialists and revolutionaries participated in the independentist coalition, but they remained peripheral nuisances, checked by pragmatic leadership that disassociated itself from highly publicized incidents of terrorism provoked during the late 1960s and early 1970s by small, conspiratorial fringe groups.

The PQ achieved a level of grass-roots mobilization unmatched in Canadian history. Card-carrying, dues-paying membership reached a peak of 175,000 in 1977. The party financed its operations and campaigns almost entirely from dues and contributions by devoted members and sympathizers, since wealthy French-speaking individuals and enterprises were overwhelmingly federalist in their sympathies. The PQ won immediate, enthusiastic, and overwhelming support from Quebec's educated youth—high school and university students, journalists, musicians, artists, and teachers as well as industrial workers. Performing artists, especially, established an exciting ambiance for the youthful and enthusiastic militants of the PQ. The decade of the 1970s was a heady springtime of assertiveness, especially for the generation that benefitted from the educational expansion and middle-class employment opportunities generated by the Quiet Revolution. To be an educated youthful French speaker in the 1970s meant that one must be in the PQ camp.

Though all PQ supporters were nationalists, many nationalists continued to adhere to the federalist option, believing that the cultural and economic interests of Quebec's majority could best be served by promoting Quebec's autonomy, but within the Canadian political and economic framework. However, nationalist sentiments drove beyond their prudential calculations the policies and actions of the federalist Liberal Party government that regained office in 1970. After agreeing at a conference in Victoria, British Columbia, to an amending formula that would have permitted Canada to "patriate" its constitution, to eliminate the need to submit proposed constitutional amendments to the British Parliament, Quebec's federalist prime minister, Robert Bourassa, was forced to withdraw his approval because of a strong and unanticipated nationalist backlash against the prospect that Quebec would lose its veto over constitutional amendments.

More consequential was Bill 22 of 1974. Introduced by the Liberals, this measure explicitly abandoned the long-standing practice of bilingualism by declaring French to be the (sole) official language of Quebec. Henceforth all French-speaking and all immigrant children—except for those who could demonstrate prior knowledge of English—would be required to attend French-language schools, thereby eliminating parental freedom of choice. All professionals would be compelled to demonstrate a working knowledge of French before they could practice in the province. All but small businesses would be required gradually to convert to French as their language of work. A new government agency was established to monitor and enforce compliance with the new language regime. The angry protests of Montreal's Anglophone community were brushed aside, heralding the end of the consociational arrangements that for more than a century had regulated relations between the two communities. Official bilingualism had been solemnly adopted in 1969 as the policy of the government of Canada—in the face of substantial grassroots grumbling by English speakers; now, to their dismay, Quebec formally turned its back on bilingual practices that had prevailed in the province for more than a century. Nationalist sentiment was in the ascendancy: both federalists and independentists supported Bill 22.

English speakers were further shocked in November 1976, when the PQ, with 41 percent of the vote, defeated a divided opposition, won a majority of seats in the National Assembly, and took over the government of Quebec. Surveys indicated that fewer than 25 percent of Francophones favored political independence, and the PQ promised not to pursue the independence option without first consulting the voters. The most dramatic enactment of the new PQ government was Bill 101, the Charter of the French Language, which incorporated the policies of Bill 22, but with much greater rigor. Corporations employing more than fifty persons would thenceforth be required to conduct their labor relations in French, communicate with government and keep records in French, and petition for *francisation* certificates committing themselves to convert their operations to the French language. The visible ambiance of Quebec would henceforth be uniquely French. Like their predecessors, the PQ government followed pragmatic capitalist-oriented economic policies in order to maintain vital access to the New York money markets, attract foreign private investment, curb the exodus of Anglophone firms from the province, and ease the adjustment to a French language regime for firms that chose to continue in Quebec.

The 1980 Referendum and Its Aftermath

The PQ cabinet provided Quebec with unparalleled intergrity and competence; it was rewarded in turn by public appreciation and respect.

Mistaking this appreciation for pro-independence sentiment and prodded by their more militant wing, the Lévesque government sponsored a referendum in 1980 that would authorize them to inititate negotiations with the government of Canada for political sovereignty with economic association. After the tumultuous and bitter debates that preceded the balloting, the "no's" won 60 percent of the vote, French speakers dividing almost equally, English speakers opposing the measure nearly unanimously. Though the PQ was rewarded the next year with a second consolation term in office and by an enhanced majority, the independence bubble had burst. Enthusiasm waned, PQ membership declined sharply, and the second Lévesque government suffered one disastrous blow after another.

The Ottawa government under Trudeau had pledged that the defeat of the 1980 referendum would be followed by a fresh effort at "renewed federalism." In the protracted constitutional discussions that followed, Trudeau and the English-speaking provincial premiers outmaneuvered and eventually isolated the Quebec delegation. Quebec's independentist government refused to accede to the new constitutional agreements, even though they included a Charter of Rights and Freedoms that confirmed French as well as English as coequal official languages of the government of Canada, entrenched the constitutional right of Canadians to demand and receive services from the government of Canada in the official language of their choice, and required all provinces to provide elementary and secondary schooling for official language minorities. The new constitution did not, however, recognize the special status of Quebec as a distinct society, a status demanded by the great majority of Quebec's federalists as well as its independentists. The federal Parliament, with the approval of the nine English-speaking provinces, proceeded to enact the new constitutional provisions despite the passionate opposition of Quebec's government.

Surprisingly, this fresh set of grievances, this "calculated insult to Quebec," failed to stem the decline of the PQ. In response to a serious budgetary crisis, the PQ government reduced the salaries and then broke the strike of teachers and other provincial employees, among the PQ's most ardent and reliable supporters. In 1985, the PQ split over a decision by the majority not to press for independence in the oncoming provincial election. The unraveling of the PQ was completed later that year when the federalist Liberal Party, after nearly a decade in opposition, regained office with a large majority. Bourassa returned as prime minister, replacing Lévesque, who then resigned as leader of the PQ.

The malaise of the independentist movement after the 1980 referendum in no way signified the demise or decline of Québécois nationalism. Nationalist sentiments, never far below the surface of Quebec's politics, can be easily aroused. All Quebec separatists and most Quebec federalists are nationalists. They refer to Quebec as their national homeland and most of its conspicuous public institutions are prefixed by the term "national" rather than "provincial": its legislature, for example, is called the "national assembly." Many regard Quebec City as the capital of their Francophone nation, whereas Ottawa serves as the capital of English Canada. Thus they are part of a Canadian state, but not of a Canadian nation. Their primary collective identity is Québécois and their primary allegiance is to Quebec.

After Trudeau resigned as prime minister, Quebec voters abandoned the federal Liberal Party in the 1984 federal elections and helped to turn over the Ottawa government to the Progressive-Conservative Party headed by the Anglophone but fluently bilingual Quebecer, Brian Mulroney. Mulroney promised a policy of decentralization and reconciliation that would enable Quebec to accede to the 1982 constitutional changes. Bourassa and his associates agreed that if the federal government and the English-speaking provinces met certain strict conditions, Quebec would be prepared to ratify the changes. These conditions included explicit recognition of Quebec as a "distinct society" with implied but vague powers to protect its integrity when threatened. They called for the devolution of certain governmental functions, including immigration, communications media, manpower development, and natural resource management from federal to provincial control, as well as the funds required to manage them. Finally, they demanded a role for Quebec's government in the appointment of federal senators and supreme court justices. In a meeting at Meech Lake in 1987, the federal prime minister and the premiers of all the provinces accepted these terms, though they still required ratification by the federal parliament and all the provincial legislatures.

In the event, by the expiration in June 1990 of the three-year deadline for ratification, two of the provincial legislatures had failed to comply. Ratification was blocked in Manitoba because of the failure of the Meech Lake accords to recognize aboriginals—Indians and Inuit—as distinct societies. Throughout Canada a popular backlash was spreading among English speakers who feared that the Meech Lake provisions conceded too much to Quebec, crippled the federal government by stripping it of financial resources needed to maintain valued public services, and exposed the majority to future blackmail from Quebec for concessions of one kind or another as their price for remaining in Canada. The atmosphere was poisoned by the refusal of Quebec's federalist government, despite promises to the contrary, to relax the provisions of Bill 178, which denied English speakers the right to display signs in the English language on their business premises. To English speakers across Canada this measure constituted a flagrant and mean-spirited violation of Canada's Charter of Rights in a country that had accepted many elements of bilingualism to order to accommodate the French-speaking minority. If Quebec is unwilling to reciprocate, why should the majority agree to special status and special privileges for Quebec, why should they agree to have "French stuffed down our throats"? Better allow Quebec to secede, if it should come to that, than face more non-negotiable threats in the future.

Quebec's nationalists argue that Bill 178 and similar unilingual policies are needed as long as French remains an "endangered language" in North America. It requires special promotion and protection even if these measures incidentally and in small ways inconvenience the minority whose language and culture face no such threat. To English-speakers in Quebec and elsewhere in Canada, however, the sign law tramples on basic human rights and symbolizes the unwillingness of Quebec's majority to reciprocate the spirit of accommodation and good will represented by the Meech Lake provisions and by the bilingual legislation that has prevailed in Canada since 1969.

Quebec was outraged by the failure of the Meech Lake process. Once again Quebec had been insulted and its reasonable aspirations trashed. Nationalist sentiment, gradually recovering from the defeat of the 1980 referendum, was so inflamed that an unprecedented 50 percent of Quebec voters responded to polls in late 1990 that they would now welcome independence. Prime Minister Bourassa responded by scheduling another referendum for October 1992 on Quebec's future status in Canada, unless Ottawa in the interim presented an acceptable set of proposals similar in substance to the Meech Lake package. Such a set of proposals was indeed cobbled together at a meeting of first ministers in Charlottetown, Prince Edward Island, in August 1992. In addition to a modified distinct society clause for Quebec and the devolution of functions similar to the Meech Lake provisions, it guaranteed Quebec a minimum of 25 percent of the seats in the federal House of Commons regardless of future population trends. It conceded to the aboriginal peoples an "inherent right to self government" in what would constitute a third level of government within the boundaries of the provinces but outside their jurisdiction. An elected and strengthened senate with equal representation of the provinces would accommodate long-standing grievances among the western provinces. A "social charter" promised the welfare state favored by the labor unions and the New Democratic party. In a referendum on October 26, 1992, this complex package was defeated by a nationwide majority of 55 percent and lost in six of the ten provinces, including Quebec. The debacle in Quebec was due to an unlikely coalition between separatists and Pan-Canadianists who opposed the Charlottetown package for entirely contradictory reasons. This time, despite the support of its federalist prime minister, a majority in Quebec rejected an initiative by English-speaking Canada designed to accommodate their collective grievances and aspirations. To some Quebec nationalists, only independence would suffice; to others, English Canada had not conceded enough. To English speakers elsewhere in Canada, the Charlottetown package yielded too much. Constitutional reform was in shambles.

Senior politicians in English-speaking Canada, concerned with maintaining national unity and often oriented more to provincial than to federal power, have been more inclined than the Anglophone public to accommodate Quebec's demands. Many of the latter come from non-British, non-French immigrant backgrounds; having acculturated to English in what they consider an English-speaking country, they have neither asked for nor been granted any form of special treatment for their inherited language or culture; they have a gut hostility to French signs on public buildings, to commercial labels in French, and to French voices on the airwaves. Unsympathetic to the idea of special status and special privileges for Quebec, they are disinclined to weaken Ottawa's ability to finance such valued public services as health, hospital care, and equalization payments to the poorer provinces. They are more willing than their political leaders to call Quebec's bluff, to contemplate Quebec's secession rather than face repeated demands for unilateral and unreciprocated concessions.

Economic Factors and Independentist Sentiments

The economic base of Francophone society in Quebec has changed significantly in the three decades of the Quiet Revolution. French-owned, French-managed, French-speaking enterprises are more prominent and dynamic than ever before. In managerial and professional employment, though not in the ownership of corporate assets, French speakers have caught up with their English-speaking counterparts. Inherited patterns of ethnic stratification in employment have been eliminated. Quebec's political elites assume that an independent Quebec could accede to the North American free trade area, thus gaining ready access to U.S. markets and shedding dependence on the Canadian economy. Many express confidence that Quebec could now manage economically on its own.

Like the economies of Canada and the United States, however, the Quebec economy was in deep recession during the early 1990s, with an unemployment rate that exceeded 12 percent. Business leaders of both linguistic communities have been warning solemnly that secession would cause further flight of corporate headquarters and of capital and skills from Montreal, the drying up of needed foreign investment, a shrinking tax base, and massive unemployment; they plead for agreements that will retain Quebec's economic unity with Canada. Given a third provincial referendum, would the Francophone majority in Quebec be ruled by their hearts which favor independence; or by their heads which caution against the economic risks of secession?

Recent Canadian experience provides no simple economic explanation for variation in the intensity of nationalist mobilization. The surge of nationalism and collective self-confidence in the 1960s, including the rapid growth of the Parti Québécois and the enthusiasm it prompted among Francophone youth, appeared to be the product of optimistic expectations in an environment of economic expansion and global decolonization, rather than a response to specific threats or grievances. Rapid demobilization followed the defeat of the 1980 referendum, which may have been influenced by the weakness of the Quebec economy. Quebec's anger and frustration over the 1981–82 constitutional negotiations did not precipitate nationalist mobilization; the nationalist recovery occurred instead during the late 1980s at a time of economic recession and pessimism. It was accelerated by another insult to Quebec, the rejection of the Meech Lake package. Nationalist mobilization has occured in times of economic optimism and of economic pessimism, in response to grievances and independently of specific threats or complaints.

Though they harbor grievances, Québécois know that they are neither a powerless nor an oppressed people. They can determine their own future through negotiated arrangements as part of Canada or as an independent entity. Their emotions and calculations are influenced by many factors, including economic prospects, specific grievances, and ideological predispositions, but they react in complex patterns that defy simple correlations. Quebec's experience provides no support for the simplistic economism that associates ethnic mobilization with economic grievances and adversity, or interethnic harmony with economic growth and prosperity.

Language Minorities: Anglophones in Quebec, Francophones Elsewhere

The clear losers from the trends unleashed by the Quiet Revolution were English-speaking Quebecers. A demographic minority of 20 percent in the early 1970s, centered in Montreal, they dominated the modern economy and lived their lives in economically and socially privileged enclaves. Most of them had never bothered to learn French, finding the language of the majority unnecessary to their careers or social lives. They identified not with their neighbors, Quebec's French-speaking majority, but with Canada's English-speaking majority. To some Francophone intellectuals, this behavior provided a classic example of residual colonialism in their midst. A growing proportion of this heterogeneous "community" was not of British stock but of more recent immigrant origin—Italians, Jews, Greeks—from Eastern and Southern Europe. They had in common with earlier arrivals—English, Scots, Irish—a commitment to English as the language and culture of opportunity in Canada and North America. Indeed, English speakers were shocked and dismayed when the federalist Liberals, for whom most of then habitually voted, enacted Bill 22 in 1974, initiating a coercive language regime that English speakers perceived to be discriminatory and to threaten their vital interests. They were embittered not only by the disregard of established consociational procedures in Quebec but also by the failure of English Canada and the Ottawa government to come to their rescue. They would have to learn to survive on their own.

Within the next few years, especially after the separatist PQ victory in 1976 and the more stringent language legislation that ensued, large numbers. of Quebec's Anglophones emigrated to other provinces of Canada or to the United States. By the end of the 1980 their numbers had shrunk by nearly a third, to fewer than seven hundred thousand. Enrollment in

English-language schools declined by 50 percent as young Anglophones left Montreal and their numbers could no longer be replenished by immigrants. The emigrants included both small and large business and financial enterprises, many of the latter moving all or parts of their operations outside Quebec. Prominently represented were young people with portable skills. Large corporations, including the multinationals, adjusted rather easily, converting their Quebec-oriented operations to French and hiring more managers with Francophone backgrounds. From the provincial government eager to maintain their economic presence and the resultant employment and revenues, they won concessions that enabled them to continue to conduct international and trans-Canadian operations in English and allow transient headquarters staff to enroll their children in English language schools.

The majority of English speakers who remained attempted to learn French and adjust their business and personal activities. As befitted an economically and socially privileged middle-class community, Anglophones were unaccustomed to organized protest or political violence, hesitant to mobilize, and unable or unwilling to employ militant confrontational tactics. They never publicly challenged the principle of French-language hegemony. Their stance was entirely accommodational, asking only that their formal legal rights as a minority be guaranteed. They were seldom able to deter the application of measures that threatened their status and interests, including the aforementioned Bill 178 which denied them the right to display English signs on their business premises. Though their organizations, notably the Quebec Alliance–Alliance Québec, proclaimed, in fluent French, their determination to remain in Quebec and participate fully in Quebec's future, their ineffectual performance did little to bolster the confidence of their anxious and angry constituents. As their numbers diminished and they lost preferential access as individuals to managerial posts in the private corporations, Quebec's Anglophone community faced the grim prospect that they would lack the numbers and the financial resources to maintain their educational, cultural, and welfare institutions. As the spectre of demographic *minorisation* was lifted from Francophones, the once proud Anglophone minority had to learn to survive as a marginalized community.

Economic discrimination was not the only concern of Anglophone youth. They were also uneasy about their minority status in an increasingly nationalist environment. Who would qualify in the future as a full-fledged Quebecer? Would full membership in Quebec society be based on ethnic or on civic criteria? Quebec's political leaders, federalist and separatist alike, urged Anglophones to stay, promising liberal rights and protection for their institutions, and, by an act of the National Assembly in 1986, guaranteeing public services in English, as long as they were prepared to comply in the public realm with the new language regime. Their skills and capital were needed and wanted. Other spokespersons for the majority were, however, much less reassuring. They suggested that only persons of Catholic and French origins, Québécois *pure laine,* would qualify as first-class members of Quebec society; others, however fluent in French, would be relegated to second-class status and could not expect, in fact, to enjoy equal political and economic rights. If, as many Anglophones feared, ethnic criteria would indeed prevail in a nationalist Quebec, they could anticipate the status only of a tolerated minority subject to informal but nonetheless real discriminatory treatment. As there were ample opportunities elsewhere in North America for English speakers, especially those with capital or advanced skills, emigration accelerated during the 1980s. The average age of the shrinking Anglophone community continued to rise as its youth departed.

The other official language minority consists of Francophones outside Quebec. They are present in all the English-speaking provinces, but in substantial numbers only in bilingual New Brunswick, where former Acadians comprise a third of the population, and in Northeast Ontario adjacent to Quebec. Elsewhere, French-Canadian communities survive in scattered enclaves, vulnerable to assimilation because their language has no economic value. In earlier periods, isolated agricultural communities led by their priests could function and maintain themselves in French. In modern urbanized societies there are few incentives and fewer means for young people to carry on those traditions. As a result, attrition rates exceed 50 percent with each passing generation.

In keeping with its bilingual policy, the government of Canada attempts to make federal services available in French to those communities, including radio transmissions, and provides subsidies to provincial governments to strengthen educational facilities in the French medium in support of the Charter of Rights and Freedoms that requires provinces to provide schooling in minority official languages where numbers suffice. Except for New Brunswick, which is formally bilingual, and Ontario, which has gradually extended public services in French, the English language provinces do not undertake to deliver services other than education in French.

Organized French-speaking communities outside Quebec oppose independence for Quebec, fearing that if Quebec should leave, Canada would cease to be a bilingual polity. In that event, the assistance they now receive from Ottawa to maintain their culture would disappear, as might constitutional protection of minority language rights. Quebec nationalists have a different perspective. They express strong fraternal sympathy for the survivors of the diaspora from Quebec, helping with school texts and curricula and with radio and television programming. They are unwilling, however, to constrain any of their own demands or aspirations in order to protect Francophones elsewhere. They argue that, except perhaps in New Brunswick and Ontario, these communities are doomed, for their language has no economic value and they lack the critical mass needed for the survival of their institutions. If they wish to participate in and contribute to a flourishing, modern French society, they are welcome to "return" to Quebec. In defense of provincial autonomy on language matters, Quebec's government actually appeared in court to challenge the right of Ottawa to intervene in Alberta and Saskatchewan on behalf of the rights of French-speaking minorities! Quebec separatists ridicule Canada's bilingual programs as symbolic sops to French speakers outside Quebec. Following the normal practice of governments, they argue, Quebec should become unilingually French, the rest of Canada unilingually English.

External Influences

External factors have influenced relations between English and French speakers. The global success of national liberation movements in the 1960s, especially in Algeria and Vietnam, helped to inspire nationalist sentiments and confidence among Québécois intellectuals and youth. The most significant external influence has been the expansive and powerful presence of the United States. The decisions of the victorious British to tolerate the Catholic faith, French-speaking institutions, and the Franco-Roman legal system in 1774 and 1791 were predicated on Britain's need to win the support of the clergy against the rebel colonies and their secular republic. Similar calculations facilitated the Confederation agreements in the 1860s, when the elites of both communities joined in common cause to prevent encroachment from the expansionist republic to the south. As long as Quebec's elites clung to the strategy of conservative survival, the United States seemed a greater threat than English Canada. With the Quiet Revolution, these calculations shifted. United States territorial expansion was no longer a concern. It was left-leaning Anglophone intellectuals, not Francophones, that agonized over their elites' "silent surrender" to economic invasion by Yankee capitalists and to American cultural imperialism. Both independentists and federalists in Quebec have actively sought and welcomed U.S. participation in Quebec's economy, investments by American-owned firms, access to U.S. money markets, and outlets for Quebec's products in the vast U.S. markets. Quebec's government vigorously supported the Canada–U.S. Free Trade Agreement of 1988 as a counterweight to the Ottawa government and to the economic power of Canadian firms. Independentists continue to espouse sovereignty-association—economic association no longer with Canada, but with the United States.

Quebec's government maintains the equivalent of a foreign ministry, insisting on the right to conduct international relations on any subject for which it is responsible under Canada's constitution. In practical terms, this insistence has meant Quebec's participation in international organizations and conferences that involve "la francophonie." Though Ottawa originally asserted its exclusive power to represent Canada and all its provinces in international forums, it has gradually accommodated Quebec's claims on matters involving French language and culture. Canadian delegations to such conferences now include representatives selected by the government of Quebec. Meanwhile, the government of France has promoted Quebec's role as an international actor, blatantly with de Gaulle's "vive le Québec libre" pronouncement at the Montreal City Hall in 1967, more subtly by treating Quebec's office in Paris virtually as an embassy, and more correctly by extravagant recognition of Quebec's participation in *la francophonie.*

French-Canadian and Québécois nationalism have not, however, depended on inspiration or support from France. For nearly two centuries, the clerical elites preferred to keep their distance from the anticlerical society that emerged from the revolution of 1789. Their secular successors correctly calculated that they could expect little tangible political or economic assistance and only limited moral support from Paris.

Conflict Management

The fathers of Confederation in the mid-1860s chose a federal polity. While promoting an integrated continentwide economy and thereby resisting encroachments by the United States, federal arrangements allowed sufficient provincial autonomy to enable the Catholic, French-speaking majority in Quebec to protect and maintain its distinctive collective identity and institutions within a dominantly English-speaking polity and economy. Federalism has provided the structural foundation for the management of Canada's ethnic pluralism in two arenas, at the level of the central state and within each of the ten provinces. The relatively open political opportunity structure in Canada, including freedom for aggrieved ethnic communities to organize, protest, and exert political influence on their behalf, has insured that most episodes of ethnic conflict, notably the demands of Québécois nationalism associated with the Quiet Revolution and its aftermath, have occurred peacefully and legally.

Until the Quiet Revolution the nine English-speaking provinces accorded few collective rights to their French-speaking minorities. Public education and other government services were available only in English; in several areas, notably Manitoba, language rights guaranteed to Francophones by federal statute were subsequently nullified and overridden by English-language majorities. Cultural survival for French-speaking communities depended on their own resources and those of the Catholic Church. Under these unfavorable conditions they were highly vulnerable to assimilation. Quebec's Quiet Revolution in the 1960s, combined with pressures from Ottawa, prompted accommodational changes in the English-speaking provinces. New Brunswick, 30 percent French-speaking, became officially bilingual in 1967. Though avoiding official bilingualism, Ontario gradually extended a full range of public services to its substantial Francophone minority. Manitoba has been compelled by the Supreme Court of Canada, after a break of nearly a century, to honor its statutory obligation to respect the language rights of its Francophone minority. The other English-speaking provinces, overcoming the initial reluctance of their constituents, have committed themselves under the 1982 constitutional amendments to provide elementary and secondary education at public expense to official language minorities where numbers warrant. These entrenched constitutional rights can be litigated in the courts, an effective method of conflict management. Ottawa allots money to implement minority official language education. French-speaking communities outside Quebec are mobilized to promote and protect their newfound language rights.

During the century preceding the Quiet Revolution, ethnic pluralism in Quebec was regulated by consociational arrangements. The French-speaking Catholic majority and the economically dominant English-speaking minority maintained their separate institutions free of interference from the other. When conflicts arose that required settlement, they were negotiated behind the scenes by the elites of both communities, English-speaking business leaders on the one hand and the church hierarchy and senior provincial politicians on the other. Measures that might offend either community or that might alter the implicit rules of this pluralist society were avoided, establishing a century-long pattern of peaceful, though economically very unequal, coexistence.

The jettisoning of this pattern of coexistence by Bill 22 in 1974 signalled the end of the consociational era and the inauguration of a new pattern of political relationships in which English speakers became a weak and ineffectual minority. Since 1867, the provincial government of Quebec has functioned as the agent of the ethnic majority that it represents. Before 1974, it was constrained by consociational understandings to accommodate the economically powerful English-speaking minority. Since 1974, these constraints no longer apply; terms of coexistence are not negotiated, they are dictated by nationalist elites in firm control of Quebec's political institutions.

Until the 1960s, the government of Canada served, in fact, as the political expression of Canada's English-speaking majority. Though the French language enjoyed legal status in the Parliament and the courts, government operated entirely in English. Francophone prime ministers, Laurier (1896–1911) and St. Laurent (1949–1957), as well as French-speaking cabinet ministers and senior civil servants functioned in English. Federal offices even in Quebec operated in English. Ottawa did little to protect the interests of French-speaking minorities. Quebec's distinctive interests could be articulated by their elected deputies in Parliament and the major parties competed for Quebec's votes. But their political weight could be and indeed was overridden in important instances, notably in the execution of the prairie-based rebel Louis Riel in 1885 and in conscription in both world wars, the latter leaving a bitter residue of resentment among Quebec's majority.

The emergence of the Quiet Revolution in 1960 was followed in three years by the return to office in Ottawa of the federal Liberal Party. Aware of their dependence on Quebec for electoral support, their leaders were also unprecedentedly sensitive to Quebec's grievances and disposed to accommodate them. At the symbolic level the Maple Leaf supplanted the Union Jack, and "O Canada," in French and English versions, replaced "God Save the King." Their inclination to reassure Quebec was enhanced by the findings of the prestigious Royal Commission on Bi-Lingualism and Bi-Culturalism which reported urgently that unless Quebec's well-founded economic and cultural grievances were attended to, Canada might not survive as a political community. An essential first step, the commission recommended, would be to equalize the status and the value of the French language throughout Canada.

In 1969, the Parliament under Prime Minister Trudeau enacted an Official Languages Act establishing French and English as coequal official languages of the government of Canada. This act included the principle that any Canadian should be able to request and receive public services from any agency of the federal government anywhere in Canada in the official language of his or her choice. To qualify for federal positions designated as bilingual, English-speaking civil servants were encouraged, at public expense, to become competent in French. To achieve "balanced participation" of members of both language communities in bureaucratic positions, special efforts were made to recruit Francophones; overall this goal was achieved by the mid-1980s, though Francophones remain underrepresented in senior managerial and scientific positions. The leaders of Canada's three major parties, Progressive-Conservatives and New Democrats as well as Liberals, have steadfastly supported bilingual programs as essential to the unity of Canada, despite considerable grassroots grumbling and opposition, especially in the western provinces, among English-speaking civil servants, and among non-French, non-British ethnic minorities. In 1988, again with all-party support, Parliament enacted an Official Languages Act that extended, clarified, and updated the earlier legislation. Federal legislation regarding official bilingualism applies, however, only to the federal government and its institutions. Except for measures entrenched in the constitution, language policies for provincial services remain under provincial control and can, as in the case of Quebec, disregard or directly contradict federal policy.

Trudeau moved decisively to confirm the "French fact" in the Ottawa government by appointing French speakers to many conspicuous cabinet-level posts and to senior positions in the civil service. Even after Quebec turned its back on bilingualism, the Ottawa government under both Liberal and Conservative regimes persisted with this instrument of accommodation. It did not formally challenge Quebec's unilingual language policies and practices, though these compromised the spirit, if not the letter, of Canada's constitution, and it allowed Quebec to "opt out" of several federal programs with full financial compensation. In many other ways it acquiesced in measures that stretched the notion of provincial autonomy, all in the interest of conciliating Quebec and reducing the appeal of the growing separatist movement.

The political elites disagreed fundamentally on what constituted the interests of Canada's French speakers, and their differences had important implications for public policy. To Pan-Canadian liberals like Trudeau, accommodating the legitimate needs and aspirations of Canada's Francophones meant the achievement, Canada-wide, of equal status for both official languages and insuring equal opportunities for all individuals throughout Canada to participate in the country's development. By Trudeau's firm antinationalist position and by opposing special status of any kind for Quebec, this formidable French-speaking Quebecer incurred the enmity of Quebec nationalists, federalist and separatist alike, who construed his opposition to special status for Quebec and his emphasis on individual rather than collective rights as a sell-out to the English majority and a death knell for a distinctive French-speaking society in North America. The cultural and economic interests of the Québécois can be protected, they argued, only by vigorous collective measures enforced by the one political authority that they control, the state of Quebec. Moreover, these necessary measures must not be constrained by the preferences or anxieties of Francophone minorities outside the homeland. What Trudeau and the English-speaking majority regarded as accommodative to the French-speaking minority, Quebec's nationalists regarded as at best irrelevant, at worst as subversive to their survival and development as a distinct people. Events surrounding the constitutional changes in 1981–82 and the subsequent failure of the Meech Lake accords confirmed their suspicions that English speakers and Pan-Canadianists were prepared to ignore and override ruthlessly the fundamental collective interests of the Québécois nation.

Prime Minister Brian Mulroney, who took office in 1984, attempted to reverse Trudeau's policy by explicitly accepting the nationalist demand for special status for Quebec. Canadian unity could be protected by formally recognizing Quebec's claims to be a "distinct society" and by meeting Quebec's demands that certain federal powers be devolved to the provinces, enhancing Quebec's autonomy but within the framework of a more decentralized Canadian state. In both the Meech Lake and the Charlottetown rounds, Mulroney persuaded the leaders of Canada's three major political parties, including the premiers of the English-speaking provinces, to concur with these constitutional changes in the interest of maintaining the unity of Canada. These initiatives were nonetheless rejected by a majority of English speakers and, adding insult to injury, were rendered moot when a majority of his own constituents repudiated Quebec's federalist prime minister in the October 1992 referendum.

In response to the Quiet Revolution, the Ottawa government ceased to function as the agent of Canada's English-speaking majority. It achieved sufficient autonomy to attempt accommodation of competing expectations about what would constitute fair and equitable patterns of coexistence: for the mobilized majority in Quebec that considers itself a distinct nation, and the English-speaking majority elsewhere in the country that regards Canada as a single polity comprising ten provinces and two major language communities in a multicultural framework. Though the constitutional changes of 1982 entrenched language rights, they failed to satisfy the broader political aspirations of Quebec's majority, including the federalists among them. Despite agonizing and exhausting efforts by Canada's political elites, Anglophone and Francophone alike, a structural formula for managing this conflict and achieving consensual terms of coexistence continues to elude them.

The results of the October 25, 1993, general election reflect a polarizing trend along the ethnic divide in Canadian politics. The Progressive-Conservative Party, which had sponsored the Meech Lake and the Charlottetown initiatives, suffered the worst electoral disaster in Canadian history, winning only two seats in the new Parliament. Capitalizing on economic discontents and on long-standing alienation from the central Canadian "establishment," including its accommodative stance toward Quebec and its support for bilingualism, the populist Reform Party took third place, winning 52 seats, supplanting the Conservatives as majority representatives for western Canada. The Bloc Québécois, campaigning on a separatist platform, swept Quebec; it garnered 54 seats, three-fourths of Quebec's deputies in the federal Parliament, achieving the status of official opposition. After nearly a decade in opposition, the Liberal Party won 177 of 285 seats and formed a government headed by Jean Chrétien, a protegé of former prime minister Trudeau. In January 1994, shortly before this book went to press, a survey of Quebec voters reported that 53.7 percent of respondents favored independence. Had a provincial election taken place at that time, the separatist Parti Québécois would have defeated the federalist Liberals by 46.6 to 40.9 percent.[1]

[1] *Montreal Gazette,* 21 January 1994, A5.

A century and a half after Lord Durhams's observation that introduced this chapter, two nations continue to war—happily by civil rather
than violent means—in the bosom of a single state. The survival of that
state remains very much in question.

7

International Migration
and Labor Diasporas

Beginning with a brief survey of labor migration since World War II, this chapter examines in successive sections the politics of several labor diasporas: Mexicans in the United States, North Africans in France, Turks in Germany, and the emergent Asian diasporas in Japan. A final section confirms and expands the general conclusions anticipated in the following propositions:

1. High-income and growing economies have a continuing and compelling need for labor; because of low birth rates this demand cannot be fully satisfied from domestic sources.

2. Low-income countries with high rates of population growth generate chronic large labor surpluses.

3. The coincidence of the two foregoing situations produces irrepressible pressures for large-scale transnational labor migration, legal where possible, illegal where necessary.

4. As the economies of democratic receiving countries become dependent on foreign labor, the diasporas establish permanent minority settlements. Democratic polities are inhibited from arbitrary treatment or summary expulsion of legally resident aliens.

5. The legal regimes, institutions, and political cultures of receiving countries confront immigrant communities with variable patterns of constraints, controls, and opportunities. Governments that define citizenship

An earlier version of this chapter appeared in the journal *Diaspora* 2 (Spring 1992), published by Oxford University Press. This version appears by permission of the publisher.

in political or cultural terms tend to be relatively open; those that define citizenship in ethnic terms tend to be relatively closed.

6. The discrimination encountered by migrant communities, combined with their desire to maintain their culture, generates political mobilization and political action that may employ both institutional and non-institutional methods.

7. The conspicuous presence and political activation of immigrant communities produce reactive mobilization and demands among segments of the receiving society to limit or roll back the status of immigrants. This tendency is exacerbated in periods of economic recession.

8. Thus, international labor migration to democratic countries brings contentious political issues to the agendas of the receiving polity.

9. The outcomes of such political processes, including eventual patterns of immigrant incorporation, depend on the propensity of diasporas to accept membership in the host society and the willingness of the latter to integrate them as full members of the polity.

10. Governments that foster integration encourage individual assimilation but tend to resist official recognition of group pluralism, multiculturalism, or minority political rights.

Labor Diasporas as Political Actors

Since the beginnings of recorded history people have migrated across political boundaries.[1] Whole communities have been expelled and forced to migrate, Jews from Spain in 1492, Acadians from Nova Scotia in 1755, Tatars from the Crimea in 1944. Africans and others have been

[1] Aside from case studies, there have been few systematic efforts to examine the political as opposed to the economic, social, and demographic implications of labor diasporas. One of the pioneers was Gary Freeman's *Immigrant Labor and Racial Conflict in Industrial Societies* (Princeton: Princeton University Press, 1979). See also William R. Brubaker, ed., *Immigration and the Politics of Citizenship in Europe and North America* (Lanham, Mar yland: University Press of America, 1989); Mark J. Miller, *Foreign Workers in Western Europe: An Emerging Political Force* (New York: Praeger, 1981) includes a section on comparative perspectives, 195–204, as does William Safran's essay "Sociopolitical Context of Ethnic Consciousness in France and the United States," in Anthony Messina, et al., eds., *Ethnic and Racial Minorities in Advanced Industrial Democracies* (New York: Greenwood Press, 1992), 67–90; Milton J. Esman "Diasporas in International Relations," in Gabriel Sheffer, ed., *Modern Diasporas in International Politics* (London, Croom-Helm, 1986); and John Armstrong, "Mobilized and Proletarian Diasporas," *American Political Science Review* 70 (June 1976).

transported across continents in bondage. Small groups have migrated
to escape religious or political persecution. Most often, however, these
movements take place in pursuit of economic opportunities and better
livelihoods. Since World War II, the rate of transnational migration has
accelerated rapidly; World Bank demographers estimate that 80 million
people work outside their country of origin and that by the mid-1990s
net annual migration across international borders will exceed 1.1 million.[2]

Labor migrations are driven by two complementary forces: the compelling need for unskilled labor in "First World" industrial and postindustrial economies, and the desperate search for livelihoods in
labor-surplus "Third World" countries. These simultaneous push and
pull forces have been strengthened by low fertility rates in the industrialized countries and the unprecedentedly high rates of population
growth in the Third World. So imperative are these demand and supply
relationships and so persistent and resourceful the migrants that the resultant labor flows, legal where possible, illegal where necessary, thwart
the enforcement of immigration controls. This exigent labor market
nexus has been facilitated by technology, especially the availability of
reliable, speedy, safe, and relatively low-cost mass transportation.

These labor migrations have not been random. They have been patterned by familiar channels traceable to earlier colonial links, established
economic networks, and geographical convenience. Commercially motivated intermediaries in both sending and receiving countries facilitate
these movements. Prospective migrants tend to be attracted to locations
where they can expect social supports from earlier arrivals and job opportunities. These channels are enlarged by services that facilitate re-
mittance of funds to families in the home country, two-way shipment of
goods, arrangements for travel back and forth, and importation of familiar foodstuffs, publications, and religious objects. Such services help
to insure, for instance, that Mexican laborers migrate to and eventually
settle in the United States, especially the Southwest, that North Africans
locate in France, Turks in Germany and Koreans in Japan. Such patterns
are never exclusive, but they help to explain why workers of certain
backgrounds tend to gravitate to and form communities in certain countries and not in others.

Public attitudes in receiving countries are at best ambivalent and often

[2]Sharon Russell and Michael Teitlebaum, *International Migration and International Trade*, World Bank Discussion Paper 160 (1992).

unfriendly to foreign workers, who, although needed, are not welcomed. The official reception varies, however, with immigration experience, legal institutions, labor market conditions, and the provenance of the migrants. In general, the greater the cultural and racial distance from the norms of the host society, the greater the hostility. Though the need for immigrant labor may be reluctantly conceded, the initial expectation is that the labor flows will be temporary and that migrants will return to their country of origin when their services are no longer needed. Thus, as sojourners, they will not constitute a permanent presence in the receiving country, a view that is often shared by the migrants themselves. If permanent residence cannot be avoided, immigration regulations may insure that immigrants and their locally born offsprings remain in the status of resident aliens. In some cases, however, they are permitted to naturalize, to participate eventually as citizens in their adopted country, especially in countries where locally born children are entitled ipso facto to citizenship. The status of immigrants can range from illegal to legal temporary, to legal permanent resident, to citizenship. The status accorded to the locally born second generation is a critical factor.

Industrialized countries develop an evolving structural need for low-cost immigrant labor. The initial demand appears in agriculture, manufacturing, and construction; for such labor, employers, often with government support, recruit workers in Third World countries. Some employers in manufacturing industries may attempt to reduce this demand by exporting jobs, building plants in low-income countries. When the initial demand for foreign workers is met, governments may curtail or even terminate legal immigration, recognizing at the same time that migrants occupy niches and perform indispensable functions in their economies. They hold jobs that citizen workers decline to fill, jobs that are considered menial and in fact become reserved in segmented or dual labor markets for immigrants, even in the face of substantial domestic unemployment. Even if manufacturing jobs are exported, jobs in agriculture and construction cannot be; moreover, there are large and seemingly inexhaustible needs for low-cost labor in the expanding service sectors of affluent economies, from restaurants, hotels, and hospitals to airport and street maintenance, household employment, and the sex industries. Since employers prefer a trained and stable work force, they pressure governments to convert immigrants to permanent resident status. When the demand cannot be met by resident aliens and their children, additional and, if necessary, illegal immigration invariably follows.

Authoritarian and democratic polities treat immigrant labor differently. Authoritarian states, of which the Persian Gulf kingdoms and emirates are examples, may demand and attract large flows of immigrant labor often from long distances. These workers are regarded as temporary. Renewed and extended contracts convey no legal rights and no prospect of ever achieving citizenship. The workers are useful only as a source of labor, they remain entirely on sufferance, they can be sent home without warning and with no legal recourse. When Yemen supported Saddam Hussein's invasion of Kuwait in August 1990, the Saudi government deported a half million Yemeni workers, some of whom had resided in Saudi Arabia for decades. In 1983, Nigeria summarily expelled a million Ghanaian workers.

Democratic governments find it difficult to treat immigrant workers in this way, especially those who have been accorded legal resident status. Even when their status is closely regulated and constrained, as in Switzerland, they are not without rights. The constitutions, laws, and conventions of democratic polities confer certain rights even on noncitizens; they can be encouraged and even bribed to return to their native countries, but they cannot be arbitrarily expelled. Even when further immigration has been terminated, family reunions are usually allowed on compassionate or humanitarian grounds. As resident aliens, immigrants are usually eligible for government- (and union-) provided welfare services. Interventions on their behalf by domestic religious, civil rights, humanitarian, and welfare-oriented organizations are reenforced by international pressures. The foreign policies of receiving countries often favor good relations with the sending country; these relations can be impaired by discriminatory or arbitrary treatment of the latter's nationals. Despite hostile or harsh treatment, then, resident alien workers and their families are not without important rights and protections in democratic polities.

Most labor migrants originally consider themselves sojourners, intending eventually to return to their home country, and many in fact do so. But because they are economically needed in the host country, because economic prospects in their home countries are unpromising, because they find the way of life in the receiving country not entirely unattractive for themselves and especially their children, and because they enjoy some rights in these countries, significant numbers choose to remain. The resulting diaspora settlements remain distinctive communities, enclaves with their own institutions and practices. Because they usually experience rejection and marginalization by their host society and because they desire to maintain elements of their culture and collective identity, they do not assimilate. In many ways, however, the first and especially the second generation acculturate, living simultaneously in two societies. Far from disappearing, their numbers increase in absolute and relative terms because their communities are demographically young and their fertility greatly exceeds that of their aging host population.

These permanently established disapora communities encounter discrimination or what they interpret as discrimination. They are relegated to housing in the poorest and most dilapidated urban neighborhoods, denied access to skilled, higher-income employment, confined to inferior schooling and other public services, and often denied opportunities for citizenship and political participation. Immigrants believe these patterns of symbolic and real discrimination to be deliberate for they often involve hostile behavior by local officials and abusive treatment by police. Meanwhile, strong sentiment may favor cultural maintenance, which members of diasporas, especially intellectuals among them, believe should not only be tolerated but supported as a basic human right by host governments.

When their aspirations appear blocked, their status disparaged, their rights denied, diaspora communities mobilize. What begin as mutual help and sociocultural associations gradually evolve into quasi-political organizations committed to defending and promoting collective interests through public relations, demonstrations, legal means and political action. Often the political entrepreneurs who assume leadership of these organizations are acculturated second-generation men or women whose career expectations have been blocked by discrimination and whose political futures can be built by mobilizing support from their communities. The divisions that invariably appear among immigrant organizations can be traced as often to competing personal ambitions as to underlying class or ideological differences.

As diaspora political organizations are activated, elements in the host society feel threatened by encroachments of despised foreigners on their neighborhoods and way of life; by competition for employment, housing, and public services; and by the sense that their society and culture are being overwhelmed and degraded by unattractive and unassimilable aliens. These sentiments generate political reactions from nativist sources. From their ranks emerge political entepreneurs who mobilize constituencies to demand that government protect society from the immigrant threat. They call for measures ranging from expulsion to severe restrictions on further immigration to curtailing access to employment, public services, and welfare benefits. These processes of political mobilization and countermobilization inevitably produce ethnic tensions and even violence at the local level, which escalate to the level of national and often international politics. Though specific patterns vary, labor diasporas invariably generate political mobilization and political conflict in industrial and postindustrial democratic polities.

Mexican-Americans in the United States

The United States is a society accustomed to receiving and absorbing large flows of immigrants.[3] Except for the native peoples who were conquered, dispossessed, and eventually reduced to impoverished dependency, no ethnic group can convincingly claim the United States as its exclusive ancestral homeland. All are of immigrant stock. There have been periods of nativism punctuated by episodes of violence in which the descendants of earlier arrivals, now native sons, protested and attempted to limit immigration by successors of less desirable origins. Racist sentiments have been present, barring the legal immigration of Asians and, from 1924 to 1965, enforcing national origins quotas that favored immigrants from northern and western Europe and discriminated against those from eastern and southern Europe. By international standards, however, the United States remains a country that accepts large numbers of immigrants from diverse ethnic backgrounds. Once admitted legally, immigrants of all origins are encouraged to "Americanize" as rapidly as possible. Naturalization after five years of residence is a simple proce-

[3]Data on Mexican Americans have been drawn mainly from the following sources: Walker Connor, ed., *Mexican-Americans in Comparative Perspective* (Washington, D.C.: Urban Institute, 1985); F. Chris Garcia, ed., *Latinos and the Political System* (Notre Dame, Ind.: University of Notre Dame Press, 1988); L. H. Gann and Peter J. Duigan, *The Hispanics in the United States: A History* (Boulder, Colo.: Westview Press, 1986); and Mario Barrera, *Beyond Aztlan: Ethnic Autonomy in Comparative Perspective* (New York: Praeger, 1988). On immigration reform the best source is Aristide R. Zolberg, "Reforming the Back Door: The Immigration Reform and Control Act of 1986 in Historical Perspective," in Virginia Yans-McLaughlin, ed., *Immigration Reconsidered: History, Sociology and Politics* (New York: Oxford University Press, 1990). The best treatment of bilingual education is by James Crawford, *Bi-lingual Education: History, Politics, Theory and Practice* (Trenton, N.J.: Crane Publishing, 1989). The vast literature on U.S. experience with immigration is epitomized in Lawrence Fuchs's recent volume, *The American Kaleidoscope: Race, Ethnicity and Civic Culture* (Hanover, N.H.: Wesleyan University Press, 1990). See also Roger Daniels, *Coming to America: A History of Immigration and Ethnicity in American Life* (New York: Harper Collins, 1991).

dure. All children born in the United States, whether or not their parents are citizens or even legal aliens, are ipso facto entitled to citizenship. Despite assimilationist pressures, immigrants and the ethnic communities they form enjoy the right to define, defend, and promote their group interests by organized political and nonpolitical means. The concept of citizenship is civic and inclusive rather than ethnic and exclusive.

Each of the many diasporas that entered the United States, including African Americans distinguished by race as well as culture, had distinctive experiences celebrated in a large literature. The largest category of arrivals during the past three decades has been "Hispanics" from the Caribbean basin. More than 60 percent of Hispanics are of Mexican origin. In its 1987 current population survey, the U.S. Census Bureau estimated that nearly twelve million of the nineteen million Hispanics in the United States were of Mexican origin; this diaspora is likely to exceed fifteen million by the turn of the century.[4]

The first Mexican Americans came to the United States, so to speak, with the territory. The conquests in the 1840s of the vast territories of the Southwest, comprising most of the present states of Texas, California, New Mexico, Arizona, Nevada, Utah, and Colorado, brought under U.S. jurisdiction an estimated hundred thousand resident Mexicans who chose to remain and accept U.S. citizenship. Over the next half-century, with few exceptions mainly in northern New Mexico, these people were dispossessed of their property, reduced to menial occupations, and excluded from political participation while their culture was ridiculed and degraded. As non-white mestizos (mixed Caucasian and Indian) Mexican Americans felt the lash of institutional racism that prevailed in U.S. society until well after World War II.[5]

Movement across the two thousand–mile border has long been a normal occurrence, as American farmers recruited low-cost labor and Mexicans sought more remunerative employment. During the first three decades of this century an estimated million Mexicans migrated to the United States, many of whom were brutally, summarily, and illegally deported during the Great Depression of the early 1930s. The migratory flow was resumed and regulated by international agreement under the "bracero" program that originated in a period of acute labor scarcity during World War II. This program assured a reliable flow of docile,

---

[4]Data reported in Daniels, *Coming to America*, 311.

[5]This history is recounted by Leobardo F. Estrada, F. Chris Garcia, Reynaldo Flores Macias, and Lionel Maldonado, "Chicanos in the United States: A History of Exploitation and Resistance," in Garcia, *Latinos in the Political System*.

low-cost workers to the farming enterprises of the Southwest and provided employment for landless Mexicans on far more lucrative terms
than were available in their country.[6] The program was extended for
more than two decades, terminating in 1964 when U.S. employers found
that spontaneous flows of manpower provided sufficient labor without
the government controls associated with the bracero program. By this
time large-scale migration from Mexico had become part of the structure
of the labor market in the Southwest. This influx was balanced by large
reverse flows, most Mexicans regarding themselves as sojourners who
would work for periods in the United States, remit money to their families, make the easy return trip to Mexico, and perhaps repeat the experience. Of each wave of migrants, however, some elected to remain in
the United States, moving out of agriculture into higher-paying manufacturing and service employment. Eighty-five percent of Mexican Americans now reside in urban areas, and 20 percent of them live outside the
former Mexican territories, mostly in midwestern cities and metropolitan
New York.

   These continuing and large-scale migrations have been prompted by
the realities of the labor market: the seemingly inexhaustible demand in
the United States for low-cost labor; the chronic poverty, low wages,
unemployment, and explosive population growth in Mexico; and a long,
poorly guarded international border that can easily be breached by resourceful and persistent migrants. Well-established receiving networks
provide basic social supports, handle remittances and similar services,
and channel workers to jobs. Those with historical memories observe
the local Spanish place names and note that the areas in which they
work were once part of Mexico.

   The U.S. immigration legislation of 1965 abandoned the national origins quota system with its offensive racial and ethnic preferences, but
it imposed for the first time quantitative limits on immigration from
Mexico and other western hemisphere countries.[7] Since the Mexican
quota does not meet the U.S. demand for labor, two categories of Mexican workers have emerged, legal and illegal ("undocumented"). Immigration controls have been evaded on an enormous scale, and many U.S.
employers prefer to hire illegals who can be more easily exploited. During the 1980s an estimated 3 to 6 million illegal immigrants, the majority
from Mexico, were working in the United States.

   The 1960s civil rights movement had important implications for the

---

   [6]Ernesto Galarza, *Merchants of Labor: The Mexican Bracero Story* (Santa Barbara,
Calif.: McNally-Loftin, 1964).
   [7]For the provisions of the 1965 Act, see Daniels, *Coming to America*, 338–45.

permanent communities of Mexican origin. Originally intended to protect African Americans, the Federal Voting Rights Act of 1965 and legislative measures, judicial decisions, and administrative enforcement prohibiting discrimination in employment, education, and other public services applied as well to other minorities, including Mexican Americans. In its wake came "affirmative action" programs providing preferential access to higher education and employment. In addition, Congress and the Supreme Court mandated bilingual education for non–English-speaking children.[8] The U.S. government and society began to demonstrate greater respect for cultural pluralism and for multicultural values than ever before. Mexican-American citizens who had been mostly passive politically, often as a consequence of intimidation, discrimination, poll taxes, and literacy tests, responded positively to the improved opportunity structure. They began to register and vote in substantial numbers, to run for office, and to win elections. Between 1975 and 1984 Mexican-American voting registration in Texas doubled, exceeding one million. The major political parties at state and national levels found it expedient to compete for their votes. As early as 1968, Mexican-American voters provided the winning margin that carried Texas for the Democratic candidate for president, Hubert Humphrey.

Though activated politically, the Mexican disapora has been less influential than its numbers would suggest. Undocumented residents cannot vote. Nor can noncitizens; because of their continuing sojourner mentality, naturalization rates among legally resident Mexican Americans are very low; at least a third are noncitizens, thus ineligible to vote. A larger proportion than among "Anglos" are young, below voting age. Skeptical of the efficacy of voting, low income people turn out to vote at low rates. Nevertheless, political participation has been increasing, abetted by federal voting rights legislation, including the 1975 amendments specifically protecting the rights of non–English-speaking citizens. Registration and voting have increased dramatically, though they remain below national averages. Mexican Americans have been elected to the governorship in New Mexico and Arizona, the mayoralty in Denver and San Antonio, to the US Senate and House of Representatives and to State legislatures. State and local elected officials of Hispanic origin totaled about four thousand in the mid-1980s, 90 percent of them in California, New Mexico, and Texas.[9]

---

[8] For details, see Crawford, *Bi-lingual Education*. See also Schmidt, Ronald J., "Language Policy Conflict in the United States," in Crawford Young, ed., *The Rising Tide of Cultural Pluralism* (Madison: University of Wisconsin Press, 1993).

[9] Reported in Garcia, *Latinos in the Political System,* 15.

Though they have identified overwhelmingly with the Democratic Party, Mexican Americans, like all diasporas, are divided in their attitudes toward public issues. Inspired by the Black Power movement and the prominence of Third World liberation fronts, militant protest dominated the mood of young Mexican Americans during the late 1960s. It was spearheaded by university students who emphasized Mexican-American/"Chicano" pride. The movement soon split into two main factions. One proclaimed the need for social revolution to redress the oppression of all exploited people, including Chicanos; the other emphasized separate development, the importance of vindicating Mexican culture and of protecting it from foreign, imperialist influences. The tactics of militancy extended from symbolic acts of violence to the formation of a separate political party, La Raza Unida, which won several local elections in Texas.[10] The militants seldom reached beyond their core student constituency, however, and by the mid-1970s they had passed from the scene. Mainline sentiment among Mexican-American citizens has proved to be neither revolutionary nor separatist but strongly pragmatic and integrationist, striving within the U.S. political system to achieve individual equality and collective dignity. Mexican Americans, led by university graduates, have learned to use both political and nonpolitical tactics, an outstanding example of the latter being the Mexican-American Legal Defense and Educational Fund (MALDEF).[11] Inspired by the NAACP and funded in part by major foundations, this organization has fought vigorously and successfully in the courts to defend the rights of Mexican Americans, including illegal aliens, to public education, nondiscriminatory employment, local housing and public services, and affirmative action; they have compelled local jurisdictions, including Los Angeles County, to redraw election districts to insure more adequate representation for Mexican Americans.

In electoral and nonelectoral politics Mexican-American organizations have a clear agenda. They combat discrimination in private sector and government employment; they protest inferior public services in neighborhood facilities and particularly in education; they challenge abusive behavior by local police and federal immigration authorities; and they

[10]This story is detailed by Carlos Munoz, Jr., and Mario Barrera, "La Raza Unida Party and the Chicano Student Movement in California," in Garcia, *Latinos in the Political System.*

[11]Detailed by Karen O'Connor and Lee Epstein, "A Legal Voice for the Chicano Community: the Activities of the Mexican-American Legal Defense and Educational Fund, 1966–1982," in Garcia, *Latinos in the Political System.*

oppose electoral procedures that reduce the political weight of Mexican-American voters. They fight aggressively for bilingual public services, including education and ballots. Despite rapid acculturation to English, as a matter of ethnic pride most Mexican Americans want government to be responsive to those who prefer to function in their mother tongue and to maintain their inherited culture. Government-supported culture maintenance is promoted by a segment of Mexican-American professionals, especially educators, who see culture maintenance as their special mission and whose employment opportunities are enhanced by bilingual programs. There has been no evidence of irredentist sentiments among Mexican-Americans, even in such formerly Mexican territories as Southern California, which will soon harbor a Mexican-American majority, nor of disloyalty to the United States, nor of active interest in the politics of Mexico. Though large numbers of illegals and many permanent residents retain Mexican citizenship, the central aspiration of Mexican-American citizens is to achieve nondiscriminatory incorporation into U.S. institutions and public respect for their distinctive culture. The constitutional protections and legal regime in the United States provide an opportunity structure that lends credibility to these aspirations. Particularly in the southwestern states, where the population of Mexican Americans continues to increase, their political weight is likely to grow.

The process of integration has not, however, been trouble-free. Nativist reaction to the Mexican "threat" has crystallized around two issues: tightening immigration controls and rolling back bilingualism by legislating English as the sole official language of the United States. Immigration reform has been prompted by the perception that the U.S. government has lost control of its borders, that its laws are daily flouted by hordes of undesirable immigrants, and that the Southwest is being overrun by foreigners who steal jobs from Americans, overwhelm welfare, educational and other public services, import drugs, AIDS, and crime into the United States, and cannot or will not assimilate into American society. Promoted by a nativist advocacy group, the Federation for American Immigration Reform (FAIR), immigration restriction became a contentious issue on the federal agenda between 1981 and 1986. Opposed to effective limits on illegal immigration was an improbable coalition of Hispanic organizations, civil libertarians, church groups, and employers, especially of agricultural labor. Labor unions that traditionally oppose large-scale immigration and Black organizations whose constituents often compete with illegal immigrants for jobs did not support tight controls, wishing to avoid suspicion of racism. The supporters of restrictions were unable to mobilize the widespread but diffuse public sentiment favoring tighter immigration controls.[12]

The Immigration Reform and Control Act that was finally adopted in 1986 provided amnesty—the opportunity for several million illegal aliens to regularize their status and become legal residents. It also penalized employers who hire illegals and provided special measures for the temporary importation of seasonal agricultural workers. More than a million and a half Mexican illegals responded to this opportunity to secure permanent resident status. This complex set of compromises will not, however, restrict illegal immigration across the Mexican border as long as the present transborder labor demand and supply conditions continue. And certainly the more open borders resulting from the North American Free Trade Agreement will further facilitate transborder flows of labor.

During the prolonged legislative contest over immigration controls, Mexican-American organizations proved to be active and effective coalition players at the federal level, beating back and attenuating legislative proposals that they considered symbolically as well as practically hostile. The government of Mexico was a minor but significant factor in these debates, for it indicated that it would regard any harsh embargo on Mexican labor as an unfriendly act that might reduce its willingness to cooperate with the United States on other issues, such as drug control.

The other nativist reaction to the growing Mexican-American diaspora has been the English Only or U.S. English campaign. Its founder, former U.S. senator Dr. S. I. Hayakawa, summarized its purpose succinctly:

> We have unwisely embarked upon a policy of so-called "bilingualism," putting foreign languages in competition with our own. . . . English has long been the main unifying force of the American people. . . . Prolonged bilingual education in public schools and multilingual ballots threaten to divide us along language lines . . . I launched a national public interest organization and named it *US English*. Its goal is to make English the Official Language of the United States and to promote the opportunity to learn English for all people of the United States. . . . We have enough problems as a nation without having to talk through an interpreter. (undated fundraising letter, circa 1990)

Hayakawa and his supporters hoped to ensure that federal funds, which since 1968 have been available for bilingual education, are used only for

---

[12]For the politics of this legislative conflict see Zolberg, "Reforming the Back Door."

transitional assistance, to help non–English speakers function in English as quickly as possible. Though most Mexican-American parents seem to accept this formulation, many of their intellectual leaders vigorously disagree. They argue that government-financed bilingual instruction should be employed to ensure culture maintenance, which they consider a basic human right.

Among English speakers there appears to be strong latent support for English Only—to ensure national unity, to require that immigrants speak "American," to prevent whole areas such as southern California from communicating in a foreign language and becoming mini-Quebecs in the "indivisible" American nation. By constitutional amendment and by ordinary statutes, eighteen state governments have declared English their official language; more are likely to follow. Referenda on this subject usually carry by large margins. At a deeper level, the attack against bilingual education and bilingual public services reflects the fear that the United States is admitting too many immigrants of the wrong kinds, that these newcomers are making excessive demands on American government and society, and that they are not trying hard enough to become truly American.

Mexican-American citizens seem to be acculturating to English at much the same rate as earlier European disaporas. As a measure of integration, 50 percent of Mexican-American marriages in Los Angeles occur outside their ethnic ranks.[13] Though more than 25 percent subsist below the official poverty line, though their high school drop-out rates exceed 40 percent, and though they continue to lag both in educational performance and in economic achievement, substantial numbers of Mexican Americans have moved into more skilled and remunerative employment, out of barrio enclaves and into the suburbs. The dearth of semi-skilled industrial jobs in the current U.S. labor market hampers the upward mobility of second-generation immigrants. The most important factor delaying their collective integration, however, is the continuing high rate of fresh, mostly illegal, immigration.

In the 1990s, economic stagnation, conspicuous acts of terrorism by illegal immigrants in the New York area, and evidence of large-scale smuggling of immigrants by criminal organizations produced a political reaction, including renewed demands that immigration laws be strictly enforced and illegal immigration curbed. These pressures have been felt by the Mexican diaspora, especially in California, where the costs of providing education, health, hospital, welfare, and housing services to

---

[13]Reported in Connor, *Mexican-Americans in Perspective*, 21.

illegal immigrants and their families are believed to contribute to large fiscal deficits and high taxes in a state already hard hit by cutbacks in federal defense spending.

More than half the Mexican Americans in the United States are now citizens. Despite many misgivings, prompted in part by lingering racist sentiments, the U.S. polity, with its inclusive civic definition of citizenship, is in the process of accommodating them as full participants in its pluralistic society. While demanding non-discriminatory opportunity and public respect for their culture and heritage, Mexican-Americans individually and collectively continue to pursue the strategy of full and equal inclusion.

Germany: Guest Workers in the Welfare State

The official, oft-repeated policy of recent governments is that the Federal Republic is "not a country of immigration" and that social and cultural pluralism is not an acceptable pattern for German society. Yet, in the late 1980s, immediately prior to unification, 8 percent of the permanent residents of the Federal Republic (West Germany) were foreigners.[14] The largest component, 1.7 million of a total 5 million, were of Turkish nationality, including about four hundred thousand Kurds. While Germany's birth rate has fallen well below replacement levels, the fertility of foreign residents remains quite high; the numbers of the latter and their proportion of the total will no doubt continue to increase, abetted by illegal immigrants whose numbers were estimated in the late 1980s conservatively at three hundred thousand. "Needed but not wanted" is the phrase that best describes the standing of "guest workers" in Germany, for they have become essential to the German economy. They are a conspicuous presence in such major industrial centers as Stuttgart, Berlin, Munich, Duesseldorf and Frankfurt (now the fourth largest Turkish

[14]Data on Germany's guest workers have been drawn from the following sources: Ulrich Herbert, *A History of Foreign Labor in Germany, 1880–1980* (Ann Arbor: University of Michigan Press, 1990), chap. 5; Ray Rist, *Guestworkers in Germany: The Prospects for Pluralism* (New York: Praeger, 1978); Rosemarie Rogers, ed., *Guests Come to Stay: The Effects of Labor Migration on Sending and Receiving Countries* (Boulder, Colo.: Westview Press, 1985)—including chap. 2, Hermann Korte, "Labor Migration and the Employment of Foreigners in the Federal Republic of Germany Since 1950," chap. 4, Friedrich Heckmann, "Temporary Labor Migration or Immigration? 'Guestworkers' in the Federal Republic of Germany," and chap. 8, Ursula Mehrlaender, "Second Generation Migrants in the Federal Republic of Germany"; and Mark J. Miller, *Foreign Workers in Western Europe: An Emerging Political Force* (New York: Praeger, 1981).

city after Istanbul, Ankara, and Izmir). Even during periods of high unemployment, indigenous workers from the Federal Republic and more
recently from the former Democratic Republic (East Germany), protected by the provisions of a generous welfare state, are unwilling to
accept the heavy, dirty, menial, boring jobs performed by foreign workers in what has become a dual labor market.

Despite heavy air attacks, German industry expanded rapidly during
World War II. Prisoners of war and conscripts from the occupied territories who manned mines, factories, and construction sites during the
war were replaced by ethnic Germans expelled from Eastern Europe and
refugees from Soviet-occupied East Germany. When the Berlin Wall
blocked this source of labor after 1961 and German industry continued
to expand, the Labor Office of the Federal Republic, on behalf of employers, engaged in large-scale recruiting campaigns in the labor-surplus
Mediterranean basin. The terms and conditions of recruitment were
formalized in international treaties. Officials of the Federal Republic and
of the labor-supplying governments—which welcomed these relatively
high-wage employment opportunities for their unemployed citizens and
the foreign exchange they would provide through family remittances—
expected that these workers would reside in Germany without their families and in a few years rotate back to their native country. If the need
for foreign workers persisted, fresh recruits would replace them. It soon
became evident, however, that rotation would not work. While they
retained family connections and sentimental attachments to their native
countries and traveled back and forth on holidays, the majority of guestworkers were not inclined to accept the bleak economic realities in their
homelands. Nor did German employers want to lose experienced workers. Though many guest workers did in fact repatriate, those who preferred to remain in Germany for indefinite periods were granted
permanent status as resident aliens and allowed to invite their families
to join them.

In 1973, the number of guest workers peaked at 2.7 million, slightly
more than 10 percent of Germany's labor force. In response to the oil
shock of that year and the resultant economic slowdown, the government suspended labor recruitment. Over the next few years, generous
government-financed payments induced about six hundred thousand
guest workers to return to their homelands, reducing the total by nearly
25 percent. But family reunions in the 1980s inflated the number of
resident foreigners to five million. Thus, in less than twenty years, individual temporary workers had become permanently domiciled family

groups who lived in the lower-rent areas of the cities in which they worked. These slum areas soon became ethnic enclaves; Germans who could afford to relocate moved out. The immigrant diasporas formed self-contained communities with their own networks of religious, social, cultural and recreational associations. New businesses catered to their distinctive needs. Meanwhile, the German state extended its welfare and educational services to the new residents, and labor unions hastened to enroll them as members. The guest workers and their families had become a permanent, if unwelcome, reality in German society.

Prevailing opinion in Germany, faithfully reflected in the posture and statements of its ruling party, the Christian Democratic Union, is that membership in the German polity should be limited to ethnic Germans. The presence of foreign workers—all evidence to the contrary notwithstanding—should be considered temporary. A 1982 survey indicated that 82 percent of respondents believed there were too many foreigners in Germany.[15] They should not be encouraged or invited to become citizens or to participate in Germany's political life. Whereas ethnic Germans "returning" to the fatherland are entitled automatically to all the privileges of citizenship, naturalization for other immigrants is a complex, exacting, and expensive ten-year process; several efforts in the 1980s to liberalize and simplify these procedures were defeated. Few immigrants choose this ordeal: the twenty thousand guest workers who opt annually for German citizenship represent less than 25 percent of the births in these communities.[16]

Acutely conscious of Germany's tragic history of racism, the main political parties agreed not to exploit immigration or resident foreigners as a political issue. Reassured by its government's stonewalling on the issue of citizenship, Germany did not witness overt anti-immigrant agitation on a significant scale until the early 1990s. The collapse of Soviet power in Eastern Europe provoked a massive flow of ethnic Germans and tens of thousands of non-Germans into West Germany, which was already experiencing significant unemployment and housing shortages. The new immigrants were mostly Poles, Croats, Romanians, and Gypsies, but quite a few came from Third World countries as well. In 1990 alone, the number of arrivals exceeded eight hundred thousand, including more than two hundred thousand non-Germans who claimed refugee

---

[15] Reported in D.W. Urwin and W. E. Paterson, eds., *Politics in Western Europe Today* (London: Longman Group, 1990), 172.

[16] *New York Times Magazine,* 15 February 1991, 81.

status under Germany's liberal asylum laws.[17] This influx overwhelmed the interparty agreement and produced widespread protests, including hundreds of incidents of violence and arson against the newcomers by gangs of skinheads and neo-Nazis. Since German public opinion holds that most of the asylees are not political refugees, but in reality economic migrants, the government intends to respond by tightening and speeding the enforcement of regulations, including deportation, against migrants who cannot demonstrate prima facie a legitimate claim to political or religious refugee status.

Terrorist incidents first directed against asylees have been extended to "foreigners" in general, including Turkish guest workers and their families. While xenophobic violence contributes to hostile antiforeign sentiment in Germany, it does not directly address the longer term, troublesome question of the political status of the five million plus legally resident aliens who will not return to their native countries but cannot be expelled. Will these persons who live in Germany, work in Germany, pay German taxes, and consume Germany's public services be invited or permitted to become full-fledged Germans? If invited, will they accept? If not permitted, will they and their progeny constitute a permanently unfranchised, segregated ethnic underclass in the German democratic welfare state?

Despite their residential segregation and their cultural distinctiveness, Turkish guest workers have attracted sympathizers and supporters within the German polity and have partly integrated into some of the institutions of German society. Their most vocal political advocates have come from the left, especially from militant young socialists who regard foreign workers as conspicuous victims of capitalist exploitation, natural allies in their efforts to radicalize the increasingly bourgeois-minded German working class. The establishment Social Democratic Party has advocated humane treatment and has opened its ranks to individual membership by foreign workers, though it continues to waffle on the question of permanent status and citizenship. Christian churches have consistently urged fairer, more humane treatment of foreign workers and their dependents by the agencies of government in the fields of housing, family services, and education and by the police and other law-enforcement agencies.

The powerful German labor movement has done the most to integrate foreign workers. From the beginning, the unions have insisted that guest

[17]*Economist*, 19 October, 1991, 58.

workers be compensated at the same rate as indigenous workers and be entitled to the same government health, pension, and other welfare and social security benefits. They have done so both to express working-class solidarity and to prevent employers from using foreign workers to undermine wage levels and labor standards. They successfully recruited foreign workers into their unions to forestall the formation of competing unions. Half of all Turkish workers have been enrolled in the mainline unions, where foreigners comprise 10 percent of total membership. Turkish workers have won union elections for membership in works councils (the German system of industrial management known as *mit-bestimmung*) and for influential positions as shop stewards. Nevertheless, foreign workers consider themselves underrepresented at the decision-making levels of the union structures. They feel that their interests and needs are often overlooked and softpedaled and that they suffer discrimination in disputes involving work rules, wage rates, and promotions. Encouraged by leftist elements within the unions, Turkish workers have taken prominent roles in highly publicized wildcat strikes, protesting employers' practices as well as the hesitation and failure of the union establishment to defend their distinctive economic interests. Its flaws notwithstanding, the labor movement is the one major institution of German society in which foreign workers actively participate.

Though guest workers are not permitted to vote even in local elections, they participate marginally in local government through "coordinating groups" that enjoy consultative status. Voting turnout is low, for foreign residents regard the groups neither as representative nor effective. Since their opportunities for institutional participation are so circumscribed, immigrant workers resort to noninstitutional channels of political expression that sometimes turn violent, including rent strikes, boycotts, and street demonstrations against charges of harassment and brutality by the police. Much of their political energy, however, has been invested in the politics of their home country.

Turkish guest workers generally live in ethnic enclaves dominated by a transplanted homeland culture; there are continuing transnational flows of personnel and information from the homeland. Denied political participation in the host country, they are encouraged both by German and Turkish authorities to regard themselves as sojourners destined one day to return to Turkey. Freedom of expression and association are available to them by the democratic rules and practices of the Federal Republic. These virtually insure not only that Turks in Germany will focus on the politics of their homeland, but also that their discontents in Germany will be captured by radical protest organizations. A substantial number of guest workers affiliate with German-based branches of Turkish political movements, especially extremist organizations of the right and the left, abetted in the latter case by leftist German activists. These groups contribute money to homeland political organizations while providing a base of operations for antiregime activists, including terrorists, who launch attacks on representatives of the Turkish government in Germany.

Prominent among the dissidents are Kurdish nationalists, who demand autonomy or even independence for their people in southeastern Anatolia. Their agitation has created a no-win situation for the Federal Republic, which is charged by the Ankara government with tolerating violent and hostile anti-Turkish activities on their soil. In March 1992, the Federal Republic suspended arms shipments to their NATO ally, Turkey, because German-supplied arms had been used in the violent suppression of Kurdish demonstrations which, in turn, had prompted protests by Kurdish guest workers in Germany. Nor are Turks unique among resident foreigners in their preoccupation with radical homeland politics. Croat guest workers have participated actively in the *ustashi*, a cryptofascist ultranationalist organization. In pursuit of the goal of Croat national independence, finally achieved in 1992, it launched violent terrorist attacks from German soil against the government of Yugoslavia.

The myth of the apolitical foreign worker preoccupied with the basic economic and social needs of his family has been exploded. Clearly, the frustrations, discontents, and aspirations of diaspora communities find expression in political action oriented both to the local situation and to their homeland. Blocked by German law from participating in institutional politics, Turkish guest workers have resorted to the noninstitutional politics of sporadic militant protest. Diaspora communities seldom wholly ignore the politics of their homelands even when they are well-integrated into the host society; when political integration is foreclosed, they are even more likely to focus their political energies on their homeland.

In an exercise of calculated self-deception, the political elites of Germany have cultivated the comforting illusion that resident foreign workers and their families will one day go home. Thus, having benefitted economically from their presence, Germany would one day again be ethnically pure, avoiding the need to incorporate individual foreigners or, worse still, the "nightmare" of multiculturalism. Their ally in perpetrating this myth has been the Turkish government, which clings to the policy of jus sanguinis—the idea that all persons of Turkish blood must remain forever Turkish—and rejects categorically the notion that Turks in Germany should be offered the option of German citizenship. A venal reenforcement of this policy is the Turkish government's recognition that more than half of Turkey's foreign exchange is earned by remittances from its nationals working abroad. In defiance of the myth of return, the Turkish presence in Germany grows daily through family reunions and high fertility. By 1995, an estimated 20 percent of the 15–19 age cohort in West Germany will be ethnically non-German, the majority Turkish.[18]

Nowhere has confusion about the future status of resident foreigners been more apparent than in public education. Education in Germany is a responsibility of the provinces (*laender*) and the curricula they offer to the children of foreign workers varies considerably. The main conflict arises between emphasis on integration into German society and preparation for eventual return to their homeland. This issue lies at the heart of the "second generation" problem. Some *laender*, notably Bavaria, emphasize culture maintenance, preparation for returning to Turkey. The children are effectively segregated, much of their instruction is in the Turkish language, and relatively few hours a week are devoted to learning German. In Berlin, by contrast, preparatory classes in German are provided for foreign children so that they can achieve transition to the standard German curriculum as quickly as possible. In all too many cases, Turkish youngsters emerge functionally incompetent in both languages. Turkish children drop out of the educational system at the appalling rate of 54 percent.[19] Their unfamiliarity with the German language, combined with a home environment where undereducated parents are unable or unwilling to help with schoolwork, produce poor performance, frustration, low self-esteem, and indiscipline in the classroom. As dropouts, they cannot qualify for the apprenticeship training that is the German route to skilled, high-wage employment. They are thus condemned to menial tasks or consigned to the criminal underworld. A substantial minority, however, does survive the German educational system, qualify for upward occupational and income mobility, and integrate economically into German society.

The second and third generations—mostly German-born—are cruelly

---

[18]Miller, *Foreign Workers in Western Europe*, 202.
[19]Rogers, *Guests Come to Stay*, 168.

cross-pressured. Their parents and the often reactionary mullahs who provide religious instruction and guide them in the Islamic way of life, urge them to resist cultural assimilation into an infidel, normless, and hostile society. Yet daily exposure to the German mass media, opportunities to participate in a more open and "modern" style of life, and the realization that their future lies in Germany, not in Turkey, impel German-born Turks toward acculturation, accommodation, even rebellion. Young women in particular feel the contrast between the constraints of traditional Muslim-Turkish society and the freedom and opportunities available to modern German women. Similar cross-pressures on second and third generations are common in diaspora communities, but they are especially acute for Turkish youth, whose status and future are ambiguous and ill-defined—by their own community as well as by their host society—and whose inherited culture is so sharply at odds with German norms and practices. Though the German government also withholds the privileges of citizenship from European guest workers and their families, they acculturate more readily and are more welcome than Turks, who are popularly regarded as reclusive, dirty, and dark-skinned, thus poor candidates for incorporation into German society. Nonetheless, Turks are now by far the largest and fastest growing contingent of resident foreigners, a settled diaspora that Germany, however reluctantly, will have to come to terms with.

The Turkish diaspora confronts German society with a severe test of its post–World War II commitment to democratic and universalistic values and its post-Holocaust rejection of racism. The Turks were invited to Germany because their labor was needed; they were then granted permanent resident status; now they are a settled community that lives, works, and pays taxes, but they are excluded from membership and participation in the German polity. Germany's international standing, its democratic pretensions and commitments, the vigilance of civil libertarian and humanist advocacy groups, and the guest workers' essential role in the German economy preclude their expulsion. Sentimental links notwithstanding, it is clear that the great majority will not voluntarily return to poverty and unemployment in Anatolia. Indeed, of all the diasporas in Germany, the Turks have been least inclined to return to their homeland. The second and third generations, increasingly acculturated, are condemned by the present impasse in German policy to subordinate status on the margins of German society. The inevitable resentment originally activated by left-wing radicals is now fostered by Islamic militants whose message is virulently antiwestern and who preach the necessity of social and cultural self-segregation from a morally corrupt and culturally hostile German society. Germany thus reaps the fruit of its ethnocentrism and residual racism, of its failure to allow a substantial, permanent, and growing diaspora to integrate into their society on dignified terms. Like it or not, Germany must soon come to terms with social and cultural pluralism, for that reality will be politicized either within or on the margins of German society.

France: North African Muslims in the Jacobin State

For more than a century, France has welcomed immigrants in order to overcome its "demographic deficit"—a low birth rate compounded by heavy manpower losses during World War I.[20] But its Jacobin tradition, dominant since the revolution of 1789, proclaims a republic that is "one and indivisible." The Jacobin concept of French citizenship has been cultural rather than ethnic; cultural-linguistic pluralism, delegitimated for France's indigenous regional minorities—Bretons, Alsaciens, Basques—could not be tolerated among immigrants. They were encouraged, indeed expected, to acculturate to the French way of life, to assimilate as individuals into French society, to evolve as quickly as possible into good Frenchmen. As individuals immigrants were welcome, but cultural and social pluralism was categorically rejected.

As candidates for immigration, White European Catholics—Italians, Spaniards, Poles—were preferred. However, the Republic's colonial misadventures, in Black Africa but especially in North Africa, opened broad channels of legal immigration to people who physically and culturally were decidedly non-European. In 1954 in a vain effort to undercut the insurrection in Algeria, France offered Algerians French citizenship and

[20]Data on France's immigrant experience have been drawn from the following sources: in Rogers, *Guests Come to Stay,* Robert J. Berrier, "The French Textile Industry: A Segmented Labor Market," and Andre Lebon, "Second Generation Foreigners in France"; in the *Annals* (May 1986), William Safran, "Islamization in Western Europe: Political Consequences and Historial Parallels," and James F. Hollifield, "Immigration Policy in France and Germany: Outputs versus Outcomes"; Miller, *Foreign Workers in Western Europe;* in Tomas Gerholm and Yngve Georg Lithman, eds., *The New Islamic Presence in Western Europe* (London: Mansell Publishing, 1988), Remy Leveau, "The Islamic Presence in France," and Annie Krieger-Krynicki, "The Second Generation of Muslim Immigrants in France"; Subrata Mitra, "The National Front in France—A Single Issue Movement" in *West European Politics* (April 1988); James G. Shields, "The Politics of Disaffection: France in the 1990s," in John Gaffney and Eva Kolinsky, eds., *Political Culture in France and Germany* (New York: Routledge, 1990).

the right to immigrate and settle in the metropole. By 1962, when Algeria finally achieved independence, more than three hundred thousand Algerians were resident in France. Most of them chose to retain Algerian nationality while continuing to live and work in France.

Economic expansion in the 1960s created an imperative need for unskilled labor which was filled by migrants from the Mediterranean Basin, mostly from the impoverished former colonies of the Maghreb—Morocco, Tunisia, and Algeria. Before legal migration was suspended in 1974, a large North-African, Arab-speaking, Muslim population had been permanently inserted into French society. Continuing flows of illegals, legally sanctioned family reunions, and high fertility rates left France by 1990 with an estimated 5 million resident foreigners, including 3.5 million Muslims, most of them North Africans. The great majority have been relegated to heavy, boring, menial, and, by French standards, low-paying jobs in declining industries such as metallurgy and textiles. Undereducated, underskilled, handicapped by limited fluency in French, and victimized by discrimination, the North African labor force has enjoyed little occupational mobility in what has evolved into a dual labor market. They occupy substandard housing in neighborhoods where the stores, eating places, newspaper presses, travel agencies, and mosques cater to their needs and accommodate the networks of recreational, social, and religious associations that emerge in diaspora communities. Immigrants and their families have enjoyed relative freedom of expression and association compromised only by the vigilance of the state security forces concerned with subversive and terrorist activities. They have been eligible for the full range of the state's social and family services, including child allowances and unemployment compensation, on a nondiscriminatory basis. Because of their marginal and vulnerable status and high rates of unemployment, they have become heavy consumers of these services.

North African Muslims were admitted to the French labor unions to avert dual unionism and to maintain competitive wage scales. They participate in union activities, though on a lesser scale than guest workers in Germany because unions are relatively weak in many French industries. Still union leadership has been relatively receptive to North Africans. Many rank-and-file French workers, by contrast, resent encroachment on their neighborhoods and housing; this resentment has triggered a number of violent confrontations since the mid-1970s.

The children of immigrant workers, subject to compulsory school attendance laws, are admitted to the standard school curriculum in the

French language with the expectation that this experience will socialize them into the French way of life and facilitate early assimilation. Preparatory courses are available for preschool youngsters, as are adaptation courses for older children to improve their facility in the French language so that they can participate more productively in the normal French-medium curriculum. Special vocational courses are offered for students who intend to terminate formal schooling after age sixteen. Because of language difficulties, the absence of parental support, and suspicion that the state's education system is undermining their religious faith, a large number of children drop out, condemned to another generation of unskilled marginality in France's dual labor market.

Foreign workers' children born in France qualify for French citizenship by demonstrating their intention between the ages of sixteen and twenty-one to accept that status. For legal immigrants with permanent resident status, naturalization, which confers all the rights of French citizenship, is a simple procedure after a five-year waiting period. Though naturalization is encouraged by the state, few North Africans, unlike earlier European immigrants, have opted for French nationality. Like Turkey, North African governments cling to the doctrine of jus sanguinis and strongly oppose naturalization. Though legal immigrants and their progeny enjoy permanent residence and work opportunities in France, North African governments regard them as nationals temporarily working abroad, remitting funds, destined one day to return. With the reluctant acquiescence of the French authorities, they exercise a measure of extraterritorial control over their subjects. Their consulates in France feel free to intervene on behalf of their nationals when the latter allege abuse or unfair treatment. The Moroccan police monitor their nationals in France to curb political activity deemed hostile by the Moroccan regime. The Algerian state organizes, patronizes, finances, and provides assistance to the Amicale d'Algeriennes en Europe (AAE), a fraternal organization with branches in all centers of Algerian settlement in France which promotes cultural, social, religious, and Arab-language programs intended to resist acculturation and assimilation and to maintain cultural and political links with the homeland. The AAE serves, incidentally, as a pro-Algerian regime presence among expatriates. Partly in response to such pressures, North Africans in France tend to focus their political energies on the politics of their homelands, often financing, sustaining, and providing safe havens for opponents of the regimes in power.

Even French-born persons of North African origin, fluent in French, no longer practicing Muslims, fully acculturated to the French secular way of life, hesitate to accept French citizenship. France does not sanction the practice of dual citizenship; naturalization would thus require second-generation North Africans to renounce their former allegiance. Some of those young people are reluctant to displease their parents; others sense that accepting French citizenship implies the embrace of an alien Christian culture and the symbolic repudiation of their Arabic and Muslim roots. Since they can in any case continue to live and work in France, they prefer not to confront this moral dilemma and not to risk a rupture with their original community. Meanwhile, increasingly militant Islamic religious functionaries urge the diaspora community not to compromise with the morally degenerate culture and practices—alcohol, drugs, sexual promiscuity, godlessness, abortion, homosexuality—of the infidel society to which they are exposed for purely economic reasons.

By not accepting French citizenship, North Africans forego opportunities to participate in French political institutions. They have found ways, however, to express their interests through noninstitutional channels. Often in defiance of the instructions of their union leadership, foreign workers have participated in a number of wildcat strikes protesting harsh work rules and discriminatory treatment. Some of the most militant and violent demonstrations by immigrant workers have involved housing arrangements in which immigrants have been pitted against local authorities, including communist mayors and councils. Immigrants have also protested racism and discrimination against foreign workers. These strikes, protests, and public demonstrations have produced numerous confrontations with the police, generating charges of police brutality and allegations that the police seek out dark-skinned, foreign-looking demonstrators for unnecessarily harsh and humiliating treatment.

On grounds of ideology or compassion, foreign workers and their families have attracted support from prominent and influential sectors of French society, countering to some degree the sentiment among 75 percent of the French public that there are too many Arabs in France.[21] The immigrants' supporters include elements of the militant but unorthodox left (the Communist Party establishment proved ambivalent on this issue), church-based welfare organizations, and civil rights activists. Prominent among the latter have been the well-established Movement Against Racism, Anti-Semitism, and for Peace, and the more militant

[21] *New York Times*, 26 December 1990, A6.

SOS Racisme, an organization that emerged in 1984 with the backing of the Socialist government to combat the racist appeal of the National Front. SOS Racisme has attracted widespread sympathy and participation from students and young professionals.

Surveys indicate that as many as 90 percent of respondents recognize that the late 1980s witnessed the spread of racism in France and that the main targets were North African, Arab-speaking, dark-skinned Muslim.[22] The backlash first appeared during the mid-1970s in working-class neighborhoods where violent clashes erupted over pressures by North African immigrants on housing and public facilities. A number of municipal governments, including several controlled by the Communist Party, sided conspicuously with French workers in these disputes. Disquiet soon spread beyond immediately affected working-class areas, as the ubiquitous presence of North Africans in urban centers produced widespread concern about a large, apparently permanent, distinctly foreign, and unassimilable element on French national territory.

Gradually the issue began to intrude on the agenda of public affairs. Rightists proposed measures to reverse the flow of undesirable immigration by cutting back entitlements to public subsidies and services, especially family allowances, by financial incentives to encourage repatriation, and by summary deportation of illegals. Leftists advocated measures to protect the civil rights of immigrants while encouraging their assimilation into French society. No voices favored cultural or social pluralism as a long-term objective and all agreed on the need to terminate immigration. When the Socialists achieved their historic breakthrough in 1981, they pledged to regularize the status of illegals already in France while curbing further immigration, eliminating financial incentives for repatriation, and facilitating assimilation by allowing permanent residents to vote in municipal elections. In response to negative public opinion, however, the Socialists soon abandoned these liberal reforms.

Public policy concerning the North African diaspora was influenced in the 1980s by the surge of a new political force, the National Front led by Jean-Marie Le Pen. Capitalizing on widespread unease over the conspicuous presence of the North Africans, the National Front became an important force on the French political scene, securing more than 10 percent of the vote in a series of national, local, and European elections, and garnering an impressive 14.7 percent in the first round of the 1988 presidential balloting. The National Front is not a single issue party,

[22]Ibid.

having succeeded in reestablishing the legitimacy in French politics of extreme rightist sentiments that had been discredited and delegitimated for a full generation by the memory of the collaborationist Vichy regime during World War II. The combination of national chauvinism, deep suspicion of foreigners, lingering anti-Semitism, integralist Catholicism, populist anxiety over perceived threats to traditional social values and to small economic enterprises—these have remobilized rightist energies in French politics and forced the "respectable" conservative parties to attempt to preempt racist pressures by moving toward the right.

The specific issue that galvanized the National Front, however, was their militant opposition to Arab, Muslim, North African immigrants. North Africans have become scapegoats for every ill afflicting French society, from unemployment to crime, drugs, and terrorism, from moral laxity to AIDS. The alleged permissiveness of successive governments, conservative and socialist alike, the National Front argues, allowed a racially exotic, religiously hostile, morally lax, parasitical, unassimilable population to invade and colonize the homeland. Genuine Frenchmen can no longer feel at home in their own country. The simple remedy is to expel the aliens and with them the ills they inflict on the French people. Nearly a third of French respondents in 1991 approved the National Front's position on immigrants.[23] The core of the National Front's voting support has come from areas affected by major North African settlement and from communities of ex-*colons,* French emigrants who were forced to abandon their former homes and businesses in Algeria. Support and sympathy for the message of the National Front are not confined, however, to these areas and these constituencies. Their France-for-Frenchmen, law-and-order, traditional values themes, and their finger pointing at the North Africans touch responsive nerves in the French body politic, evoking latent racist and xenophobic fears, attracting support even from former Communist voters. As the Socialist moderate left became identified as the establishment during the 1980s while the Communist Party collapsed, the National Front became the magnet for diffuse discontents and protests against high levels of crime, unemployment, and other socioeconomic ills.

After a series of violent encounters in the spring and summer of 1991 between the police and bands of young North Africans, Jacques Chirac, former prime minister and presidential candidate and leader of the respectable right, felt obliged to express his sympathy for the French

---

[23] *Economist,* 2 November 1991, 46.

worker living next door to a noisy, filthy North African immigrant with his four wives and twenty children, surviving comfortably on monthly welfare payments of eight thousand dollars financed by hard-pressed French taxpayers.[24] In a similar effort to fend off raids by the National Front on his moderate conservative constituency, former president Giscard d'Estaing solemnly warned his countrymen against the North African "invasion." In response, the Socialist government announced that it would tighten its controls on illegal immigrants, chartering aircraft to speed thair expulsion. The conservative coalition that won control of government in 1993 promised more rigorous controls on immigration, the summary deportation of illegal aliens, restrictions on the rights and status of resident aliens, and limits on their entitlements to welfare services. Thus French policy has been driven in a rightward and xenophobic direction and the issue of immigrants and resident foreigners has remained high on the public agenda.

The North African diaspora, 3.5 million strong and growing, has become a permanent if unwelcome presence. In France's dual labor market its labor will continue to be needed as long as current welfare practices enable unemployed Frenchmen to avoid the heavy, menial jobs these immigrants perform. The moderate center in French public life is not likely to sanction abusive treatment of legally resident North Africans or their forcible expulsion. Even supporters of such draconian measures would be reluctant to impair France's relations with the states of North Africa and the wider Arab world and to compromise the long-standing strategic objective of French diplomacy to be a bridge between Europe and the Arab-Muslim world.

France confronts a resident diaspora that refuses to behave like its European predecessors. Earlier immigrants were eager to become Frenchmen. The North Africans are more inclined to cling to their inherited culture; even the second generation, born in France, French-speaking, hesitates to accept French citizenship and its privileges, though it is readily available to them. Their ethnic distinctiveness is now reinforced by an aggressively assertive religious activism that preaches the incompatibility of Islam with the infidel societies of Europe and enjoins the faithful who are compelled to live in France for economic reasons to segregate themselves in separate communities, to refuse all but the most essential accommodations to French secular culture, and to reject social and political integration into French society. Where Europe had evolved patterns of separation between church and state, between the

[24]New York Times, 23 June 1991, 9.

sacred which are matters of individual conscience and the profane which are the domain of public policy, Islam has not recognized these institutional distinctions. Europe has yet to spawn a reform movement that would limit Islam to the private beliefs and practices of the faithful, while allowing them to participate in a national civic culture and in the activities of a secular state.[25] Thus ethnic pride and Islamic militancy have combined with the opposition of North African governments to inhibit the absorption of immigrants and their locally born progeny into French society.

There has been no satisfactory response to this dilemma. Immigrants have been expected to acculturate and assimilate as individuals; cultural and social pluralism have never been legitimate or acceptable options in Jacobin France. The emerging reality, however, is precisely a substantial and permanent diaspora that appears to reject French culture and insist on a separate status. French elites still hope that the pulling power of French culture and the rewards of French citizenship will prove irresistible to the third generation, if not to the second.[26] Those who maintain their faith in France's civilizing mission refuse to contemplate the permanent presence in their midst of large communities unwilling to accommodate to French culture and society, that demand formal or de facto recognition of separate minority status on French territory. The National Front would resolve France's unwelcome pluralism by expelling the immigrants, the French establishment by assimilating them. Neither may be responsive to the current North African–Muslim challenge.

Japan: Racial Purity in the Global Village

A central theme in Japanese culture is that Japanese are a homogeneous and unique people.[27] Membership in Japanese society has been and

---

[25]The *New York Times* of 24 January 1992 reported a new Islamic center at St. Leger de Fougeret which hopes to develop and propagate a European form of Islam compatible with full participation in a secular French society.

[26]This position is argued vigorously by Christian Jelen in *Ils feront de bons Francais: Enquête sur l'assimilation des Maghrebins* (Paris: Robert Laffont SA, 1991). In spite of high rates of unemployment, academic failure, and criminal delinquency, Jelen finds evidence that North Africans born in France, following the lead of a professional elite that has successfully assimilated, have begun an irreversible process of acculturation and integration as individuals into French society. This process has happened, he believes, in spite of the racism of the extreme right, the misguided tolerance by the left of multicultural heresies, and the mischievous efforts of North African governments to exercise extraterritorial political and religious influence over expatriates on French territory.

[27]The best English language source on Koreans in Japan is Changsoo Lee, and George

should remain a function of blood lineage; only ethnic Japanese, members of the Yamato nation, should qualify for the privileges and responsibilities of citizenship. As the society is closed to outsiders, so should participation in that society's public affairs in the framework of the state. The Japanese concept of citizenship is ethnic, not civic. This ideology is enforced by certain institutions, principally the family register (*koseki*), which insures the continuity of the lineage and which the eldest son of every family is duty-bound to maintain. Inclusion in the *koseki* confirms an individual's status as an ethnic Japanese; those who cannot produce a copy of a family register containing their name are excluded informally from many of the privileges of membership in Japanese society. Japan's political elites are committed to perpetuating and protecting the myth of racial exclusiveness, and there is no evidence that public opinion disagrees.

Japan's low current fertility rate, 1.57 in 1989 per adult female, is 25 percent below the replacement rate and continues to decline.[28] A function of affluence, high levels of female education and participation in the labor force, cramped housing, and the unavailability of household help, the low birth rate presages a declining population and a declining labor force. Japan's dynamic economy is already beset by acute labor shortages. Yet the government, while admitting skilled foreigners for temporary residence on a case by case basis, routinely rejects, as a matter of established policy, all requests for admission of unskilled workers, even on a temporary basis. Medium and small enterprises are closing, often forced into bankruptcy, because of the unavailability of cheap labor. The Food Service Association of Japan recently petitioned the government, unsuccessfully, to admit six hundred thousand workers to staff the hard-pressed restaurant industry. Instead of relying on foreign workers, government strategy for coping with the labor shortage includes such measures as encouraging the transfer of labor-intensive industries to low-wage Third World countries, automating activities that cannot be ex-

de Vos, *Koreans in Japan: Ethnic Conflict and Accommodation* (Berkeley: University of California Press, 1981). For more recent scholarships, see Keitaro Oguri, "Resident Koreans Are Native Speakers Too," *Japan Quarterly* 37 (October–December 1990); and S.S. Ryang, "Ethnopolitical Community of 'North' Koreans in Japan," *International Migration* 28 (March 1990). On illegals, see Philip Martin, "Labor Migration in Asia," *International Migration Review* 25 (Spring 1991), who summarizes a November 1990 conference on cross-national labor migration in Asia sponsored by the UN Center for Regional Development, Nagoya. *Japan Echo* for spring 1990 carried a symposium on immigrant labor, including articles by Watanabe Toshio, Nishio Kanji, and Shimada Haruo.

[28] *Economist,* 26 January 1991, 26.

ported, and using existing domestic labor resources more efficiently, including women and retired workers.

Looming over the minds of Japan's policymakers and opinion leaders is the spectre of an uncontrollable flood of migrants from their impoverished and overpopulated Asian neighbors, an invasion that could overwhelm, undermine, and permanently alter Japanese society. Any concessions that would legally admit unskilled workers would expose Japan to this nightmare. Foreign workers could not easily be repatriated once Japanese employers learn to depend on them; once workers achieved permanent status, their families would have to be admitted. Japan would then be confronted with the unwelcome presence of large numbers of foreigners who could be neither assimilated nor expelled. Senior politicians, including former prime minister Nakasone, have publicly ascribed low educational performance in the United States, its declining, noncompetitive economy, and its appalling crime rates to its unassimilated non-European minorities. Nor do Japan's elites wish to confront the problems created in Europe by the presence of large labor diasporas. Internationally oriented intellectuals and civil libertarians who urge their countrymen to abandon their ethnic exclusiveness and embrace a more cosmopolitan view of Japan's international obligations have had no discernible effect on public policy.

Japan's elites explain their aversion to the admission of foreign workers by unhappy experiences with their Korean diaspora. During the First World War, Japan's manufacturers and mine owners recruited and imported workers among their Korean colonial subjects. Later, during the Pacific War, large numbers of Koreans were brought to Japan, under conditions approaching slavery to overcome severe labor shortages. At the time of Japan's surrender, their numbers approached two million. With the collapse of the Japanese economy, they faced unemployment and destitution. More than a million were repatriated to South Korea and in the subsequent two decades another three hundred thousand moved to North Korea. A significant minority, however, chose to remain in Japan and were accorded the status of resident aliens. They experienced severe discrimination in employment, housing, education, and eligibility for public welfare services. In response to hostility and rejection by Japanese society, substandard educational performance, and limited life chances, many drifted into crime. They became prominent soldiers in the ranks of the notorious criminal syndicates, the *yakuza,* fulfilling the conventional Japanese stereotype that Koreans are by nature not only lazy and parasitical but criminal as well.

The majority of Koreans, segregated from Japanese society, organized autonomous networks of businesses and associations to meet their social and economic needs. The most important associations became highly politicized and preoccupied with events in Korea, especially the question of national reunification. The largest association, directly assisted by the Japan Communist Party, adopted a version of leftist nationalism oriented to the North Korean Stalinist regime. The Japanese government allowed them to operate their own schools and publish their own newspapers and journals, subject, however, to close police surveillance. The minority association, oriented to the regime in South Korea, espoused a version of rightist nationalism but did not attempt to maintain completely separate institutions. Their children attended Japanese public schools and acculturated to the Japanese language and lifestyles. By the early 1970s, most Koreans were Japan-born and many of the more militant communists had accepted repatriation to North Korea. The political energies of those who remained gradually shifted from intense concern with their former homeland to asserting their interests and claiming their rights as a minority in Japan.

Today the Korean minority is seven hundred thousand strong, 85 percent of them born and raised in Japan. All speak Japanese, many as their household language, earn their livelihoods and pay taxes in Japan, and have no intention of "returning" to Korea. Some have adopted Japanese names; despite the social obstacles, many have taken Japanese spouses. But very few have accepted naturalization. Even as citizens of Japan, their formal, legal status would, they believe, be insufficient to allow them to pass as Japanese or to prevent discrimination and rejection. They are not prepared to contemplate second-class citizenship and in the process pay the moral and psychological price of abandoning their community. Most of them prefer the more assertive strategy of maintaining their minority status and pride while insisting on nondiscriminatory access to education, employment, and public services.

The status of Koreans in Japan continues to be a concern of the South Korean government, which maintains close diplomatic, security, and economic links with Japan. Though it has not succeeded in protecting, by international agreement, the rights to permanent residence of second and subsequent generations born in Japan, the government of Korea has made it clear that good relations with Japan depend on fair and respectful treatment of its resident Koreans. This position was emphasized in a public address by President Rho when he visited Japan in May 1990. Meanwhile, with the reluctant acquiescence of the Japanese authorities, the bankrupt North Korean regime continues to receive annual remit-tances estimated at $600 million from sympathizers reputedly connected with criminal syndicates in Osaka. These funds may help to finance North Korea's nuclear weapons facilities.[29]

Given Japan's compelling need for labor and the unresponsive posture of its government, it is hardly surprising that illegal immigration became a fact of life beginning in the mid-1980s. Illegals are conservatively es-timated at two to three hundred thousand. Labor brokers in Japan con-tract with Japanese employers to provide foreign workers; their counterparts in the various Asian countries recruit prospective migrants and arrange documents and passage for which the migrants pay well. Surveys indicate that the Japanese public, aware of current labor short-ages, expects the number of illegals to increase. If demand and supply factors were allowed to supplant what has, in fact, become an under-ground labor market, Japan could readily absorb two to three million foreign workers. Together with their families they would constitute about the same proportion of Japan's population as foreign workers and their families in Germany and France.

Filipina immigrants have gained important niches in the burgeoning entertainment and sex industries and are active in the nursing profession. Heavy, dirty jobs in construction and in metallurgical factories are filled increasingly by Pakistanis, Bangladeshis, and Chinese. The major air-ports contract for cleaning and janitorial activities with foreign firms. Hospitals, hotels, and restaurants urgently need low-wage labor. There is a large latent demand for household labor. On the demand side, Japan has begun to replicate the dual labor market phenomenon common in other affluent economies, for Japanese will no longer accept certain types of low-wage jobs that are considered arduous or menial. On the supply side, the market response is lagging because of government barriers, but these barriers are being circumvented by the illegal networks that now operate with the support of Japanese employers. Many employers ac-tually prefer to have foreign workers on illegal terms since they are vul-nerable to exploitation and fall outside the purview of protective legislation.

The topic of immigration and foreign workers has been surrounded by official taboos; unrecognized, it cannot exist. The police, however, concede that since the scale of illegal immigration exceeds their enforce-ment capacities, they often turn a blind eye to what many Japanese

[29]*International Herald Tribune,* 2 November 1993, 1.

consider an economic necessity as long as the migrants avoid criminal activity. The police do tangle frequently with the illegals; an embarrassing incident in 1989 involved the leak of an internal National Police Agency memorandum describing Pakistanis as filthy, foul-smelling, afflicted with epidemic skin diseases, and inclined to lying while invoking the name of Allah. The government publishes no data on illegal immigrant workers or on their living and working conditions. There is no evidence that the illegal Asian communities have become politicized.

The racist flavor of the Japanese government's resistance to foreign labor is underscored by its willingness, based on the doctrine of jus sanguinis, to admit Brazilian citizens of Japanese ethnic origin as unskilled guest workers. (Brazilian-Japanese complain bitterly, however, about discrimination and second-class treatment.[30] The bottom line is that in the face of a declining domestic labor supply and exigent demand for workers, the Japanese government clings to the doctrine of racial exclusiveness. This stance is possible only because it tolerates the large and growing presence of an illegal underworld of foreign workers. To expel them, even if such a measure could be implemented, would disrupt important sectors of the Japanese economy, antagonize employers, and upset relations with Asian countries with which Japan maintains important economic and diplomatic relations. Having achieved by economic penetration the 1930s vision of a Greater East Asia Co-Prosperity Sphere, it would be awkward to inform countries that accept Japanese products and Japanese investment that their nationals are unwelcome as workers in Japan and subject to summary deportation if apprehended. With the closing of the Persian Gulf labor market, Asian countries look increasingly to Japan to provide employment opportunities for their nationals whose remittances, in turn, contribute badly needed foreign exchange. Racial exclusiveness is not an acceptable posture for any state these days, particularly one that aspires to international leadership.

The Japanese government strategy for avoiding foreign labor is predicated on the notion that jobs can be transferred overseas by investment, and much of this has indeed occurred. But this strategy cannot apply to sectors such as agriculture, construction, and transportation, which are inherently local, nor to the numerous small industry and service activities that tend to flourish in an expanding affluent economy. Japan, like it or not, is well on its way to hosting large numbers of foreign workers simply because their labor is needed. The next step will be to acquiesce,

[30] *New York Times,* 13 November 1991, 1.

perhaps informally, in their permanent status, in part because frequent turnover is an undesirable cost for employers, and then to yield to compassionate claims for family unification. Since Japan's government is exposed to international scrutiny and respectful of human rights, it cannot treat guestworkers inhumanely, even if their formal status is, to use the American euphemism, "undocumented."

Once this stage is reached, Japan's government can only with great difficulty and embarrassment continue to ignore this large and growing underground phenomenon. Once the status of foreign workers has been legalized, Japanese policy will face the choice between encouraging assimilation or acquiescing in cultural and social pluralism on Japanese national soil. The former would imply the end of racial exclusiveness based on blood lineage, the latter the reluctant sharing of Japan's living space with permanent diaspora communities who will invoke Japan's democratic constitution to demand separate but equal rights and treatment for themselves.

Will this scenario be realized? Or can Japan, alone among the affluent democratic economies, innovate ways of satifying imperative domestic demand for foreign workers while refusing to recognize their existence as social and political communities?

The Political Dynamics of Labor Diasporas

Demographic pressures—low birth rates in affluent countries, explosive population growth in nearby Third World countries, the availability of safe and cheap transportation, strong, continuing demand in rich countries for low-cost, docile labor—have sustained powerful incentives and opportunities for large-scale migratory movements from impoverished Third World countries to affluent industrial and postindustrial economies. Third World governments welcome this safety valve for their unemployed citizens, as well as the precious foreign exchange the emigrants provide through family remittances. Often these governments continue to claim the emigrants and their progeny as subjects. Under conflicting pressures from employers and nativists, governments in receiving countries tend to be more ambivalent; under conditions of economic recession they may completely ban legal immigration and facilitate the repatriation of resident aliens. National borders these days tend, however, to be porous. Where strong demand prevails in industrial countries, Third World emigrants are prepared to incur substantial risks and costs; where legal entry is blocked, determined emigrants discover and exploit illegal channels.

In affluent democratic polities, the formation of labor diasporas follows a standard sequence. As immigrants occupy niches in the domestic economy that indigenous workers, even the unemployed, refuse to fill, the economy becomes dependent on their services. Eventually many foreign workers are awarded permanent status as resident aliens. Family reunions become unavoidable, as spouses, children, and collateral dependents join the breadwinner. Soon settled disapora communities emerge, residential enclaves with all the accoutrements of permanent communities: their own businesses, newspapers, religious centers, and recreational and mutual aid associations. Because they are foreigners, with low income, inferior status, and few influential connections, they encounter hostile, discriminatory, and often abusive treatment by employers, landlords, merchants, bureaucrats, and police. Language handicaps and unsupportive home environments for youth tend to produce substandard school performance, high dropout rates, and delinquent behavior, which inhibit job mobility and condemn many to the status of an ethnic underclass. A minority, however, become skilled workers, professionals, and businessmen and manage to rise into the middle class. From their ranks emerge the spokesmen and political entrepreneurs of diaspora communities. Though life is often frustrating in the host country, few immigrants, especially among the second generation, opt to return to the barren economic prospects of their country of origin.

Even when foreign workers become a problem to their host governments, when they experience unemployment or when their unwelcome presence generates a xenophobic political backlash, democratic governments cannot summarily expel permanent residents or deprive them of economic rights or public services. Such behavior is prohibited by their constitutions and legal systems or by the commitment of their political culture to basic human rights. Domestic supporters and advocates for the underprivileged, civil libertarians, church groups, labor unions, and humanitarian societies, are prepared to defend their rights. Furthermore, arbitrary or abusive treatment of their nationals is certain to provoke strong negative reactions from states with which the host government desires to maintain friendly relations. In response to xenophobic pressures, however, governments can erect strict barriers to legal immigration, limit the entitlements of resident aliens, and attempt more rigorous enforcement of laws against illegal immigrants.

Once they acknowledge the reality that diasporas will constitute permanent presences in their midst, host governments face a limited set of choices for managing their political status. The first of these strategies is to facilitate assimilation by individuals, the usual practice in polities that define citizenship by civic rather than ethnic criteria. This inclusive strategy is implemented by encouraging acculturation, especially language fluency; promoting occupational and residential mobility by banning discrimination in employment, housing, and education; awarding citizenship by simple naturalization procedures and automatically by birth. Citizenship, in turn, provides members of diasporas with incentives for integration and with political and judicial resources for promoting and defending individual and group interests. Cultural maintenance becomes the responsibility not of the state but of the ethnic community through voluntary efforts. This pattern of incorporation by individual assimilation is practiced in the United States and has been the traditional method in France. In contemporary France, however, the implementation of this strategy has been complicated by the unexpected reluctance of most North Africans to acquire French nationality, implying as it does the acceptance of membership in a secular and non-Muslim society that they consider hostile to their heritage.

The second strategy is to recognize and tolerate ethnic pluralism as an unwelcome reality, but to pursue a pattern of apartheid that denies citizenship to substantial numbers of permanent residents. Such polities continue to define citizenship in ethnic terms. Individuals in these diasporas can exist into the third and fourth generations in political limbo, participants in the economy, taxpayers and recipients of public services, but forever foreigners, political pariahs on the margins of society. Germany and Japan attempt to protect ethnic purity by thus excluding their substantial and growing labor diasporas.

The third strategy, official multiculturalism, would recognize ethnic diasporas as distinct communities empowered to manage their own institutions, including schools, in their own language and to conduct internal affairs, such as family relations, property transactions, and minor criminal matters, in their own tribunals according to their own legal traditions. They might be represented in the political and administrative institutions of the state as an officially recognized minority in proportion to their numbers. Group incorporation with minority privileges is the polar opposite of individual assimilation. Some such pattern of institutional pluralism has been proposed by spokesmen for Muslim North

Africans in France. A version of cultural and institutional autonomy is advocated by some scholars as necessary to preserve Hispano-Mexican traditions for Mexican Americans in the American Southwest.[31]

With the possible exception of Canada, officially sanctioned multiculturalism on their national territory has not been recognized for immigrant people by any of the governments of democratic countries.[32] Though it will be vigorously resisted, this pattern of social and political pluralism is likely to be claimed in the future by representatives of diasporas who insist that the maintenance of their collective identity and distinctive culture is a basic human right that must be respected by governments and accommodated by formal political arrangements.

The initial impulse for labor migration is overwhelmingly economic, but once diaspora communities become established they find it necessary to articulate collective interests and aspirations. They mobilize politically, usually dividing internally along ideological or class lines. The longer a diaspora is established, the more likely are its members, especially the second and subsequent generations, to draw away from the old country and focus on local needs. When formal political channels are closed to them, they resort to such noninstitutional methods as strikes, boycotts, and demonstrations that sometimes turn violent. When citizenship is available and accepted, diaspora communities can employ the full range of political instrumentalities, voting and coalition formation, legislative lobbying, judicial interventions to influence policy and administration on their behalf. Where, as in the case of Mexican Americans in southern California and Texas, their numbers are sufficient to affect the outcomes of elections they can become a significant political force.

Diasporas, in turn, stimulate nativist political backlash at local and national levels. Locally, indigenous people fear that their neighborhoods have been invaded and their quality of life endangered by unwelcome, unwashed, and crime-prone foreigners. Political entrepreneurs emerge to capture that market, to persuade their fellow citizens that they must act

---

[31] See reference to Mario Barrera in note 3.

[32] The government of Canada fosters multiculturalism for diasporas, financing community centers, scholarships, publications, radio and TV broadcasts and similar facilities to enable immigrant communities to maintain their cultural heritage within the Canadian "mosaic." They are not, however, recognized as political communities and they enjoy no minority political or official language rights. Jean Leonard Elliott and Angie Fleras, *Multiculturalism in Canada: Problems and Prospects* (Pacific Grove, Calif.: Brooks Cole-Nelson Canada, 1991).

to protect their rights and interests, to curb the foreigners, to regain control over their own community. The status of foreign workers thus escalates to the agenda of national politics. Labor diasporas become scapegoats for such problems as unemployment, high taxes, welfare abuse, and crime. Demands to control or roll back immigration can attract significant public support and threaten the status and security even of permanently resident foreigners. During the economic recession of the early 1990s, ethnic backlash against immigrants roiled the politics of European democracies, including Germany and France, even though it was clear that these economies would be seriously disabled without the services of workers from their large labor diasporas.

Two factors critically affect the processes by which labor diasporas are incorporated into contemporary democratic polities. The first factor, political opportunity structure, is the relative openness or restrictiveness of the host polity to the acceptance of immigrants as citizens. The second factor is the relative willingness or reluctance of immigrants to acculturate and accept membership in the host polity. Both factors are variable and reflect distinctive political developments in individual countries. They help to explain, however, divergent experiences of immigrant diasporas in affluent democratic polities. Polities that cling to ethnic definitions of citizenship provide more restrictive opportunity structures for immigrants than those that define citizenship in civic terms. Diasporas whose values accord with those of the host culture are inclined to integrate. Those, on the other hand, whose inherited values and practices conflict with those of the receiving society tend to be reluctant to integrate. Thus militant Islam inhibits integration among members of Muslim labor diasporas in Europe.[33]

The main interest of students of ethnic politics has been the struggles of indigenous peoples in their ancestral homelands claiming the right of self-determination—greater autonomy from the central state or outright independence—and the responses of the state to their demands. A different but equally important manifestation of ethnic pluralism stems from labor diasporas, the outcome of contemporary migration to the affluent democratic polities of Europe, North America, and Japan. This chapter has outlined the political issues and dilemmas, transnational as well as domestic, that labor migration and the ensuing disaporas produce in contemporary democratic states.

[33]See William Safran's article, cited in note 20 above.

The Stakes in Ethnic Conflict

Ethnic communities coexisting at the local level may compete for jobs, land, trading opportunities, housing, and control of neighborhoods. Such conflicts may be contained by tacit understandings or by mutual accommodation, but they frequently erupt into violence. Though local authorities may regulate minor clashes, those that are severe and persistent tend to escalate to the level of the state. Modern states establish and enforce rules that distribute political, cultural, and social values important to mobilized ethnic communities. When values are allocated by other processes such as custom, coercion, or markets, the state may intervene to modify or replace these processes when the outcomes are deemed to be detrimental to social order or prejudicial to the interests of ethnic groups that are able to influence the behavior of government. When competitive market processes in the economy and in higher education appeared to favor Chinese over Malays, the Malay-dominated state intervened to modify the rules of allocation. The government of Canada moved to revise its language policies when prevailing practices were believed to threaten survival of the polity.

States establish or acquiesce in the rules of allocation and deploy substantial resources; therefore, the main prizes in ethnic conflicts are influence over the outcomes of policy or, where possible, domination of the state and its agencies.[1] Where domination or influence are impracticable objectives, ethnic communities must make the best of minority status or

---

[1]Paul Brass, ed., *Ethnic Groups and the State* (Totowa, N.J.: Barnes and Noble, 1985); also Donald Rothschild, ed., *State and Ethnic Claims: African Policy Dilemmas* (Boulder, Colo.: Westview Press, 1983).

attempt to withdraw de facto or de jure from the state's jurisdiction. Since state institutions often incorporate diverse interests and viewpoints and maintain complex links with elements of society, this pluralism provides opportunities for representatives of ethnic communities and factions of these communities to exert influence on government. Afrikaner extremists, for example, exercised considerable influence on the state security forces whose activities compromised negotiations initiated by their government to replace the apartheid regime.

Where the state has been created or captured by a particular ethnic community and operates as an agent of that community, that state becomes a party to ethnic conflicts, especially when prevailing rules, practices, or allocations are challenged by ethnic competitors. The cases of Malaysia, Israel, and South Africa under Afrikaner rule illustrate patterns of ethnic hegemony that prevail in many countries. In some polities, Canada for example, governments enjoy sufficient autonomy that they can credibly attempt to mediate and accommodate the demands of competing ethnic constituencies. South Africa today is in the process of transition from a state controlled by and for a racial minority to one that confers equal citizenship on all residents. In the new South Africa the state will be the arena in which conflicting ethnic interests and demands are promoted and adjusted; it is not yet clear whether that state will enjoy sufficient autonomy to mediate between the parties.

The centrality of the state in the management of ethnic conflicts is unaffected by regional or global economic integration. Though they have lost some control of economic policy, contemporary states are in no danger of withering away. They retain vast powers over political, cultural, and economic matters vital to their competing, constituent ethnic communities. The impersonality of large bureaucratic structures and the harsh consequences of market forces, including the inequitable division of economic resources, create fresh needs for community that are often filled by ethnic organizations and movements among both immigrant diasporas and homelands peoples. The disintegration of multinational states, such as the Soviet Union and Yugoslavia, eliminates neither states nor ethnic conflicts. Successor states become new arenas for the pursuit and the regulation of conflicting ethnic claims by civil and by violent means. Economic integration notwithstanding, states and their agencies remain arenas, targets, and usually parties to ethnic-based conflicts.

In this chapter, I examine what is at stake in the challenge and response relationships between mobilized ethnic communities and governments that manage the affairs of the state.

Recognition and Respect

Mobilized ethnic communities strive for the respect of outsiders, especially of those in positions of authority. This observation applies particularly to subordinated communities whose members have experienced rejection, contempt, and denial of collective respect by members of more powerful and more prestigious communities. Ethnic intellectuals rediscover, recreate, and even invent glorious histories, heroes, literature, and myths to buttress the self-esteem of their people and compel the respect of outsiders. Formal recognition as a distinct people may be a necessary prelude to fair treatment. French Canadians demand recognition as one of Canada's two "founding races" and formal constitutional status as a "distinct society." Hispanics in the United States insist on bilingual education as a symbol of official esteem for their origins and culture as much as for instrumental reasons. Public displays of Hannukah menoras beside Christmas trees connote to some American Jews societal respect for their community and its traditions. The campaign for "multiculturalism" on university campuses in the United States reflects this demand for respect. Black Consciousness, Black Pride, and Azania proclaimed self-respect among an oppressed people and demanded recognition of their collective dignity by outsiders, especially South African Whites.

Meanwhile, denial of recognition is a weapon in the hands of ethnic adversaries. For decades, the English denigrated and disallowed the use of the Welsh language. A generation of Israeli politicians refused to acknowledge Palestinians as a nationality. Malays continue to remind Malaysia's Chinese citizens that they are immigrants, not native sons, and to deny the Chinese language official recognition and status in government or in secondary and higher education. For Malaysian Chinese, economic affluence cannot compensate or substitute for denial of collective respect.

A struggle for collective recognition and respect is likely to emerge where an ethnic minority believes its status has been denigrated by those in authority. They may be willing to invest considerable resources to gain the symbols of collective respect. Though such recognition, when achieved, may in fact be essentially symbolic, subordinated ethnic groups understand that they cannot otherwise be serious participants in negotiations with other ethnic groups or with agencies of the state. One instrument of conflict management is to yield conspicuous formal evidence of such respect, as, for example, the designation of Martin Luther King Day as an official holiday in the United States.

Cultural Goals

One significant dimension of recognition is the status of language.[2] Language, the classic marker of ethnic identity, is one of the principal bonds of community. The status of language conveys both symbolic and instrumental significance. Whether a language appears on public buildings and public signs, is disseminated over the airwaves, serves as a medium of instruction in public schools, can be used in transactions with government reflects the status and the respect accorded to its community. The relative official status of languages can symbolize ethnic equality or domination and subordination. From an instrumental perspective those who attend school, take examinations, compete for employment, and transact with government in their native tongue enjoy a considerable advantage over those who must function in a second language. Thus language policy can be a subject of bitter controversy and a weapon in ethnic conflicts, but it can also be a sign of respect, recognition, and accommodation.

Malays have used language policy as a weapon by which Malays symbolize and reenforce their hegemony in a country where they constitute a slim demographic majority. The message to the Chinese minority of 35 percent is unmistakable: their language has no value in education or government. The state patronizes and promotes the Malay language and Malay culture. Preservation of Chinese language and culture in Malaysia becomes the private responsibility of Chinese communities. Similarly, by rejecting and abandoning an established bilingual regime, by aggressively expanding the role of French in government, education, industry, and the professions and by simultaneously circumscribing the role of English, Quebec's Francophone nationalists have confirmed the dominance of French in all sectors of Quebec society and the subordinate status of English. Their policy threatens the survival of English-speaking institutions and has induced a third of Quebec's Anglophone community to leave the province.

By contrast, in an effort to appease its French-speaking minority and thereby assure the survival of Canada as a polity the government of Canada has attempted to enhance the position of the French language by according it equal official status with English. That these efforts at

---

[2] For the effects of language policy on ethnic conflict, see Brian Weinstein, ed., *Language Policy and Political Development* (Norwood, N.J.: Ablex Publishing Corp., 1990); also William R. Beer, and James E. Jacob, eds., *Language Policy and National Unity* (Totowa, N. J.: Rowman and Allanheld, 1985).

accommodation failed in their intended purpose and were treated with disdain by Quebec nationalists is one of the ironies of recent Canadian history. British policy in South Africa was more successful. Abandoning their policy of aggressive anglicization in the wake of the Boer War, the British conceded equal official status to Afrikaans, the language of the defeated Boers, a gesture of reconciliation that enabled Afrikaner politicians to participate in the new Union of South Africa.

Conceding official status to a minority language at the national or regional level can be a useful measure of accommodation, but it may not be sufficient. Israel's willingness to treat Arabic as an official language has not been sufficient to reconcile its Palestinian minority to Israeli rule. Though religious freedom and official status for their language are welcome, Palestinians believe that their legitimate aspirations extend far beyond cultural autonomy.

As an instrument of policy, the status of language is subject to change. During the Franco dictatorship the Catalan language was proscribed, its use criminalized. Following the transition to democracy, Catalan achieved recognition as the paramount official language of the new regional government of Catalonia. Language has ceased to be an issue between the Spanish state and the Catalan regional minority. During the half century of Soviet rule in the Baltic states Russian was the dominant language; once independence was restored, the Baltic national languages were accorded exclusive official status, despite the protests of their substantial Russian minorities who had refused to learn the local languages. Their predicament reflected the abrupt shift in their status from membership in the dominant society to unpopular and vulnerable minorities.

Political Goals

The political goals of mobilized ethnic communities can be classified as hegemony, autonomy, and inclusion.

Hegemony entails control of the apparatus of the state and the ability to frame and enforce the rules and practices that govern the relative status and opportunities of ethnic communities as collectivities and of their members as individuals. The concept of hegemony can also be extended to efforts to expand the borders of the polity in order to redeem ethnic kinfolk and the territory they occupy from foreign rule and in-

corporate them into the ethnic homeland.[3] Examples of irredentist pol
itics are the successful campaign of the Serb elites to realize a Greater
Serbia after the breakup of the Yugoslav federation, and the failed efforts
of Somalia to wrest the Ogaden with its Somali majority from Ethiopia
in the late 1970s.

Ethnic hegemony can be exercised by processes and policies of exclusion, subordination, or preference. Other ethnic communities can be excluded from membership and participation in the polity; they remain
subjects of the state but not citizens. Such was the fate of non-Whites in
South Africa prior to the abandonment of apartheid. Thus, too, the Turkish diaspora is effectively excluded from the German polity. A less draconian form of exclusion may apply to ethnic communities as collectivities
but not necessarily to individuals. The policy may deny official recognition to the claims of ethnic minorities for collective political recognition or
cultural rights but permit and even encourage acculturation and assimilation of individuals into the dominant society. Society will thus be gradually homogenized as individuals abandon their native communities and
join the ethnic mainstream. Having regained national independence in
1991, the Estonian state has limited citizenship to persons whose forebears prior to 1940 were Estonian nationals, defining citizenship in ethnic
terms and, in effect, excluding Russian "colonists" who had moved to Estonia and taken up residence during the Soviet period. Under international pressure, the Estonian government is considering liberalization that
would permit ethnic Russian residents who have learned the Estonian language to be naturalized as individuals, but Russians as a collectivity would
not be granted minority political or cultural rights.

The most common expression of political hegemony is the subordination of ethnic minorities. Recognized as ethnic communities and endowed with some rights, they are nevertheless consigned de jure or de
facto to inferior status. While Palestinians in the Occupied Territories
are excluded from political rights, their kinfolk in Israel proper are citizens with formal rights to voting, office holding, and access to the courts
and to public services. As a practical matter they are a powerless and
suspect minority, excluded from decision-making roles in the Israeli government. They have no access to official sources of capital or credit, and
they experience discrimination in the provision of most public services,

[3]Naomi Chazan, ed., *Irredentism and International Politics* (Boulder, Colo.: Lynne Reinner, 1991).

including education and municipal amenities. In Malaysia, Chinese enjoy citizenship, their ethnic political organizations are recognized as legitimate participants in the political process, and a Chinese political party, the MCA, is admitted as a junior partner in government. Nevertheless, Malay hegemony and Chinese subordination are firmly enforced by Malay control of the apparatus the state and by a monopoly of its symbols, including the status of Islam as the state religion, Malay as the sole official language, and a Malay sultan as head of state.

Finally, hegemony can be expressed by preferential measures that can be construed as reverse discrimination. Thus, the Afrikaner government used public funds to foster Afrikaner-owned businesses and Afrikaner employment in state enterprises, opportunities unavailable even to non-Afrikaner Whites, however worthy or needful. Bumiputera policies and practices in Malaysia provide formal preferences for Malays in higher education, employment in government and in the private sector, government contracts, and the allocation of capital, credit, and licenses. Those ineligible for preferences regard them as ethnically discriminatory, in effect if not in intent. Preferences for members of the dominant community arc common practices in ethnically hegemonic regimes; bumiputera preferences in Malaysia are unusual only to the degree that they have been explicitly stipulated and formalized.

Where hegemony is not a feasible aspiration, ethnic communities often opt for autonomy. The ultimate autonomy is de jure separation from the polity, the achievement of political independence and hegemony in a new state, which often entails, however, the subsequent subordination of ethnic minorities in their midst. Secession is usually a high-risk option, regarded as revolutionary by state elites who consider it their responsibility to preserve the territorial integrity of their state and are likely to counter attempts at secession with severe repression that may result in lengthy insurgencies or bloody civil wars. The failed Ibo campaign for independence from Nigeria produced more than a million casualities. The indecisive Tamil struggle for an independent Eelam in Sri Lanka has been particularly brutal; Since 1983 more than fifty thousand lives have been lost and 1.7 million people, 10 percent of the population, have been displaced. For more than thirty years the Eritreans waged a costly but eventually successful armed struggle for independence from Ethiopia.

The recent peaceful dissolution of the former Czech and Slovak Federated Republic (Czechoslavakia) and the likelihood that Quebec's secession from Canada could be accomplished without bloodshed do not nullify the general proposition that the pursuit of self-determination through secession is likely to be resisted by force. The argument that independent statehood for minorities may create economically unviable entities has been undermined by the economic successes of small countries such as Singapore, Mauritius, Switzerland, and Denmark. Economic specialization and the lowering of trade barriers create opportunities for small states. Scottish and Quebec nationalists are therefore convinced that their economic futures would be secure as independent states by membership, respectively, in the European Union and the North American Free Trade Area.

Territorial autonomy is a milder form of self determination in a federalized relationship that preserves the boundaries of the state. Where an ethnic community is geographically concentrated, a two-tiered federal structure permits a large measure of regional self-government, plus the opportunity to participate in the affairs of the central state. Federalism facilitates the sharing of two collective identities, regional and national; participation at the center conveys a role in decision making in executive as well as legislative institutions. Canada would not be conceivable without the federal arrangements that have provided the French-Canadian majority in Quebec with political space for substantial self-government; but Canada also demonstrates the inherent tensions between the center and component units in federal systems. The combination of unredressed grievances and experience with regional self-rule may inspire aspirations for full sovereignty. Thus territorial autonomy may be a prelude to eventual attempts at secession. In ethnically plural states federalism may provide a thin and unconvincing subterfuge for highly centralized regimes; in the former Soviet state, for example, federal arrangements lacked legitimacy and became vulnerable to fragmentation once the central regime was weakened.

Regional autonomy has, however, stabilized relations between Catalans and the Spanish state and between Walloons and Flemings in Belgium. Violence was averted between Austria and Italy when, after extended negotiations, Italy conceded regional autonomy to its German-speaking minority in their South Tyrolian enclave. In a structurally similar situation, the Armenian government has been under pressure to annex the enclave of Nagorno-Karabakh in Azerbaijan which is populated by ethnic kinfolk, even though that territory shares no border with Armenia. The Armenian-assisted Karabakh rebellion has persisted for five years, resulting in thousands of casualties, an estimated hundred thousand refugees, and enormous economic costs among all the participants. Ancient animosities between Armenians and Turks (Azeri being a Turkic-speaking people), and between Christians and Muslims, have inhibited so rational a settlement as regional autonomy that has effectively stabilized relationships in South Tyrol.

If an ethnic minority is not concentrated in a particular territory, another form of autonomy may be available. Cultural autonomy allows minority ethnic communities to operate, at public expense, their own institutions in their own language and even to maintain tribunals that apply their own legal system in disputes among members of their community. The millet system under the Ottoman Empire institutionalized cultural pluralism; its vestiges remain in Lebanon and elsewhere in the Middle East. A form of cultural pluralism has allowed English speakers to operate their own schools and hospitals in Quebec and Muslims in Israel to have separate schools in the Arabic medium and tribunals that apply Muslim law to relations among Muslims. Spokesmen for the North African dispora in France demand similar autonomy for Muslims—an affront to the Jacobin tradition of France as one, indivisible, secular state. Where populations are ethnically mixed and cultural pluralism can be tolerated as public policy, it can be an effective method of conflict management.

A frequent political objective of ethnic communities is inclusion on a nondiscriminatory basis in the body politic. There are two distinct processes of inclusion. The first establishes the right of individual members of a previously disadvantaged community to participate fully and equally in the institutions of government and society. Immigrant diasporas commonly demand the elimination of all barriers, formal and non-formal, to full participation as individuals, but this demand can arise also in deprived indigenous communities such as African Americans in the United States and non-Whites in South Africa. Civil rights movements insist on eliminating discriminatory rules and informal practices in employment, housing, education, and the economy as well as in government. Indeed, one important faction among Malaysian Chinese is less interested in cultural pluralism than in equal inclusion. Their slogan, a "Malaysian Malaysia," serves as a code word for the elimination of bumiputera preferences, the ending of all forms of discrimination, the inclusion of non-Malays as individuals with equal access to all the institutions of government and society—in effect a nonviolent revolution in Malaysia. Individual inclusion does not necessarily imply assimilation; ethnic communities, by voluntary means, may attempt to maintain their culture, sometimes, as in Canada's program of multiculturalism, with state assistance.

A second kind of inclusion refers to collectivities rather than to indi-viduals. The polity is conceived not as an aggregation of atomized in-dividuals, but as a federation of coexisting ethnic communities, some of which may have been excluded or subordinated in the past but are en-titled to be incorporated into the polity as collectivities in consociational or power-sharing arrangements. Consociational arrangements may be sought where territorially based federalism is not feasible. They normally involve such practices as government by multiethnic elite cartels, repre-sentation of participating ethnic communities in the decision-making in-stitutions of the state, allocations by demographic proportionality, self-managed institutional pluralism, and veto power over matters deemed harmful to the vital interests of any participating community.

Some of these power-sharing arrangements operated in Malaysia be-fore 1969, in Lebanon before 1975, and informally in Quebec before 1974. In each case they broke down and were abandoned because they failed to satisfy important factions in one of the participating commu-nities. Despite these instances of instability, the idea of power sharing continues to appeal to spokesmen for ethnic minorities that fear exclu-sion or subordination under majoritarian rule. In South Africa, Whites as well as Inkatha have urged power-sharing arrangements in order to protect minority rights, as have Palestinians in Israel. Though a British-sponsored power-sharing proposal failed in Northern Ireland in 1974, similar schemes continue to surface as the most likely way out of that otherwise endless conflict.

The beginning of wisdom for observers and analysts of ethnic conflict is to recognize that ethnic communities are seldom monolithic actors. Inevitably they contain factions based on class cleavages, kinship rival-ries, personal ambitions, or ideological differences. Bottom-line issues may unite all factions—for Québécois the paramount status of French in their homeland, for South African Blacks the elimination of apartheid, for Palestinians in the Occupied Territories escape from Israeli rule. Be-yond these areas of consensus, organized factions within ethnic com-munities may clash over goals as well as tactics. The secular PLO and the fundamentalist HAMAS hold incompatible images of a future Pales-tinian state. Quebec nationalists dispute so fundamental a goal as their future relations with Canada, and those that favor secession disagree over tactics to achieve it. Elements associated with Inkatha and the ANC engage in bloody internecine warfare, while PAC and the ANC clash over the role of the Communist party and the future status of Whites in postapartheid South Africa. In Malaysia during the late 1980s, UMNO split into two bitterly contending factions, a split based largely on competing personal ambitions. In all cases, factions compete for power, influence, and support among their constituents; for control of the community's resources; and for the right to speak for them in relations with outsiders. Internal struggles may consume as much time and energy of faction chiefs as do relations with the state and with ethnic adversaries.

Internal conflicts may create improbable coalitions across ethnic boundaries, sometimes formal, often tacit. Witness the tacit electoral entente between the Malay Party Islam and the secular Chinese-dominated Democratic Action Party to undermine their common antagonists the UMNO and its junior partner the MCA. The adage that politics makes strange bedfellows is no better illustrated than in the expedient cross-ethnic coalitions that emerge even in intense, long-lasting, and violent conflicts. What may prove to be a marriage of convenience between ancient enemies, the ANC and the NP, has been activated in large measure by their common interest in outmaneuvering foes within their respective ethnic communities. Politics do not stop at the water's edge of ethnic communities.

Factionalism and factional competition are dynamic processes in ethnic communities. Elites that fail to deliver may be challenged and eventually displaced even within the same organization, as the Youth League challenged and replaced the older leadership of ANC in the 1940s, radically altering the organization's program as well as its tactics. Changing circumstances and new outlooks may result in the formation of new factions, for example, the 1982 defection from the National Party of Afrikaner right wingers, who formed the new Conservative Party to fight for orthodox apartheid. One faction may be displaced by another: in 1960, the modernizing Liberals defeated the traditional nationalists in Quebec and launched the Quiet Revolution; in 1976, the separatist Parti Quebec defeated the federalist Liberals. Internal factional battles over tactics in the mid-1980s contributed to the PQ's electoral debacle in 1985 and the resignation of its long-time leader, René Lévesque. Factional struggles for power often persist even during periods of maximum stress and danger for their community, as during Israel's war of independence when the "revisionist" Irgun faction insisted on its own military operations in defiance of instructions from the provisional government, which then proceeded to attack and sink a ship carrying a cargo of arms to the dissident faction.

Economic Goals

Economic values may be vital to mobilized and competing ethnic communities. These include access to higher education, employment opportunities, and control of economic assets, such as land and capital.

Elementary and secondary education have achieved the status of entitlements in most contemporary states, especially in urban areas, even where governments cannot afford to universalize them. The issue most likely to agitate ethnic communities is the medium of instruction. They may demand that publicly financed education be available in their own language and that their representatives have a role in the management of schools, including choice of teachers and curriculum content. The clumsy attempt to impose Afrikaans as a compulsory medium of instruction precipitated the Soweto insurrection in 1976. Chinese in Malaysia have campaigned without success for publicly financed Chinese-medium secondary schools; the government replies that national unity requires a single medium of communication and that all instruction must therefore be in the national language, Malay. The government of Quebec compels the children of immigrants to attend French-medium schools, contrary to the wishes of parents and despite protests from Anglophones that this policy violates individual rights and risks the viability of the English-medium school system.

Still more controversial is the question of access to higher education, a scarce value often perceived in zero-sum terms. Higher education is crucial to social mobility, furnishing the credentials that qualify individuals for positions in government and in the prestigious and lucrative learned professions. Ambitious parents, especially from urban middle-class and educated backgrounds, are especially sensitive on this issue; persons from these backgrounds are likely to be leaders, activists, and attentive supporters of ethnic political movements. Black and Hispanic spokespersons in the United States demand "affirmative action" programs that provide positive preferences for university admission to their constituents who have been severely underrepresented in the past. To many Whites the skewing of admissions and of financial assistance, especially to professional schools, amounts to de facto quotas and constitutes reverse discrimination.

As a result of shifting the language of qualifying examinations and of instruction from English to Malay and reversing the rules governing university admissions from individual competition to ethnic preferences,

Malay enrollments leaped from about a third to three quarters of the total. Thus many more qualified non-Malays were denied access to higher education. This constitutes a bitter grievance among Chinese, a reminder of their second class status. On the other hand, Israel's agreement to expand higher education in the Occupied Territories produced Palestinian graduates with high expectations but very few opportunities for professional employment and plenty of time for nationalist agitation. The four universities in the Territories became centers of militant Palestinian opposition to Israeli rule.

If ethnic groups clash over criteria for access to higher education, access to employment, especially to positions that depend on higher education, is an even more loaded issue. This applies especially to government jobs which in many countries combine power, prestige, security, and middle-class income with opportunities to supplement salaries by perquisites and corrupt practices. In Malaysia entry to the higher civil service is strictly regulated by quotas of four Malays to one non-Malay; for other positions informal preferences apply both in recruitment and promotion. Civil service positions in Quebec, 98 percent of which are held by persons of Francophone background, are effectively closed to their English-speaking but tax-paying compatriots. Arabs are similarly excluded in Israel, as Blacks have been in South Africa. No doubt the postapartheid transition will witness a vigorous effort among newly enfranchised Blacks, especially ANC activists and cadres, to gain access to middle-class civil service positions. Since South Africa's financial plight will not permit rapid expansion of the state sector, White incumbents are likely to feel vulnerable, exacerbating ethnic tensions associated with the transition. Whites are likely to insist on maintaining "standards," while Blacks will demand preferential access to achieve a more "representative" set of state bureaucracies.

In ethnically conflicted systems, the most sensitive sector of the state bureaucracies are the security services, the police, and above all the military. The security forces, particularly the officer corps, are the ultimate arbiters of politics. Except for limited participation by the Druze and Bedouin minorities, the Israel Defense Forces are entirely Jewish. The Malaysian army at all ranks is Malay except for a handful of non-Malays in technical and noncommand positions. Comprising 40 percent of the population, Serbs held more than 80 percent of the officer positions in the Yugoslav National Army. The officer corps in South Africa, one of the mainstays of the apartheid regime, has been exclusively White as have Army conscripts, though non-Whites have had a substantial presence in the lower ranks of the police. The latter have been reviled by Black militants as collaborators and traitors and have been prominent victims of social and physical abuse, including assassinations and "neck-lacing."

Hegemonic ethnic regimes are careful to tightly control the security forces, usually by excluding or limiting the participation of outsiders and dissident factions from their own community. Where ethnic competition is more diffuse, as in the United States, recruitment criteria and practices may disregard ethnic factors, in the hope that these will result in ethnically representative security forces. The Canadian defense establishment aims explicitly for "representative participation" among Anglophones and Francophones in all ranks and includes a number of units in which French is the language of communication and command. The more adversarial ethnic relations, the more certain that access to the security forces will be biased and even monopolized in favor of the dominant ethnic community.

When an ethnic group gains control of the state, important economic assets are soon transferred to members of that community, the bulk to elites, though rank-and-file members usually participate in the redistribution. The new dominant group appropriates land and housing as members of the defeated community abandon the territory, are driven out, or are forced to sell at sacrifice prices. During the colonial era, large tracts of Malay land were transferred to British corporations for "development"; in the 1980s, most of these assets were reacquired through purchase by the Malaysian state for the eventual benefit of Malay investors, especially those with sufficient resources to buy shares at discounted prices. Following its war of independence, Israel distributed abandoned Arab land and houses to Jewish immigrants. After World War II, the government of Czechoslovakia expelled its German minority from the Sudetenland and distributed the land and other assets to fellow Czechs.

When an ethnic community controls the state apparatus, it generally defines access to and control of economic assets in ways calculated to benefit its constituents. In addition to land and natural resources, such assets include factories, capital, credit, and licenses to operate commercial and financial enterprises and to practice professions and trades. If members of the dominant community possess the skills needed to compete successfully under market processes and disciplines, market rules may be allowed to prevail. Members of other ethnic communities may then participate in the competition and acquire a share of the wealth. Despite informal processes of discrimination, this policy has provided opportunities for upward mobility for members of immigrant diasporas in most Western European countries and in North America.

When, however, members of the politically dominant ethnic community appear to lack the competitive skills or to have been excluded from opportunities to acquire the necessary contacts or experience, governments supersede market processes of competition and manipulate the rules governing access for the benefit of their ethnic constituents. Similar preferential methods were employed by the Afrikaner regime after 1948, by the Quiet Revolution regime in Quebec after 1960, and by the Malay regime under its New Economic Policy after 1970.[4] The governments expanded facilities for higher education and implemented employment preferences in government, state enterprises, and even private business. The state acquired economic assets to be operated for and by members of the politically dominant ethnic community; some were subsequently transferred to them (privatized) on favorable terms. Government-controlled capital, credit, and contracts were reserved for and allocated to firms operated by members of the preferred community.

By systematic intervention, the state increased access by members of their community to economic assets and opportunities while maintaining capitalist structures and without confiscating or expropriating the assets of ethnic competitors. In South Africa, Canada, and Malaysia, aggressive government intervention succeeded in enhancing the participation of disadvantaged ethnic communities in modern economic roles as owners and managers of industrial, financial, and commercial enterprises. Similar preferential measures will likely be attempted by the postapartheid government of South Africa on behalf of the severely disadvantaged Black majority. (Militant African nationalists in fact demand nationalization, in effect expropriation, with the possibility that some of these assets might later be privatized to Africans). Members of economically more successful ethnic communities, excluded from these preferences, consider themselves victims of government-sponsored discrimination and demand limits to the scope and duration of such practices.

"Middle-man minorities" that move into peasant societies and occupy the economic space between the military-political-landlord ruling elites and peasant masses may gain prominent or even dominant positions in commerce, finance, credit, manufacturing, and especially in retail trade and small-scale lending.[5] In some cases they have been employed as ec-

[4]Milton J. Esman, "Ethnic Politics and Economic Power," *Comparative Politics* 19 (July 1987): 395–418.

[5]John Armstrong, "Mobilized and Proletarian Diasporas," *American Political Science*

onomic agents of ruling elites, operating trading monopolies and serving as tax farmers. Though initially they may be welcomed for the economic services they provide they remain socially apart from the indigenous community, practicing endogomy and maintaining their inherited culture. Sooner or later they attract the envy and resentment of indigenous competitors and especially of ambitious politicians who build constituencies by attacking the exploiting "foreigners" in their midst. This pressure may result in measures intended to limit the scope of their economic activities, and they may become victims of officially inspired discrimination, extortion, scapegoating, and even pogroms. Jews and Greeks in Eastern Europe, Chinese in Southeast Asia, and Indians in eastern and southern Africa have suffered this fate. Zulu mobs pillaged and massacred Indians in the Durban area of South Africa in 1949; in 1972, Idi Amin expelled Uganda's Asian minority, confiscated their wealth, and distributed it to his followers, destroying Uganda's economy in the process. The targeting of Korean retail merchants in the Los Angeles riots in 1992, though lacking official inspiration or sanction, was an instance of apparently spontaneous violence against members of a middle-man ethnic minority.

Economic values, then, are important stakes in competition and conflict among ethnic groups.[6] There is likely to be an economic dimension to most ethnic conflicts. When they cannot be managed at the local level, when they reach the agenda of the state, ethnic-based allocations may be implemented by expropriation or, in more stable conditions, by market processes or administrative redistribution. The western liberal individualist tradition celebrates market processes as the normal methods of allocating values, producing both efficiency and justice among competing individuals and firms. According to this canon, the only proper way to allocate scarce opportunities for higher education and employment is by individual competition according to objective rules—no preferences, no discrimination. Access to economic resources should be governed by market processes open to all competitors on equal terms.

But what of the ethnic consequences of individual competition and mar-

Review 70 (June 1976): 393–408. Edna Bonacich, "A Theory of Middleman Minorities," *American Sociological Review* 38 (October 1973): 583–94.

[6] On the economic dimensions of ethnic conflict, see Donald Horowitz, *Ethnic Groups in Conflict* (Berkeley: University of California Press, 1985), "Economic Interest," 105–35; and S.W.R. Samarasinghe and Reed Coughlan, *Economic Dimensions of Ethnic Conflict: International Perspectives* (New York: St. Martin's Press, 1991).

ket processes? What if, as in Malaysia, members of the Chinese minority score consistently higher on qualifying exams for university entrance, win most of the places in universities, and thereby dominate the learned professions and government employment? When, under market processes, non-Malays gain control of most of the banks, manufacturing enterprises, construction companies, and commercial firms in the private sector, should Malay elites meekly acquiesce in economic subordination? Or should they attempt to use the powers of government to rectify their disadvantaged status by revising the rules of access and by administrative intervention?

Individual competition and market processes tend to reward those who enter the level playing field with superior resources. This applies to ethnic collectivities as well as to individuals. Advocates for ethnic groups that lose out in individual and market competition often ascribe failure to disabling past injustices, institutionalized discrimination, or informal processes by which initially successful ethnic competitors monopolize their advantages and effectively exclude others from employment, capital, credit, market access, and managerial experience. The solution, whenever possible, is to change the rules governing access so that individual competition and market processes yield to administrative methods of allocation that privilege, at least temporarily, members of the previously disadvantaged community and improve or even guarantee them access to higher education, middle class employment, and opportunities to own and manage businesses. The previously advantaged ethnic community then contends that such preferential measures victimize and discriminate unfairly against them and urge that they be discontinued.

What ensues are conflicts between representatives of ethnic groups who believe that their members benefit from individual competition and market processes and those who believe their constituents need the encouragement and protection of preferential rules that may include numerical proportionality. Both assert their case in the name of fairness, fairness among individuals or fairness among ethnic communities. Interethnic consequences rather than ideological principles are likely to determine the processes by which valuable economic opportunities and resources are allocated in societies characterized by competitive ethnic mobilization.

Multiple Grievances, Multiple Goals

In this chapter I have analyzed the stakes and values that are contested in ethnic conflicts. In real life, ethnic conflicts combine cultural, political, and economic grievances and goals, but in variable proportions that may change over time. At a particular moment, one element may be prominent, another latent, only to resurface at a later date. The more intense the mobilization, the tighter the boundaries, the more likely that fresh issues will sustain the conflict.

Cultural dimensions have been prominent in Malaysia and Quebec because of the centrality of language as an issue. Though cultural matters have been marginal to the struggles in South Africa and Palestine, they could arise in the future over the relative prominence of European and African symbols in the postapartheid state and the fundamentalist-secularist conflict among Palestinians. Economic issues are manifest in most ethnic conflicts, but they, too, may be latent for extended periods. Though French Canadians were aware of their economic subordination, their economic grievances were submerged for more than a century until the Quiet Revolution brought them to the fore. Political issues, involving the boundaries of the polity, terms of inclusion and participation, and relative power, are inherent in ethnic disputes once they reach the agenda of the state. Yet their relative salience may change. Whereas the grievances and demands of the North African diaspora in France had focused on economic and cultural matters, their political status became politicized by the inflammatory rhetoric of the National Front. Particular grievances, demands, and goals in ethnic conflicts are empirical questions that depend on the strategies and reactions of participants, their internecine struggles, and transnational influences that are not readily predictable. There have been numerous attempts at explanation after the fact, but no recorded predictions of the radical reversal of strategy among French Canadians in 1960, among Malays after 1969, or among Afrikaners after 1989, and their consequences for ethnic coexistence and conflict in these polities.

A common, often dogmatic, "explanation" ascribes all conflicts, including ethnic conflicts, to economic causes. As the underlying elements in all conflict are said to be economic, so must the methods of management be economic as well. The tendency to transmute political to economic issues and to reduce all conflict to economic origins is shared by Marxists, with their materialistic interpretation of history, and liberal individualists, with their image of man as economic maximizer. If "rational" individuals are motivated mainly by economic incentives and economic goals, collectivities such as ethnic communities must be similarly motivated. That professional economists should perceive the world as a series of markets and seek to explain all behavior in terms of competitive quests for material advantage is not surprising; that other social scientists should embrace this paradigm, some in the name of "rational choice," indicates how vulnerable they are to simplistic explanations of complex phenomena.[7]

That such views persist in defiance of the weight of evidence to the contrary suggests that economism is less an explanation than an ideology, influential nonetheless both among academics and laymen, similar in that respect to the Freudian preoccupation with sex as the master explanation of human behavior. To argue, for example, that the Israeli-Palestinian struggle is basically about economic values, or that the Quiet Revolution is mainly about employment opportunities for educated Quebecois, or that Malays are concerned primarily with closing the economic gap utterly trivializes and distorts the meaning and the stakes of these conflicts. I do not consider the subject worth debating. Equally unconvincing is the Marxist version of economic determinism that reduces all "antagonistic contradictions" (conflicts) to class origins. Some ethnic conflicts include elements of class stratification; class reenforces ethnicity as the source of cleavage, for example, in South Africa. But I know of no case where interethnic class solidarity has blunted or overcome ethnic lines of cleavage or survived polarization along ethnic lines; normally the main front-line fighters on all sides of violent ethnic conflicts—Northern Ireland, Bosnia, Sri Lanka—are proletarians. In conflict situations ethnic solidarity supersedes class differences. By reducing ethnic conflicts to expressions of underlying class antagonisms, this vulgar version of economic determinism defies the weight of historical and contemporary evidence.

A more limited but much more interesting proposition claims that economic growth is the most useful, reliable, and available solvent to ethnic conflicts. Since World War II the notion that economic growth mitigates social conflicts has become an article of conventional wisdom, shared alike by scholars, politicians, and laymen. Simply put, when there is more to go around, everybody benefits, material grievances and anxieties are assuaged, incentives for conflict are reduced, and an environ-

---

[7]There are numerous examples of writings that attempt to trace ethnic conflict to economic causes. Among them are Michael Hechter, *Internal Colonialism: The Celtic Fringe in British National Development* (Berkeley: University of California Press, 1975), and Andre Gunder Frank, *Dependent Accumulation and Underdevelopment* (New York: Monthly Review Press, 1979).

ment is created that is conducive to group accommodation.[8] When this idea gained currency it was meant to apply to class tensions between owners and workers but was soon extended to cover a wider range of conflicts. By the late 1960s, when ethnic discord appeared to be over-shadowing class conflict as a threat to social order, economic growth was conveniently available as the main solvent for these conflicts as well. One of the first deliberate efforts to apply this insight as public policy was the New Economic Policy in Malaysia, designed in 1969–70.[9]

Although the utility of economic growth for the management of ethnic conflict is commonly asserted and appeals to common sense, it has never been convincingly demonstrated. There are three incompatible propositions that attempt to explain this relationship.[10]

The first proposition posits economic growth as a facilitator and maybe even a necessary condition for the successful management of ethnic conflict. Scarcities invariably provoke competition, but increasing the material resources available to society makes it possible to provide incremental material rewards to members of all ethnic groups. Everyone benefits in this positive-sum game of growth with redistribution, and no individual or group need be deprived or harmed. Grievances and claims can be accommodated at no real cost to any of the competing ethnic parties. Economic gains need not be distributed equally or even proportionally among ethnic groups. Indeed, this is the very point: more can be provided—in job opportunities, business licenses, credit, housing—to the relatively disadvantaged, mitigating their grievances and satisfying their aspirations for material improvement and distributive justice without penalizing the economically advantaged. Thus, economic expansion and only economic expansion provides the means to benefit all, albeit at differential rates.

Though material conditions may not, according to this perspective, be the sole issue dividing ethnic groups, they inevitably form the root of

---

[8]H. W. Arndt, *The Rise and Fall of Economic Growth* (Melbourne: Longman Cheshire Press, 1978), traces the history of the idea that economic growth contributes to social peace.

[9]For a good statement and application of this position, see Just Faaland, J.R. Parkinson, and Rais Saniman, *Growth and Ethnic Inequality: Malaysia's New Economic Policy* (New York, St. Martin's Press, 1990).

[10]For a more extended statement of this position, see Milton J. Esman, "Economic Performance and Ethnic Conflict," in Joseph Montville, ed., *Conflict and Peacemaking in Multiethnic Societies* (Lexington, Mass.: Lexington Books, 1990).

much societal conflict. Material scarcities generate struggles for shares, since the benefits that accrue to one mobilized competitor are perceived to come necessarily at the expense of others. Conditions of economic stagnation or slow growth, not to mention decline, hinder the management of any kind of societal conflict. Vigorous economic growth, conversely, creates a social climate of optimism and generosity that can generate intergroup trust, facilitate mutual accommodation, and enhance peaceful and consensual regulation of ethnic conflicts. Ethnic groups whose cultural or political aspirations are thwarted may be appeased by improved economic opportunities or material welfare, but only if economic growth makes these incremental resources available. Following this logic, a group of Jewish-American businessmen considered raising funds to promote autonomous economic development for Palestinians in the West Bank in the naive hope that this might divert their energies from political protest to the pursuit of material affluence, reduce violence, reconcile them to Israeli rule, and blunt the campaign for a Palestinian state.

The second proposition predicts that economic growth accentuates and aggravates ethnic conflict. Whatever other benefits economic growth may bring to society, reducing ethnic tensions is not one of them. This pessimistic assessment draws from the celebrated social-psychological concept of relative deprivation. Though economic expansion may produce real improvements in material conditions, its more important effect is to shift aspiration levels. People who once acquiesced in deprived economic conditions because they could visualize no practical alternative now begin to reassess their prospects and possibilities. Their aspiration levels rise. No longer are they content to compare their improved circumstances with their previous experience and be grateful for improvement, for their reference group has shifted. They now compare their present conditions and opportunities with those of groups who are materially better off than they and ask by what right the others should be so privileged. Perversely, then, as their objective conditions improve, they become more dissatisfied because their aspirations outdistance their achievements.

As their grievances mount, so does the stridency of their demands. When the target of these demands is another competing or hostile ethnic group, they are readily perceived by the ethnic competitor as a threat to its own fully deserved and hard-earned social, economic, and occupational status. The competitor then mobilizes to protect its position, inflaming preexistent ethnic antagonisms and increasing the likelihood of conflict. Thus during the 1960s, the substantial economic progress of American Blacks did not assuage their grievances; instead, as their reference group shifted, the gap between them and Whites became more apparent and more unacceptable. Meanwhile the economic progress of Blacks loomed as a competitive threat to the status and opportunities of many Whites, who responded by throwing their political support to anti-Black politicians such as George Wallace and Richard Nixon.

Advocates of the relative deprivation school regard as simply naive the notion that economic growth is likely to mitigate ethnic or any form of societal conflict. Even if there were enough growth to go around, to make a significant difference, its distribution would be problematical and probably conflictual. Moreover, the growth-producing-satisfaction hypothesis ignores the main psychological consequences of economic expansion—the shift in aspiration levels and reference groups that generates fresh dissatisfactions and grievances in the wake of economic growth. These dissatisfactions breed hostility, not positive-sum contentment, and they diminish individual and collective propensities for accommodation and compromise. Thus, in ethnically divided societies, economic growth is more likely to exacerbate than to mitigate group conflict.

The third proposition, essentially agnostic on this relationship, argues that economic growth is essentially irrelevant to the management of severe ethnic conflict. The foundations of ethnic conflict are not economic but cultural and especially political: Whose country is it? Which groups shall control the central government? How shall minorities be represented and participate in national politics? How much autonomy shall be conceded to regionally based minorities? Which language or languages should enjoy official status in education and in government operations? These critical political issues involve the competitive status, rights, and dignity of ethnic collectivities. On such often nonnegotiable issues men and women may be prepared to put their lives on the line, as they have in South Africa, Palestine, Sri Lanka, and former Yugoslavia.

Compared to these issues, economic concerns are trivial, usually derivative of these more basic political issues. Neither economic growth nor economic stagnation can fundamentally affect the course or the outcome of conflicts that are waged for different and higher stakes. The core of this proposition is that economic performance seldom explains and economic means are seldom effective in resolving the more dangerous and violent instances of ethnic conflict. Thus economic factors are irrelevant to the management of conflicts that originate from other, mainly political causes.

There are indeed economic dimensions to most instances of ethnic conflict, including all the cases examined in this book. Where the intensity of conflict is moderate, economic expansion along with astute distributions of the increments of growth may alleviate conflict. The conditions under which economic distress exacerbates conflict and economic growth mitigates conflict are less apparent. In Canada, economic expansion in the 1960s aroused great expectations among Québécois. It fueled their propensity to demand enhanced status for the French language, increased participation in modern economic roles, and even independence for Quebec. In that case economic growth had the effect of exacebating conflict. Recession in the late 1970s deflated the belief that Quebec could prosper economically on its own and contributed to the defeat of the 1980 referendum. Economic recession, which might have been expected to exacerbate ethnic conflict, in this case actually diminished its intensity. A similar sequence could be observed in Scotland.

In Malaysia, two decades of rapid economic growth and an aggressive interethnic redistributional program designed to end the identification of race with economic function and thereby enhance "national unity" have not mitigated interethnic tensions. Though they have shared in the benefits of economic expansion, Chinese remain embittered by the discriminatory effects of government policies and by the continuing stigma of second-class citizenship. Similarly, the belief among many South African White liberals that enhanced economic opportunities would mitigate Black grievances proved to be false, as many of the beneficiaries of these opportunities became militant enemies of the apartheid regime. Improved economic prospects only aggravated their sense of political and social oppression. Recession in the United States in the early 1990s did not appear to threaten the Mexican-American diaspora, but rising unemployment and economic anxieties in France in the late 1980s were believed to have contributed to the rise of the racist National Front.

One of the effects of economic growth may be to disrupt established relationships within ethnic communities, producing unexpected consequences for interethnic relations. The occupied West Bank furnishes a case in point. There the poorest, least educated, lowest status proletarian elements among the Palestinians have, because of opportunities for wage labor in Israel, achieved material standards of consumption far beyond those previously attained in their society. Their material prosperity, in turn, has undermined the status and power of the traditional landed gentry whose education, political connections, control of employment, and clientelistic practices had long insured their dominant position in Palestinian society. Yet the youthful educated class found professional opportunities blocked both in Israel and the dependent economy of the West Bank. Not sharing in economic prosperity, they became leaders and activists in the *intifada* revolt against Israeli rule, the most militant fighters for Palestinian nationalism and self-determination. Thus differential distribution of the benefits of dependent economic growth among Palestinians affected the course of ethnic conflict on the West Bank. It neutralized the working class whose relatively comfortable standard of living depended on employment in Israel; it undermined the authority of the conservative gentry class whose notables some Israelis hoped would be induced to cooperate with the occupation regime; and it radicalized those who were unable to participate in the new prosperity.

This excursion into economic variables demonstrates how difficult it is to explain or predict the effects of economic trends on ethnic-based conflicts. We cannot expect with reasonable assurance that economic expansion will mitigate ethnic tensions or serve as a solvent for ethnic conflicts. (Whether significant and sustained economic growth is a feasible option for public policy is yet another matter.) This uncertainty applies both to short-run economic cycles as in Quebec and to long-term structural changes as in Malaysia. Even if the stakes were primarily economic, the interethnic effects of economic growth are uncertain because of distributional disputes that intensify conflict. Economic distress might be expected to aggravate the grievances that prompt ethnic mobilization, but evidence on this subject is inconclusive. Prosperity is supposed to create a political environment that facilitates compromise and accommodation; our cases do not confirm this expectation. A statistical analysis of political conflicts in sixty-one countries found no correlation whatever between politicized ethnicity and interethnic economic inequality, no surprise to those who take an agnostic position on this issue.[11]

Where so many factors intrude on ethnic conflicts, general or dogmatic statements about causes and effects must yield to the contingent nature

---

[11]Reported by Steven Majstorovic, "Political Ethnicity and Economic Inequality: A Subjective Perspective and Cross-National Examination," presented to the International Political Science Association Conference at the University of Colorado, Boulder, July 14–16, 1993.

of these relationships. Analysts and participants must be sensitive not only to economic factors, but to an array of cultural and political causes and stakes in ethnic conflicts which often occur in combinations and none of which can, a priori, be assigned pride of place. In every instance analysis and explanation become empirical tasks.

9

Outcomes and Prospects

In Chapter 1 I reviewed the running debate between "primordialists" and "instrumentalists".[1] Primordialists argue that ethnic identity and solidarity are deep, historically based collective loyalties that persist over generations. Instrumentalists hold that ethnicity is a malleable sentiment, that boundaries as well as content adapt to new situations. The most extreme instrumentalists consider ethnic solidarity nothing more than a myth, "constructed" and manipulated cynically or opportunistically in pursuit of advantages, mostly material, by individual promoters and activists.

Evidence presented in this book demonstrates the simultaneous presence of both primordial and instrumental elements. In every case there is a clear historical, cultural, and institutional base for community that distinguishes the collectivity from relevant outsiders and antagonists: Malays from Chinese, Palestinians from Israelis, Turks from Germans, Chicanos from Anglos. These are not imagined communities, they are as real as any social collectivity. Efforts to "construct" an ethnic identity from empty cultural materials usually fail, like the attempt in the 1960s to regenerate an "Occitanian" identity in southern France, for the label conveys no legitimate meaning to its intended constituents. The one constructed identity encountered in our cases, that of "Coloureds" in South Africa, was imposed by the South African state and is unlikely to survive the passing of apartheid.[2]

---

[1]The best treatment of this dispute is the article by James McKay, "An Exploratory Synthesis of Primordial and Mobilizational Approaches to Ethnic Phenomena," *Ethnic and Racial Studies* 5 (October 1982). For additional references, see note 8, Chapter 1.

[2]On the "social construction" of ethnic identities, see note 16, Chapter 1.

Yet ethnic collectivities do contain dynamic and opportunistic features. They adjust to changing conditions and situations. In response to the Chinese threat, Bugi, Javanese, and Minangkabau identities were combined into Malay; the several Sino dialect communities merged into Chinese; but Chinese never become Malays or Malays Chinese. Those boundaries persist. Despite deep-seated antagonisms on the subcontinent, Hindus and Muslims in South Africa became "Indian." Their new ethnic category assumed fresh functions in response to common discrimination. Where opportunities permit, individuals may move into or out of ethnic communities. Thus a Daniel Johnson can become the militant leader of a Québécois nationalist party, but no person with a Chinese name could possibly lead a Malay political organization. Boundaries may shift. The clear distinctions that formerly separated Afrikaners and Anglos, the latter already a heterogeneous category, have begun to erode. Designations may change—from Catholic to French Canadian to Québécois, from Colored to Negro to Black to African American—in response to changing self-definitions and aspirations, but the collectivity itself remains.

Ambitious or cynical politicians and publicists may attempt to exploit ethnic grievances to advance their own careers, but unless they respond to genuine grievances and aspirations they find no following. Nor are all ethnic politicians unscrupulous power maximizers; the Mandelas, Ben Gurions, Lévesques, Tunku Abdul Rahmans—and many lesser ethnic politicians—are motivated by more than self-serving personal ambition. If not, their constituents would desert them. Activists may attach themselves to an ethnic movement in order to protect or enhance personal economic interests: educated Québécois to secure professional and managerial posts in the civil service and the English-owned corporations, Chinese capitalists to protect their stakes in the Malaysian economy, Chicano intellectuals to win positions in bilingual education. But only the most cynical observer could maintain that these are what Québécois nationalism, Malaysian Chinese activism, and Mexican-American solidarity are all about. Every social movement attracts individuals and groups who seek selective material benefits. But to argue that mass constituencies can be mystified or hoodwinked to contribute funds, loyalty and support to a movement from which they derive no psychological or material benefits and whose rewards and opportunities are monopolized by a select handful of self-serving manipulators is to miss entirely the effects of socialization into an ethnic community and the force of collective dignity and efficacy that bind individuals to their ethnic roots.

Thus, while ethnic identity and solidarity are adaptive realities, responsive to changing needs and circumstances, while they provide scope for individual ambition as well as for collective resentments and aspirations, they are neither mere vehicles for material opportunism nor infinitely fluid and malleable. At the core of all significant ethnic political movements are distinctive historical and cultural experiences whose meaning has been not "constructed" but interpreted by their leadership to respond concretely to the threats and the opportunities their community confronts. Rooted in distinctive experiences, cultures, and institutions, ethnic identities and solidarities are more likely to persist as collectivities than to dissolve into the dominant mainstream. Some ethnic collectivities are maintained by a combination of internal solidarity and external rejection: Chinese are not welcome as bumiputera, Palestinians are not acceptable as Jews, Turks cannot aspire to become Germans. Others, like Québécois, have confronted the real possibility of assimilating as individuals into the Anglo-Canadian mainstream; some have accepted this option, but the great majority have chosen, at some economic cost, to endure and if possible to flourish as a separate people.

Evidence of the primordial dimension of ethnic solidarity is the failure of crosscutting identities and interests to mitigate ethnic conflicts. Interclass tensions exist in all ethnic communities. Malay landlords squeeze their tenants and landless workers, substituting machinery for labor and driving down real wages; no love is lost between Chinese workers and Chinese employers. Yet there is no cross-ethnic solidarity among workers or capitalists from these two communities. Québécois workers chose to form their own labor unions rather than associate with pan-Canadian or North American English-speaking unions. A similar course was followed by Black students in South Africa who broke away from a student organization that they believed was dominated by White liberals, even though its stance was militantly antiapartheid. Despite common economic interests and ideological commitments, cross-ethnic organizations seldom emerge; those that do cannot survive the intensification of ethnic tensions.

There is furthermore a pronounced tendency for members of ethnic communities to maintain separate, parallel institutions. Exceptions do occur: the South African Communist Party insists on a single organization open to members of all races, the Catholic church in Quebec attempts to bridge the interethnic gap. The more intense the conflict, the fewer common institutions or cross-cutting memberships. But even where tensions are relatively moderate and conflict is waged by civil methods, as in Quebec, separate institutions—the "two solitudes"—are the norm. Therefore strategies of conflict management that seek to capitalize on common interests across ethnic boundaries and on cross-cutting memberships usually fail. Success with this strategy is likely to be limited to countries such as the United States where the legal system and the dominant culture emphasize individual incorporation into the polity.

Why do ethnic communities mobilize for collective action? They may function for extended periods as apolitical societies performing community rituals, maintaining their institutions and cultural practices, providing mutual assistance and protection. They expend the considerable effort required to mobilize for political combat in order to resist perceived encroachments by other ethnic communities, to protest grievances stemming from unfair treatment by the state and its agents, or to seize opportunities to improve their collective status and life chances. Decisions to mobilize may upset extant distributions of power within an ethnic community and entail unwelcome behavioral changes. For that reason they are unlikely to be accepted casually and are certain to generate internal divisions and conflicts.

As societies are more likely to be activated by threats than by opportunities, the perception of serious threat is the most common precipitator of mobilization. Malays mobilized rapidly in 1946 to resist the threat of Malayan Union, the end of the special position of Malays in their own country, and the spectre of Chinese domination. The Chinese counter-mobilization, after the defeat of the Malayan Union scheme and in the face of the imminent termination of the colonial regime, aimed to secure some rights for the Chinese minority in a Malay-dominated polity. Palestinians mobilized to resist the threat of further dispossession and permanent subordination and, hopefully, to recover some of what had been lost, including their collective dignity and self-respect. French Canadians mobilized against threats to the survival of their Catholic and French culture and sustained that defensive mobilization for two centuries. The remobilization of the Quiet Revolution, however, was intended to capitalize on opportunities to improve their unsatisfactory, relatively deprived situation. Afrikaners mobilized originally to resist the threat of cultural anglicization and economic marginalization, and then to realize the opportunity to convert their demographic majority to political domination. Mexican Americans mobilized to resist discrimination, demand collective respect, and capitalize on opportunities for upward economic mobility.

Mobilization is not a spontaneous process. Indeed, spontaneous activation without an organizational base is likely to dissolve, as in the case of the Los Angeles riots in the spring of 1992. Mobilization is inspired and managed by ethnic entrepreneurs, usually a network of individuals who share a common view of the predicament of their people, the outcomes to which they are entitled, and the processes by which an unsatisfactory present can be converted to a desired future. There is usually a division of labor among ethnic entrepreneurs between articulators and organizers, between dreamers and practical men. The intelligentsia, usually produces ethnic entrepreneurs, educated individuals with enough imagination and leisure to conceive alternative futures and with the verbal skills needed to communicate the movement's ideology and inspire support. Clergymen (Malan, M.L. King), journalists (Herzl, Lévesque), lawyers (Mandela, Tunku Abdel Rahman), medical doctors (Habash, Mahatir), professional students (Arafat) are prominent in the leadership ranks of ethnic movements, but circumstances may confer this role on others.

Malay nationalism was incubated among Malay schoolteachers, but when their community faced an imminent crisis it was scions of the Malay aristocracy who mobilized the movement that defeated the Malayan Union proposal, took control of the United Malays' National Organization, and created an independent Malay-dominated polity. Chinese mobilization was managed by prominent English-speaking members of the business community who were acceptable to the departing British and to the Malay leadership after the Malayan Communist Party, inspired and led by Chinese intellectuals, had unleashed an insurgency that failed. Such exceptions notwithstanding, the intelligentsia normally produces the men and women with the imagination, leisure, and communication skills required for the role of ethnic entrepreneurs.

Every ethnic movement produces an ideology that facilitates mobilization by defining the collective identity and justifying the movement in terms of higher order values. Notions of divine will, national destiny, or fundamental justice can inspire the contributions of activists and the support of constituents, as well as convince sympathetic outsiders of the validity of their cause. Ideologies adopted by ethnic enemies may be mirror images: both Zionists and Palestinians proclaim their exclusive right to recover the homeland of their people through autoemancipation. A movement may be beset by competing ideologies, the ANC promoting a nonracial, nontribal democracy; PAC insisting on Africa for Africans;

Inkatha urging respect and self-determination for the component tribes or nations of South Africa. Ideologies may of course reflect changes in collective self-definition and aspirations; thus the emphasis on Catholic survivalism for the French-Canadian minority shifted to secular modernization for the dominant majority in Quebec. Ideologies proclaim a people's entitlement, as chosen people (Afrikaners, Israelis), native sons (Malays, Palestinians), majorities (South African Blacks, Québécois), or citizens (Malayan Chinese, Chicanos). Ideology emphasizes the need to organize and struggle to realize these rights and to overcome enemies who block their path. In short, ideology is essential to achieving the internal focus and coherence that are required for purposeful collective action.

Ethnic entrepreneurs must gather the resources needed for their struggle. These resources may include superior numbers, territorial concentration, potential voting strength, money, weapons, organizations, legal rights, and external support. The process of resource mobilization is specific to the objective circumstances of each ethnic community. Afrikaners had some external supporters, the ANC many more. Voting strength was a key potential resource for Afrikaners, Malays, and Québécois, but was unavailable to Palestinians, South African Blacks, and Turkish guestworkers in Germany. The PLO and the Malayan Chinese have been able to command large sums of money, while the ANC and Labor Zionists were chronically impecunious.

Securing control of existing community institutions, the resources they control and the allegiances they command is a crucial objective of ethnic entrepreneurs. Networks of Black churches provided the organizational core for the Black civil rights movement in the American South; mosques have served as privileged sanctuaries for propagating the message of Palestinian nationalism; community savings institutions were tapped to supply Afrikaner and Québécois nationalists. In the absence of existing institutions new ones must be laboriously built, such as the Jewish National Fund for land acquisition, the Confederation of South African Trade Unions (COSATU) for disciplined Black labor militancy, and the Mexican American Legal Defense and Educational Fund (MALDEF) to promote Mexican-American interests in the courts.

Whatever the availability of resources and relative success in mobilizing them, much depends on strategy, the ability of entrepreneurs to convert resources to action. Credible strategies cannot outrun the availability of resources needed for implementation. Should a movement capitalize on opportunities to pursue its goals legally? Thus the Zionists patiently built their institutions under the British mandate, Afrikaners concentrated on mobilizing an electoral majority, and Malayan Chinese attempted to employ their financial strength as junior partners in the Alliance and the National Front to moderate Malay economic nationalism. But when legal remedies are closed, resources must be deployed to support more feasible strategies, including civil disobedience, disruptive protest, terrorism as practiced by the PLO, and armed struggle as reluctantly embraced by the ANC.

Choice of strategies is constrained by three variable factors: the internal coherence of the movement, the availability of resources, and the opportunity structure. Strategies may reflect the need to moderate internal divisions even at the cost of weakening the external enemy, as with Arafat's lengthy delay in accepting UN Resolution 242. The opportunity for Québécois to pursue their goals by electoral means effectively foreclosed the alternatives. Not only would violence have cost more, but it would have been unacceptable to their own constituents. The earlier failure of revolutionary violence conducted by a faction of their community convinced Malayan Chinese that, despite the constraints imposed by their opportunity structure, they are better off working within its limitations than resorting to costly and risky armed struggle or disruptive protest. The ANC, on the other hand, encountered such a closed opportunity structure under apartheid that they had no real choice of strategy except to resort to armed struggle.

Opportunity structures are more likely to affect choices of strategies and means than to determine goals. The outcomes sought by mobilized ethnic communities are often products of deep-seated historical and ideological aspirations. The Zionist goal of a Jewish homeland challenged a very improbable opportunity structure; however, their practical strategies of gradually implanting settlements and building institutions took the realities of the opportunity structure very much into account. In general, states with capacities to penetrate their societies, extract revenues, and deploy coercive forces (so called "strong states") are difficult targets for ethnic movements and provide strong incentives for ethnic organizations to operate within the rules of the polity. Where grievances exceed certain thresholds of frustration, however, ethnic militants may challenge such strong states as Israel, South Africa, and Northern Ireland. Alternatively, "weak states" provide strong temptations for dissident ethnic movements because the risks of militancy are smaller and prospects of success appear greater. The weakness of several of the successor states of the USSR has provided favorable opportunity structures for challenging the prevailing ethnic distribution of power often by violent means.

Where feasible, homelands people tend to seek hegemony in an existing polity for example Afrikaners and Malays. More often circumstances prompt such peoples to opt for territorial autonomy and self-determination, as we have observed in the cases of Québécois, aboriginals in Canada, and Palestinians after 1988. For immigrant diasporas—Malayan Chinese, Indians in South Africa, Mexican Americans in California and Texas, and Algerians in France—hegemony and autonomy are unattainable. They campaign instead for nondiscriminatory inclusion as individuals, plus respect for their distinctive cultures. Indigenous nonterritorial peoples, such as Gypsies and American Blacks, demand nondiscriminatory inclusion along with respect for their culture and way of life. Internal factional conflicts erupt over variable outcomes within these broad classes of goals: Should Quebec autonomy take the form of independence or of enhanced federalism? Should Black hegemony be manifested by nonracial majoritarianism or by racially exclusive nationalism? Should Malayan Chinese emphasize cultural pluralism or nondiscriminatory individualism? Internal disputes over outcomes may be played out through the entire gamut of tactics ranging from intense debate and electoral competition to civil disobedience and internecine violence.

Ethnic communities seldom operate as monolithic formations. They are vulnerable to segmentation into factions that attempt to impose their values on the collectivity, compete for control of the community's resources, and seek recognition by outsiders as the authoritative representatives and spokesmen for the community. Factional conflict is inherent in ethnic politics, and though it extends possibilities for alternative leadership and membership participation, it may impair the ability of ethnic communities to deal effectively with outsiders, including ethnic antagonists and hostile governments. Ethnic communities nonetheless do share common interests and can function as entities, just as a state can function in interstate politics despite competition within its leadership and agencies. Internal divisions must be appreciated by analysts and practitioners alike, but their importance should be evaluated in perspective. Ethnic communities tend to share bottom-line concerns that factional leaders must respect if they are to sustain their credibility: for Québécois, the paramount status of the French language; for Palestinians, the end of Israeli rule; for Malays, the maintenance of bumiputera privileges. These bottom-line concerns enable them, despite internal divisions, to maintain solidarity, mobilization, and ability to deal with outsiders. Important internal divisions appear in every case examined in this study; they have affected the course of mobilization, impaired performance, and complicated strategies of conflict, without, however, nullifying the bonds of ethnic community or preventing concerted political activity.

Once a mobilized ethnic movement achieves a major interethnic goal, internal cleavages become more prominent. The achievement of a Palestinian state will certainly witness intense conflict among Palestinians between secularists and Islamists. The end of apartheid will bring conflicts within the dominant Black majority among partisans of African hegemony, those who desire a centralized, nonracial, majoritarian democracy, and proponents of a federation of ethnic communities. As one set of issues is resolved, lines of cleavage may be redrawn, but there can be no end to politics in human affairs.

The State and Conflict Management

The state, which regulates the relative status and rights of ethnic communities within its territorial jurisdiction, will continue to be both the main arena and the main prize of ethnic conflicts. There are, of course, limits on the capacities of individual states to perform this function. Constitutional structures, such as federalism, restrict the powers available to the central government. Canada serves as a good example. With few exceptions, control over language and education is assigned to provincial governments. The Canadian state's policies apply only to the institutions and activities of the central government. Recent efforts by the central government to seize the initiative have been thwarted, first by two provincial governments in the Meech Lake debacle, later in the Charlottetown package, by popular referendum. The Canadian state simply does not command the constitutional power to fully regulate ethnic conflict.

Other states may lack the administrative or coercive means to enforce policies regarding ethnic relations. United States immigration laws are routinely violated and evaded; illegal immigrants are employed in willful violation of law. Since the majority of illegal immigrants come from Mexico, the effect is to expand the numbers and the resources of the Mexican-American diaspora. Many states lack the means to impose their will on ethnic minorities. For three decades, the Burmese state has been attempting to Burmanize its refractory ethnic minorities, primarily by military means, at high cost and with limited success. The Philippine state has been unable to win the allegiance or to subdue its Moro minority in the South. The writ of the Peruvian state is not respected in its Quechua-speaking regions. Nor is it clear how far the authority of the post-Soviet Russian state extends over its several regional ethnic minorities, some of which, including Tatars and Chechyns, have proclaimed their sovereignty and independence. Such instances notwithstanding, the crucial role of the state in regulating interethnic affairs remains the rule.

Much depends on the image of the polity that is held by the ruling elites and the definition of the state that is reflected in constitutions, laws, and policies. The first of these defining principles is the question of entitlement to membership in the polity. By what criteria are citizens to be distinguished from resident aliens? Specifically, shall entitlement to the rights of citizenship be determined by ethnicity or by birth and residence in the territory; is citizenship an ethnic or a civic concept? If the doctrine of jus sangunis applies, as in Germany and Japan, then permanent residents of other ethnic origins, including those born on its territory, can expect to remain aliens, to be excluded from the status and the rights of citizenship, while ethnic kinfolk outside the state's borders enjoy the right to "return" at any time and be admitted as citizens. By contrast, where jus soli is the controlling doctrine, as in the United States and France, citizenship is defined in civic terms, permanent residents are encouraged to choose naturalization, and persons locally born are ipso facto citizens or may qualify with few obstacles.

This sharp distinction is often blurred, compromised, and complicated in practice. Some countries recognize two de facto levels of citizenship: full citizenship for members of the dominant ethnic community, constrained membership for others. Malaysia is an example. As bumiputera, Malays enjoy rights not available to compatriots of other ethnic origins. Malay immigrants from Indonesia are readily admitted and incorporated as citizens; Chinese refugees desiring to immigrate are rigorously excluded. Similarly in Israel, Jewish citizens possess rights, opportunities, and responsibilities unavailable to Arab fellow citizens. In both cases citizenship confers substantial but by no means equal rights or status. If Quebec should attain independent statehood, would all citizens despite their origins share equal status, access, and opportunities, or would persons of French-Catholic stock enjoy privileged status as the only authentic Québécois, while citizens of other backgrounds would be marginalized, subject to repeated and not very subtle reminders of their second-class status?

The fact that citizenship is defined in civic terms, open to individuals of diverse origins, does not guarantee equality of status or treatment. Blacks in the United States, formally citizens since 1868, were for nearly a century denied the fruits of citizenship, with the acquiescence of the government in Washington. Governments often tolerate informal but nonetheless effective patterns of exclusion and discrimination practiced by agencies of the state as well as by employers, financial institutions, and real estate interests. The victims may be citizens, but because of their unpopular ethnic provenance they receive little official concern. When discriminatory practices against certain categories of citizens do arouse public concern, governments may intervene by civil rights measures that assert equal rights and access for all citizens. They may even institute affirmative action programs that provide privileged access, especially to education and employment, to help victims overcome the effects of previous unequal treatment. Where the definition of citizenship is ethnic, minorities can look forward to continued exclusion or unequal treatment; where the criterion is civic, informal patterns of unequal treatment can be combatted and perhaps overcome.

A second and related issue, defined by state policy, is the relative precedence assigned to individual rights and to the rights of ethnic collectivities. From the liberal perspective, all rights inhere in individuals, who enjoy the freedom to choose any group, ethnic or otherwise, with which they desire to identify and affiliate. Membership is voluntary, not ascriptive, and ethnic collectivities are neither patronized nor restricted by the state. They are self-organizing, self-financing, and free to function as long as their members are prepared voluntarily to maintain them. Under the rubric of multiculturalism, as in Canada, they may receive minor support from the state to maintain inherited cultures, but such collectivities remain voluntary associations and confer no distinctive status, rights, or disabilities on their adherents.

The practical consequence of assigning legal and moral precedence to individuals is to encourage individuals of all ethnic origins to acculturate and eventually to join the dominant mainstream. Though assimilation is not imposed, it is facilitated, for the rewards in psychological security and material opportunity provide strong incentives. Assimilation is normally promoted and welcomed by state elites who regard a more homogeneous population as easier to manage than a pluralistic, polyglot society and a beneficial outcome of the process of nation-building. The policy of the Jacobin state disparaged all subnational identities; all residents of the hexagon were expected to become good Frenchmen, citizens of the indivisible nation. Though complicated by racial differences, individual assimilation has been the policy in the United States. Bilingual education has been implemented not to perpetuate ethnic cultures, but to ensure equal protection of the laws and to help integrate individual students into the English language mainstream. The United States has, however, shown greater tolerance than France for voluntary associations that provide mutual assistance, foster the perpetuation of inherited cultures, and mediate between the individual and the state.

The opposite policy privileges the ethnic collectivity over the rights of individuals. A federalized state may enable this policy by providing a territorial base for self-determination by an ethnic minority, including control over its members. In Quebec, Francophone parents are forbidden to send their children to English language public schools. Individual freedom of choice is constrained in order to insure cultural security for the collectivity, to protect it from the threat of demographic "minorisation." (By contrast, thousands of English-speaking parents elsewhere in Canada voluntarily enroll their children in French-immersion programs, as their cultural security is not at risk.) Similar policies directed at immigrants and English speakers as well as at French Canadians are designed to protect the ethnic collectivity even at the cost of individual rights. A dramatic example is the proscription of outdoor signs in English on business premises operated by Anglophones and serving Anglophone customers.

Where territoriality is not an option, institutionalized cultural pluralism can recognize, promote, and protect minority group rights. Such recognition usually entails official status for minority languages, education in that medium, and availability of electronic media for broadcast services in that language. The minorities treaties enforced by the League of Nations attempted to institutionalize such practices to protect the rights of ethnic minorities in the new states of Eastern Europe after World War I.[3] Muslims in India are permitted to adjudicate disputes in tribunals that apply Sharia law, a privilege demanded by some North Africans in France. Group recognition may also extend to political rights: Malaysia permits Chinese to operate explicitly Chinese political parties; the U.S. government has promoted preferential treatment for designated "minorities" in public employment, higher education, and government contracts. Under the apartheid system where every person was assigned officially and compulsorily to an ethnic category, unequal

---

[3] Inis Claude, *National Minorities: An International Problem* (Cambridge: Harvard University Press, 1955); and Hans Kohn, "Minorities," *Encyclopedia Britannica* (1965 ed.), vol. 15, 542–53.

group rights were not only recognized but rigorously enforced by the state on large numbers of unwilling persons. With the impending liquidation of the apartheid system, ethnic affiliation will become a matter of individual choice, but it is not yet clear what status and rights will be available to ethnic collectivities. Some Whites demand guaranteed quotas for political representation of their minority community; the Zulu Inkatha Freedom Party not only claims the right to culture maintenance but also demands constitutionally recognized regional homelands where Zulu and other nations (including, if they desire, the Afrikaner "tribe") can exercise political and cultural hegemony.

Where ethnic boundaries are tight, formal status for ethnic collectivities follows and is likely to be consensual. The religious, language, and educational rights of Palestinians in Israel are accepted by all parties. More controversial are the relative political rights and economic opportunities available to minorities, a continuing grievance of Palestinians. A further disputed issue is the right of a state to empower an ethnic community to discipline its members and encroach on their individual freedom of choice. Malays are not free to convert to Christianity, nor are French Canadians in Quebec free to educate their children in English, nor, until recently, could Afrikaans-speaking Coloureds legally achieve the status of Afrikaner. Are these instances violations of individual rights or expressions of the legitimate power of government to protect the integrity, survival, and well-being of ethnic collectivities?

Despite efforts like those of the League of Nations to defend the collective rights of ethnic minorities, the principal tendency in international forums, especially those sponsored by the United Nations, has been to conceive human rights in individual terms. The effect has been to universalize the liberal individualistic conception of human rights and the goal of non-discriminatory individualism—in short, to promote assimilation.[4] Recently the pendulum has begun to swing, with gradual recognition that the intensity of ethnic hostilities may preclude individual assimilation as a viable goal. For example, Armenians in their ethnic enclave of Nagorno-Karabakh will never assimilate into the Turkic Azeri majority in Azerbaijan; if they are to remain in that state their collective

[4]See Vernon Van Dyke, "Justice as Fairness: For Groups," *American Political Science Review* 69 (June 1975): 607–14; and "The Individual, the State, and Ethnic Communities in Political Theory," *World Politics* 29 (April 1977): 343–69. Also Jack Donnally, *Universal Human Rights in Theory and Practice* (Ithaca: Cornell University Press, 1989); Hurst Hannum, *Autonomy, Sovereignty, and Self-determination: The Accommodation of Conflicting Rights* (Philadelphia: University of Pennsylvania Press, 1991).

rights as a separate people will have to be recognized and safeguarded. The operative question becomes the terms of coexistence among ethnic collectivities, especially the treatment of minorities.

Indeed, the single most important human rights concern has become the relative status and rights of ethnic collectivities, not of atomized individuals. After setting out in the mid-1970s to vindicate individual human rights, the Conference on European Security and Cooperation (CSCE) has gradually accepted the collective rights of ethnic or national minorities as the appropriate focus for international concern and for action by the international community in defense of human rights. The Concluding Document of the CSCE's 1991 Conference on National Minorities committed participating states to recognize and protect the rights of national minorities, rights that encompass not only cultural pluralism—language, religion, education—but also political pluralism. The latter include regional autonomy and proportionality in political representation and government employment, while specifically excluding separation or other changes in internationally recognized borders. How the collective rights stipulated in these emerging norms can, when endangered or violated, be vindicated and enforced by international intervention has yet to be resolved by the CSCE or other international organizations.[5]

The principal responsibility for managing ethnic conflicts rests not with international organizations, but with states whose elites set the rules governing the relative status and rights of ethnic communities under their jurisdiction. Ethnic communities themselves and voluntary associations may contribute to the moderation and regulation of tensions, but the failure or inability of the state to preempt or control ethnic conflict may lead to protracted violence, as in the Indian Punjab and Burundi, or even to all-out civil war as in Sri Lanka, Lebanon, and several of the post-Soviet republics. Once rules and practices are institutionalized, ethnic conflict becomes a challenge-response process, ethnic communities or major factions among them making claims on the state for changes in prevailing rules and practices. The state, in turn, responds with accommodative measures, coercion, or combinations of both. Since state elites are seldom autonomous in matters relating to ethnic policy, their propensity to accommodate may be constrained by their estimate of the willingness of their own ethnic constituencies to acquiesce in such measures. Israel's Labor coalition hesitated at first to embrace an accommo-

[5] Milton J. Esman and Shibley Telhami, eds., *International Organizations and Ethnic Conflict* (Ithaca: Cornell University Press, forthcoming).

dational initiative with the PLO, recognizing that their hard-right opposition would mount a maximal effort to derail it and, in the process, drive them from office.

Where state and ethnic communities agree about desired outcomes—for example, Mexican Americans and the U.S. government jointly supporting the goal of non-discriminatory individual inclusion—conflicts are likely to concern methods and timing and to be amenable to mutual accommodation. Where desired outcomes of government and an ethnic community are incompatible—for example Greater Israel versus a Palestinian state—the conflicts involve fundamental issues that cannot readily be compromised. Normally the state commands sufficient power to maintain the existing order, as in all the cases examined in this study, even when ethnic conflicts produce severe stresses for the polity. State elites may, however, modify rules and practices at the margin in order to appease minorities and reduce the costs of enforcement. When such costs become prohibitive, as in South Africa, the stage is set for fundamental revision of the structures of the polity and the terms of coexistence. Where the state loses control of ethnic relations, the consequence is likely to be protracted violence and civil war, as in Bosnia, Sri Lanka, and Sudan.

Outcomes desired by state elites either promote the homogenization/depluralization of society, or they accept ethnic pluralism as a permanent and legitimate reality. Depluralization can be accomplished by such coercive and draconian measures as genocide, mass expulsions (ethnic cleansing), and population transfers. History offers all too many examples: Bosnia during the 1990s, Nazi Germany during the 1940s, the nineteenth-century decimation and forced removal of American Indians, England's dispossession of the Irish during the seventeenth century. Because it involves loss of territory, secession is seldom acceptable to state elites even when it might contribute to their goal of depluralization. The recent negotiated dissolution of Czechoslavakia is the exception. More typical were Nigeria's military repression of the Ibo-Biafran secession and the refusal of Serbia to contemplate the secession of its province of Kosovo, even though 90 percent of its inhabitants are ethnic Albanians who consider themselves victims of Serbian oppression.

The classic approach to depluralization is the encouragement of individual assimilation—Gallicization, Americanization, Arabization, Russification. This goal may be implemented by coercive measures, such as banning minority languages, or, more commonly, by positive incentives that encourage and reward members of ethnic minorities to acculturate, leave their native community, and join the national mainstream. Individual assimilation has been the favorite formula of liberals and Marxists for the depluralization of society and the elimination of ethnic differences as an undesirable political and social problem.

State elites may, however, accept ethnic pluralism as a permanent and unavoidable reality. This policy may be implemented coercively by excluding minority communities. The state deploys its powers to confer on one dominant ethnic segment a monopoly of political participation, economic opportunity, and cultural prestige. The practice of apartheid in South Africa was a pure instance of the formal exclusion of ethnic majorities, but it is hardly unique. Indians in Peru have been similarly excluded, as have Gypsies in Rumania and Palestinians under military rule in the Occupied Territories. Members of ethnic collectivities so excluded can respond by acquiescence, emigration, civil disobedience, or violent protest and insurgency—methods that have all been tried by Palestinians and South African Blacks.

The more common process of nonconsensual conflict management is to subordinate minorities. Unlike exclusion, a policy of subordination generally offers the minority some rights, although they are inferior to the rights enjoyed by members of the dominant community. Malaysian Chinese, as citizens, enjoy significant entitlements, including the right to participate in politics and to hold high offices, but their political rights are structurally inferior to those of Malays. Though they enjoy considerable freedom of enterprise and their per capita incomes are higher than those of Malays, they nevertheless experience significant state-sponsored discrimination in the economic and educational arenas. Likewise, Palestinians in Israel are citizens, but their opportunities in all fields are severely constrained by their ethnic status. Turks in Germany are effectively barred from citizenship, but as resident aliens they have access to valuable educational, health, and welfare services and, through labor unions, to collective bargaining rights. For generations, Francophones outside Quebec, though citizens of Canada and of the province in which they resided, were accorded no collective recognition or rights. Many chose to extricate themselves from their predicament by assimilating into the English language mainstream, but those who retained their French-Canadian identity and solidarity considered themselves a subordinated ethnic minority.

In all such cases, collective subordination is the consequence of state policy, not a natural or accidental outcome or the product of consent. But because such subordinated communities do possess some valuable rights, they are more inclined to express their discontents and aspirations by peaceful protest and political pressure than by violence. Subordinated homelands people may, however, spawn factions that are prepared to resort to violence and even terrorism to achieve complete independence, for example, the Sri Lankan Tigers, the Irish Republican Army, and the Basque ETA.

Accommodative and consensual approaches that accept pluralism as legitimate and permanent include federalism/regional self-government, cultural pluralism, electoral coalitions, and systems of power sharing. Canadian federalism was one effort to achieve mutual accommodation, originally by yielding provincial self-government to the French-Catholic majority in Quebec, a century later by establishing official bilingualism that conferred equal status on both the English and French languages and entitled all Canadian citizens anywhere in Canada to services from the federal government in either official language. This well-intended policy having fallen short of its sponsors' intentions, Canada is now in the throes of efforts to invent new consensual arrangements for ethnic accommodation and coexistence. Regional self-determination has provided an accommodative solution to the demands of the Catalan minority in Spain, German speakers in Italy's South Tyrol, and the larger ethnic collectivities in India. However, federal solutions involving hostile ethnic collectivities are not easily achieved or sustained. The agreement brokered in 1972 by the Emperor of Ethiopia between the Arab-Muslim government in Khartoum and the southern peoples lasted barely a decade before it collapsed in a renewed civil war.

Accommodative methods may occur separately or in combinations, an example of the latter being the carefully crafted pattern of ethnic regionalism and central power sharing that has evolved in Belgium. Indeed, power sharing is a common accommodative prescription for ethnically divided societies. Several of the cases we have examined here offer variations on the consociational theme, including cross-ethnic elite coalitions, proportionality in office holding and government employment, self-management of community institutions, and mutual vetos over decisions believed to involve the vital interests of either community. Within Quebec, informal consociational arrangements between Anglophone and Francophone elites operated for more than a century until they were repudiated by militant Québécois politicians in the early 1970s. The Alliance system in Malaysia was a more formal power-sharing bargain between Malay and Chinese elites. Though it preserved the peace in that conflict-prone polity for fifteen years, the system was abandoned by Malay elites after the communal riots of May, 1969. Power-sharing arrangements are subject to continual strain and vulnerable to breakdowns. Moderates who are prepared to compromise in order to maintain the consociational system are challenged and often outbidden by militant politicians in their own ranks. Power sharing is likely to survive only where the political culture fosters interethnic tolerance and mutual respect, as in Switzerland and Belgium. Yet, where ethnic lines are tightly drawn and cross-cutting pluralistic politics seem unlikely, power sharing offers accommodational and consensual alternatives to majoritarian, exclusionary, or domination-subordination patterns of conflict management. Where the parties are more or less equally matched and capable of inflicting unacceptable damage on each other, power sharing may constitute a viable process of mutual deterrence.

Governments may attempt to foster moderation and accommodative behavior among ethnic communities while recognizing the long-lasting quality of ethnic solidarity. Multiethnic coalitions can insure that ethnic communities or factions within them participate in government. Such arrangements tend to be more fluid than formal power-sharing compacts, allowing for larger numbers of participants and for shifting memberships.[6] The danger is that politicians seeking a minimum winning electoral coalition may fail to include representatives of important ethnic communities or factions, depriving them of influence over policies and participation in patronage and exposing the government to destabilizing charges of discrimination and exclusion. In military or single-party regimes, where control of the state is decided by non-electoral processes, ruling elites may be careful to include representatives of constituent ethnic communities in decision-making roles to reassure them that their status is respected and that they share in benefits provided by the state. Such coalition arrangements require continuous delicate political management to appease mutually suspicious constituents.

Electoral systems in which politicians depend on votes only from coethnics tend to reward ethnic extremists who assert maximal demands. Systems in which politicians seeking election must appeal to members of more than a single ethnic community and depend on their electoral support generally produce more moderate politics and reward accommodative politicians with cross-ethnic appeals. Thus relatively peaceful

---

[6]On the utility of multiethnic electoral coalitions for managing ethnic conflicts in Africa, see James R. Scarritt, "Communal Conflict and Contention for Power in Africa South of the Sahara," in Ted Robert Gurr et al., eds., *Minorities at Risk: A Global View* (Washington, D.C.: U.S. Institute of Peace Press, 1993).

consociational politics prevailed in Lebanon for more than three decades. The Nigerian constitution of 1979 required that political parties eligible to contest elections have units in two-thirds of the states, they faced disqualification if their symbols or appeals were directed to a single ethnic group, and a successful candidate for the state presidency was required to receive at least 25 percent of the vote in at least two-thirds of the states. The intended effects of such electoral engineering are to foster inclusive, nonethnic politics, proscribe electoral chauvinism, and reward ethnically moderate and accommodative politicians.[7] Majoritarian systems, by contrast, though formally democratic, can exacerbate conflict. In Northern Ireland for a half century the highly mobilized Protestant majority in the Stormont legislature selected entirely Protestant cabinets; though represented in that legislature in proportion to their numbers, the Catholic minority was systematically excluded from decision-making roles in government. Grievances stemming from this process of institutionalized discrimination and exclusion precipitated the "troubles" that since 1970 have cost more than three thousand lives. Despite the legacy of centuries of hatred, power sharing may yet prove to be the way out of this impasse.

Patterns of conflict management can be epitomized by this simple matrix diagram:

GOALS/METHODS	*Coercive*	*Consensual*
Homogenization	Genocide Expulsion, "cleansing" Population transfers Forced assimilation	Induced assimilation
Accept Pluralism	Exclusion Subordination	Federalism Cultural pluralism Power sharing Ethnic coalitions Reducing political salience

State elites that employ methods listed in the "coercive" column can expect resistance consistent with the capabilities of the threatened com-

---

[7]For a discussion of electoral engineering on behalf of political moderation in ethnically divided societies, see Donald Horowitz, "Making Moderation Pay: The Comparative Politics of Ethnic Conflict Management," in Joseph Montville, *Conflict and Peacemaking in Multiethnic Societies* (Lexington, Mass.: Lexington Books, 1990).

munity. Segments of disadvantaged communities, with considerable sympathy and support among their constituents, may resort to violence or armed struggle, as in South Africa, or they may, like Chinese in Malaysia and Palestinians in Israel, opt for civic methods of resistance because the opportunity structure affords some possibility for improvement and peaceful resistance avoids the high costs to them of violent repression. The methods listed in the "consensual" column provoke conflicts more amenable to negotiated, nonviolent outcomes. Disagreement generally focuses on such issues as how much autonomy to allot to a federalized unit or how to apply the principle of proportionality in power-sharing arrangements. Complicating such conflicts are disputes between competing factions of an ethnic community, as in Quebec. Governments may find it expedient to combine coercive and consensual methods, employing them simultaneously or alternately in response to changing pressures and opportunities. The Israeli government, for instance, subordinates Palestinians politically and economically but respects their cultural autonomy. Quebec's government employs both coercive measures and reassurance in relating to its Anglophone minority.

Internal and External Forces

As the forces that precipitate ethnic mobilization and ethnic conflict are dynamic, patterns of ethnic coexistence are frequently unstable. Transborder migrations, as outlined in Chapter 7, prompted mainly by economic pressures and incentives, produce diasporas whose presence and demands become political issues in host countries. The retreat of European colonialism removed the power that had imposed interethnic peace on the plural societies of Asia and Africa, leaving indigenous ethnic communities, as in Malaysia and Palestine, to compete for power and to battle out or negotiate a new political order. The dissolution of multinational polities, such as the former Soviet Union and Yugoslavia, produced similar threats and uncertainties, compelling ethnic communities ("nationalities") to mobilize. They needed to promote their competitive claims, defend their interests, and attempt to shape a new order compatible with their collective aspirations. Internal resistance and external pressures may force a hegemonic structure, such as the apartheid regime in South Africa, to reconfigure relationships among component ethnic communities. As we have seen, more subtle ideological influences and economic forces prompted renewed militancy among French Canadians.

Disturbances in a status quo may be caused by demographic, economic, military, ideological, or political forces, including initiatives by ethnic communities themselves. Such disturbances disrupt existing expectations and relationships, altering the political environment in ways that threaten some ethnic communities and provide opportunities for others, privileging, however, those that succeed in mobilizing effectively to promote their competitive interests. Few ethnic conflicts, civic or violent, can be definitively settled or "resolved." Recent breakthroughs in South Africa and Israel promise more equitable and peaceful patterns of coexistence, but they do not signal the end of ethnic conflict. Though circumstances change, ethnic communities persist, and relations among them must be managed. As changes are inevitable, so are the uncertainties and conflicts they occasion; these provide incentives for ethnic communities to mobilize and to sustain their mobilization.

The processes and the outcomes of ethnic conflicts are influenced by both domestic and external forces. The main arena for ethnic activism is the domestic polity, the main goal is hegemony, autonomy, or equitable inclusion in the state. But state borders tend to be porous, and embattled ethnic communities are inclined to reach out for moral and material assistance to sympathetic entities beyond their borders. These outsiders may include ethnic kinfolk (diasporas), ideological sympathizers, friendly governments, and international organizations. Such entities may, for reasons of their own, take the initiative to involve themselves in ethnic conflicts in foreign countries, offering diplomatic support or material assistance in the form of money, supplies, sanctuaries, or weapons.[8]

In fact, transnational or international forces intrude on most contemporary ethnic conflicts. Some intrusions are obvious and consequential. The antiapartheid struggle in South Africa became embroiled in Cold War politics: the Soviet camp provided important diplomatic and ma-

[8] Gabriel Sheffer, ed., *Modern Diasporas in International Politics* (London: Croom-Helm, 1986); Naomi Chazan, ed., *Irredentism and International Politics* (Boulder, Colo.: Lynne Reinner, 1991); Manus Midlarsky, ed., *The Internationalization of Communal Strife* (London: Unwin and Hyman, 1992); Milton J. Esman, "Ethnic Pluralism and International Relations," *Canadian Review of Studies in Nationalism* 17/1–2 (1990): 83–93; Esman and Telhami, eds., *International Organizations and Ethnic Conflict*; Stephen Ryan, *Ethnic Conflict and International Relations* (Aldershot, Eng.: Darmouth Press, 1990); Paul Smith, ed., in collaboration with K. Koufa and A. Suppan, *Ethnic Groups in International Relations* (New York: New York University Press, 1991); Daniel Patrick Moynihan, *Pandaemonium: Ethnicity in International Politics* (New York: Oxford University Press, 1993); Astrid Suhrke and Leila G. Noble, eds., *Ethnic Conflict in International Relations* (New York: Praeger, 1977).

terial support to the antiapartheid forces, while the United States and its allies protected the South African government. Sustained and unremitting pressure from the international antiapartheid coalition led to moral and political isolation of the South African regime and eventually to economic sanctions that contributed significantly to the abandonment of the apartheid system. All sides in the Palestinian conflict have actively solicited and received external assistance; their strategies have been constrained, in turn, by the requirements of the external parties that provide vital assistance. Although Malay-Chinese relations have been relatively free of external interference and the same may be said of the protracted but peaceable Flemish-Walloon confrontation in Belgium, most ethnic conflicts include often critical external dimensions that affect the struggle and the outcome. Some instances are as transparent as the shipments of weapons from members of the Irish diaspora in North America to the Irish Republican Army, or the dispatch of seventy thousand Indian Army troops to neighboring Sri Lanka in a bloody, failed effort to settle the Sinhalese-Tamil conflict, or the post–Gulf War U.S. military operation on behalf of Iraqi Kurds, or the threat by the President of the Russian Federation to intervene in the successor states of the USSR to defend the rights of beleaguered Russian minorities.

Some transnational influences are more subtle. Anglophone-Francophone relations have been influenced for more than two centuries by the presence of the United States on Canada's long southern border. The original concession by the victorious British to their conquered French and Catholic subjects in the Quebec Act of 1774 was designed to preclude the latter's association with the rebellious American colonies. Confederation in the 1860s was similarly intended to protect British North America from the aggressive and expansionist upstart empire to the south, which represented a common threat to both British and French elites. Contemporary Quebecois separatism is attempting to capitalize on the U.S. presence. In order to safeguard the living standards of their constituents, their slogan "sovereignty-association" originally called for economic association with Canada in tandem with the achievement of political independence. The U.S.-Canada Free Trade Agreement, which the separatists enthusiastically supported, has suggested an alternative option: political sovereignty combined with economic association not with the rump of Canada but with the United States. An independent Quebec with unrestrained access to the U.S. market would have little economic need for a shrunken Canada. Though the U.S. government has been a passive observer of this development, its mere presence continues to exert a powerful influence on the strategies of the main actors in the confrontation between Anglophones and Francophones, Canada and Quebec.

In this era of instant communication, cheap transportation, and economic integration, domestic ethnic conflicts are open to external intervention and to the accompanying danger that such conflicts might spread beyond the borders of a single state. The Bosnian conflict could ignite a full-scale Balkan war. Though territorial states remain the principal arenas and targets of ethnic conflict, the potential and the reality of external intervention are readily incorporated into the strategies of ethnic elites. External sympathizers and foes alike are often more than willing to become involved diplomatically, economically, even militarily, often for opportunistic reasons not directly related to the actual conflict. An example was India's decisive assistance in 1971 to Bengali nationalists in neighboring East Pakistan, its strategic purpose being the territorial dismemberment of India's principal regional enemy.

Increasingly, international organizations, notably the United Nations, have attempted to intervene in violent ethnic conflicts in humanitarian, peacemaking, and peacekeeping roles. They have sometimes succeeded in limiting violent conflicts, as in Palestine and Cyprus. In many other situations, such as the brutal struggle in Sudan and the Chinese oppression of Tibetans, international organizations have not attempted to intervene. In Bosnia, the hesitant initiatives of the European Union and United Nations to provide humanitarian assistance and to curb the slaughter and "ethnic cleansing" have proved futile. Successful intervention by international organizations requires agreement among their more influential members and a willingness by the warring parties to accept mediation and suspend hostilities.

Ethnic Solidarities: Legitimate? Rational?

Here we expand on a theme first addressed in Chapter 2—the rationality of ethnic activism. Ethnicity has become the main preoccupation of international organizations, but many western social scientists and opinion leaders continue to have difficulty accepting ethnic solidarity as a legitimate expression of politics.[9] Its prominence and persistance are re-

---

[9] For examples of the unwillingness of many social scientists to regard ethnic solidarity as a legitimate expression of politics, see Orlando Patterson, *Ethnic Chauvinism: The Re-*

proaches to the predictions of liberals, Marxists, and modernizers that it is destined to and indeed ought to disappear. Some are inclined to ignore it, others to ridicule it, still others to dismiss ethnic activism as irrational because they associate ethnic with primordial, primordial with emotional, and emotional with irrational. On the moral plane they charge that ethnic solidarity challenges the autonomy of the individual, which liberal thinkers associate with enlightenment and modernity, and imprisons the individual in ascriptive collectivities, throwbacks to earlier stages of human development that are vulnerable to mystification and manipulation by self-serving, unscrupulous, fanatical demagogues.

On the political plane, they argue, ethnic activism promotes mindless glorification of the in-group, fosters paranoid suspicion and hatred of outsiders, unleashes savage violence, and thwarts the civilized give-and-take of politics. Politics, they believe, should properly reflect the competitive pursuit of relative advantage by individuals or associations based on "rational" economic or ideological interests. The violence that often accompanies ethnic activism perpetuates ancient animosities that are irrelevant to and utterly remote from the real concerns of modern civilized societies: Protestant-Catholic in Northern Ireland, Hindu-Muslim in India, Serb-Croat-Muslim in Bosnia, Xhosa-Zulu in South Africa. The conflicts and the solidarities that produce them, so the argument goes, are atavistic and irrational, for the bloodshed and suffering far exceed the possible benefits of victory to either party and utterly defy reasonable efforts at restraint and settlement. In this era of global economic integration, ethnic solidarity, nationalism, and political fragmentation of all kinds are condemned as aberrations, perverse, dysfunctional, and retrograde.

For a balanced perspective on this issue, we must first recognize that not all ethnic activism is violent. Indeed, violence is often a minor element in ethnic politics. But since ethnic solidarities often draw on deep layers of emotion and passion they may erupt into violence. Though inhumane, collective violence is not ipso facto irrational. As political actors, ethnic collectivities select goals and devise strategies and tactics to implement them. These goals may include such scarce, competitive, and consequential values as control of territory, relative power, status, and wealth. Though some goals pursued by ethnic communities may appear to outsiders to be unjust (apartheid) and the methods cruel (eth-

---

actionary Impulse (New York: Stein and Day, 1977), and Stephen Steinberg, *The Ethnic Myth: Race, Ethnicity, and Class in America* (New York: Atheneum, 1981).

nic cleansing) or uncivilized (terrorism), they cannot be summarily dismissed as irrational unless the methods are incompatible with the goals, or unless the means displace the goals and become ends in themselves.

Ethnic conflicts are rooted not in misperceptions of reality but in the unreconciled goals of mobilized communities; they are rooted in politics and not, as some observers argue, in psychopathology. Analysts therefore err when they treat such conflicts as a form of collective mental illness. In most cases, including those examined in this book, it is quite possible to identify the goals of the antagonistic parties and the methods by which their collective interests are pursued. The actors or factions among them may miscalculate, their judgment may be flawed, their language may be strident, they may perpetrate or tolerate atrocities, but they are not for those reasons engaged in irrational or psychopathic behavior.[10]

I have argued that ethnic solidarity and ethnic activism are rational forms of organization and behavior and that this premise is essential both to appreciating these phenomena and to humane management of the conflicts they produce. Ethnic solidarity is a response to and a means of coping with basic human needs for affiliation, security, opportunity, and meaning; otherwise ethnic communities could not continue to evoke the allegiance and the substantial psychic and material investments of their members. The collective pursuit of recognition and respect, material welfare, cultural security, and political advantage are rational goals even though the means employed may be extreme, the processes of conflict may become ends in themselves, and fanatical and criminal elements may attach themselves to ethnic organizations, as in Bosnia and South Africa. Ethnic communities mobilize in collective defense or in competitive pursuit of scarce values. Ethnic activism is thus an expression of politics, where the function of politics is construed as the assertion and promotion of competitive interests. One might deplore the activation of ethnic solidarities and wish they would disappear so that individuals might respect one another as individuals and go about the "rational" business of improving their material and cultural well-being. But hard facts cannot be exorcised; they must be confronted.

[10]For psychiatric interpretations of ethnic coflict, see Ronald J. Fisher, *The Social Psychology of Intergroup and International Conflict Management* (New York: Springer Verlag, 1990); V. D. Volkan, J. V. Montville, and D. A. Julius, eds., *The Psychodynamics of International Relationships* (Lexington, Mass.: Lexington Books, 1991); Jay Rothman, *From Confrontation to Cooperation: Resolving Ethnic and Regional Conflicts* (Newbury Park, Calif: Sage Publications, 1992), especially chapter 4, "Conflict Management Epistomology and Training."

In attempting to understand and explain the pervasive reality of ethnic activism there is little to gain by assuming an Olympian stance that dismisses ethnic solidarities as illegitimate and the concerns and behavior of its participants as absurd or irrational. A much more fruitful point of departure for appreciating what has become the main source of violent conflict in the contemporary world is to accept the actors' own definition of who they are, what is at stake, and what they wish to achieve. This is not an argument for suspending moral judgment in specific instances of conflict, but a caution against arriving at such judgments a priori before reviewing and weighing the evidence.

Aside from the defense of borders, the main function of government is to manage conflicts, thereby ensuring domestic order. Governments may attempt to manage ethnic conflicts by the sheer exercise of state power for the purpose of maintaining order, usually in the interest of the dominant ethnic community. Alternatively, as elaborated earlier in this chapter, governments may attempt more consensual methods, capitalizing on opportunity structures that facilitate and reward civic methods of promoting ethnic claims, such as bargaining behavior and compromise. Like much of what governments do, the employment of superior state power will continue to characterize the management of most ethnic conflicts and under some conditions there may be no feasible alternatives. But, where consensual and accommodative methods are attempted, those most likely to be effective will be diplomatic rather than psychiatric, in recognition of the essentially rational motivations of ethnic activism.

My purpose in this book is neither to glorify nor to deplore ethnic solidarity and ethnic activism, but to recognize ethnic solidarity and ethnic conflict as pervasive, persistent, and important dimensions of contemporary human affairs. The bulk of scholarship on ethnic politics resides in case studies, many of high quality. Comparative description and analysis, however, are indispensable to the development of theory.[11] Yet the complexity of the circumstances in which ethnic politics are played out and the number of variable factors that affect processes and

[11]Useful bibliographies are available in comparative studies of ethnic pluralism and conflict, including James G. Kellas, *The Politics of Nationality and Ethnicity* (London: Macmillan Education Ltd. 1981); Joseph V. Montville, ed., *Conflict and Peacemaking in Multiethnic Societies* (Lexington, Mass.: Lexington Books, 1990); Joseph Rothschild, *Ethnopolitics: A Conceptual Framework* (New York: Columbia University Press, 1981); Anthony D. Smith, *The Ethnic Revival in the Modern World* (Cambridge: Cambridge University Press, 1981); and R. A. Schermerhorn, *Comparative Ethnic Relations: A Framework for Theory and Research* (New York: Random House, 1970).

outcomes preclude the development of general theory. Partial theory explaining some expressions and dimensions of ethnic politics are nonetheless possible as this book indicates. Examples are Chapter 7, which explains the politics of labor diasporas, and the several chapters that analyze the processes of mobilization among homelands peoples, following the conceptual scheme in Chapter 2. The discussion earlier in this chapter imposed intellectual order on the complexities of conflict management, a necessary prelude to the development of theory.

Similar searches for partial theory provide the most fruitful strategy for clarifying and understanding the various expressions of this complex, baffling, but consequential form of collective human behavior. This is entirely compatible with a normative outlook that searches for consensual, humane, and civil methods of alleviating and managing such conflicts and achieving viable accommodation, while accepting the ineluctable reality of ethnic solidarity. The task of understanding, explaining, mitigating, and managing ethnic conflicts is a challenge that is likely to command the attention of students and practitioners of public affairs well beyond the lifespan of most of those who consult this book.

Selected Bibliography

General

Barth, Fredrik, ed. *Ethnic Groups and Boundaries: The Social Organization of Cultural Differences*. London: George Allen and Unwin, 1969.

Brass, Paul, ed. *Ethnic Groups and the State*. London: Croom Helm, 1985.

Esman, Milton J., ed., *Ethnic Conflict in the Western World*. Ithaca: Cornell University Press, 1977.

Esman, Milton J., and Itamar Rabinovich, eds. *Ethnicity, Puralism, and the State in the Middle East*. Ithaca: Cornell University Press, 1988.

Freeman, Gary. *Immigrant Labor and Racial Conflict in Industrial Societies*. Princeton: Princeton University Press, 1979.

Glazer, Nathan, and Daniel Patrick Moynihan, eds. *Ethnicity: Theory and Experience*. Cambridge: Harvard University Press, 1975.

Gurr, Ted Robert. *Minorities at Risk: A Global View of Ethnopolitical Conflicts*. Washington, D.C.: U.S. Institute of Peace Press, 1993.

Horowitz, Donald L. *Ethnic Groups in Conflict*. Berkeley: University of California Press, 1985.

Kedourie, Elie, *Nationalism*. London: Hutchinson, 1960.

Kellas, James G. *The Politics of Nationalism and Ethnicity*. London: Macmillan Education, 1991.

Kohn, Hans, *The Idea of Nationalism*. New York: Macmillan, 1945.

Lijphart, Arend. *Democracy in Plural Societies*. New Haven: Yale University Press, 1977.

Miller, Mark J. *Foreign Workers in Western Europe: An Emerging Political Force*. New York, Praeger, 1981.

Milne, R.S. *Politics in Ethnically Bipolar States*. Vancouver: University of British Columbia Press, 1981.

Montville, Joseph V., ed. *Conflict and Peacemaking in Multiethnic Societies.* Lexington, Mass, Lexington Books, 1990.

Moynihan, Daniel Patrick. *Pandaemonium: Ethnicity in International Politics.* New York, Oxford University Press, 1993.

Rogers, Rosemarie, ed. *Guests Come to Stay: The Effects of European Labor Migration on Sending and Receiving Countries.* Boulder, Colo.: Westview Press, 1985.

Rothschild, Joseph. *Ethnopolitics: A Conceptual Framework.* New York, Columbia University Press, 1981.

Schermerhorn, R. A. *Comparative Ethnic Relations: A Framework for Theory and Research.* New York: Random House, 1970.

Smith, Anthony D. *The Ethnic Origins of Nations.* Oxford: Blackwell, 1986.

——. *The Ethnic Revival in the Modern World.* Cambridge: Cambridge University Press, 1981.

van den Berghe, Pierre L. *The Ethnic Phenomenon.* New York: Elsevier, 1981.

Young, Crawford. *The Politics of Cultural Pluralism.* Madison: University of Wisconsin Press, 1976.

Malaysia

Arasaratnam, Sinnappah. *Indians in Malaysia and Singapore.* Kuala Lumpur: Oxford University Press, 1970.

Bedlington, Stanley S. *Malaysia and Singapore: The Building of New States.* Ithaca: Cornell University Press, 1978.

Embassy of Malaysia, Washington D.C. *New Development Policy.* 17 June 1991.

Esman, Milton J. *Administration and Development in Malaysia: Institution Building and Reform in a Plural Society.* Ithaca: Cornell University Press, 1972.

Faaland, Just, J. R. Parkinson, and Rais Saniman. *Growth and Economic Inequality.* New York: St. Martin's, 1991.

Hussin Mutalib, *Islam and Ethnicity in Malay Politics.* Singapore: Oxford University Press, 1990.

Jesudason, James V. *The State, Chinese Business, and Multinationals in Malaysia.* New York: Oxford University Press, 1989.

Kiran Kapur Datar, *Malaysia: Quest for a Politics of Consensus.* New Delhi: Vikas, 1983.

Means, Gordon P. *Malaysian Politics: The Second Generation.* Singapore: Oxford University Press, 1991. This book includes an exhaustive bibliography of relevant publications in the English language.

Milne, R.S., and Diane K. Mauzy. *Malaysia: Tradition, Modernity, and Islam.* Boulder, Colo.: Westview Press, 1986.

———. *Politics and Government in Malaysia.* Revised edition. Vancouver: University of British Columbia Press, 1980.

Purcell, Victor. *The Chinese in Malaya.* Singapore: Eastern Universities Press, 1960.

Roff, W.R. *The Origins of Malay Nationalism.* New Haven: Yale University Press, 1967.

Scott, James C. *Weapons of the Weak: Everyday Forms of Peasant Resistance.* New Haven: Yale University Press, 1985.

Vasil, R. K. *Politics in a Plural Society: A Study of Non-Communal Political Parties in West Malaysia.* Kuala Lumpur: Oxford University Press, 1971.

Von Vorys, Karl. *Democracy without Consensus: Communalism and Political Stability in Malaysia.* Princeton: Princeton University Press, 1975.

Wan Hashim. *Race Relations in Malaysia.* Kuala Lumpur: Heinemann, 1983.

South Africa

Adam, Heribert. *The Opening of the Apartheid Mind: Options for the New South Africa.* Berkeley: University of California Press, 1993.

Adam, Heribert, and Hermann Giliomee. *The Rise and Crisis of Afrikaner Power.* Cape Town: David Philip, 1979.

Brewer, John D. *After Soweto: An Unfinished Journey.* Oxford: Oxford University Press, 1986.

Buthelezi Commission. *The Requirements for Stability and Development in Kwa Zulu and Natal.* 2 vols. Durban: H and H Publications, 1982.

Cell, John. *The Highest Stage of White Supremacy: The Origins of Segregation in South Africa and the American South.* Cambridge: Cambridge University Press, 1982.

Davenport, T.R.H. *South Africa: A Modern History.* Toronto: University of Toronto Press, 1978.

David, Peter. "South Africa: Between Two Worlds." *The Economist: A Survey of South Africa.* March 20, 1993.

Ellis, Stephen, and Tsepo Sechaba. *Comrades against Apartheid: The ANC and the South African Communist Party in Exile.* Bloomington: Indiana University Press, 1992.

Gerhart, Gail. *Black Power in South Africa: The Evolution of an Ideology.* Berkeley: University of California Press, 1978.

Giliomee, Hermann. *Negotiating South Africa's Future.* New York: St. Martin's, 1989.

Giliomee, Hermann, and Lawrence Schlemmer. *Up Against the Fences: Poverty, Passes, and Privilege in South Africa.* Cape Town: David Philip, 1985.

Greenberg, S.B. *Race and State in Capitalist Development.* New Haven: Yale University Press, 1980.

Horowitz, Donald. *A Democratic South Africa? Constitutional Engineering in a Divided Society.* Berkeley: University of California Press, 1991.

Lewis, Garth. *Between the Wire and the Wall: A History of South Africa's "Colored" Politics*. New York: St. Martin's, 1987.

Lodge, Tom. *Black Politics in South Africa Since 1945*. Johannesburg: Raven Press, 1983.

Murray, Martin. *South Africa: Time of Agony, Time of Destiny*. London: Verso Press, 1987.

Nolutshungu, Sam. *Changing South Africa*. Cape Town: David Philip, 1983.

Price, Robert M. *The Apartheid State in Crisis: Political Transformation in South Africa. 1975–1990*. New York: Oxford University Press, 1991.

Rentete, Johannes, and Hermann Giliomee. "Transition to Democracy Through Transaction? Bilateral Negotiations Between the ANC and NP in South Africa." *African Affairs* 91 (October 1992): 516–542.

Schrire, Robert. *Adapt or Die: The End of White Politics in South Africa*. South Africa UPDATE series. New York: Ford Foundation and Foreign Policy Association, 1991.

Slabbert, F. Van Zyl. *The Dynamics of Reform and Revolt in Current South Africa*. Three lectures delivered at the Institute for a Democratic Alternative for South Africa, Cape Town, 1988.

Study Commission on U.S. Policy Toward Southern Africa. *South Africa: Time Running Out*. Berkeley: University of California Press, 1981.

Thompson, Leonard M. *A History of South Africa*. New Haven: Yale University Press, 1990.

Welsh, David. *Democratic Liberalism in South Africa: Its History and Prospects*. Middletown, Conn.: Wesleyan University Press, 1987.

Israelis and Palestinians

Almog, Shmuel. *Zionism and the Arabs*. Jerusalem: Historical Society of Israel and the Zalman Shazar Center, 1983.

Aronson, Geoffrey. *Creating Facts: Israel, Palestinians and the West Bank*. Washington, D.C.: Institute for Palestine Studies, 1987.

Ben Rafael, Eliezer, and Stephen Sharot. *Ethnicity, Religion, and Class in Israeli Society*. Cambridge: Cambridge University Press, 1991.

Benvenisti, Meron. *Conflicts and Contradictions*. New York: Villard Books, 1986.

Benvenisti, Meron (with Ziad Abu-Zayed and Danny Rubenstein). *The West Bank Handbook: A Political Lexicon*. Jerusalem: The Jerusalem Post, 1986.

Cohen, Mitchell. *Zion and State: Nation, Class and the Shaping of Modern Israel*. Oxford: Basil Blackwell, 1987.

Freedman, Robert U., ed. *The Intifada*. Miami: Florida University Press, 1991.

Gresh, Alain. *The PLO: The Struggle Within: Toward an Independent Palestinian State*. London: Zed Books, 1988.

Harkabi, Yehoshafat. *Israel's Fatal Hour*. New York: Harper and Row, 1988.

Heller, Mark A. *A Palestinian State: The Implications for Israel.* Cambridge: Harvard University Press, 1983.

Heller, Mark A., and Sari Nusseibeh. *No Trumpet, No Drums: A Two-state Settlement of the Israeli-Palestinian Conflict.* New York: Hill and Wang, 1991.

Hilal, Jamil. "PLO Institutions: The Challenge Ahead." *Journal of Palestine Studies* 23 (Autumn 1993): 46–60.

Hilterman, Joost R. *Behind the Intifada: Labor and Women's Movements in the Occupied Territories.* Princeton: Princeton University Press, 1991.

Lissak, Moshe, and Daniel Horowitz. *The Origins of the Israeli Polity.* Chicago: University of Chicago Press, 1978.

Lustick, Ian. *Arabs in the Jewish State: Israel's Control of a National Minority.* Austin: University of Texas Press, 1980.

Mandel, Neville I. *The Arabs and Zionists Before World War I.* Berkeley: University of California Press, 1976.

Metzger, Jan, Martin Orth, and Christian Sterzing. *This Land is Our Land: The West Bank Under Israeli Occupation.* London: Zed Press, 1980.

Mishal, Shaul. *The PLO under Arafat: Between Gun and Olive Branch.* New Haven: Yale University Press, 1986.

Muslih, Muhammad. *The Origins of Palestinian Nationalism.* New York: Columbia University Press, 1988.

Peretz, Don. *The West Bank: History, Politics, Society and Economy.* Boulder Colo.: Westview Press, 1986.

Sandler, Shmuel, and Hillel Frisch. *Israel, the Palestinians, and the West Bank.* Lexington, Mass.: D.C. Heath, 1984.

Smith, Charles D. *Palestine and the Arab-Israel Conflict.* New York: St. Martin's, 1988.

Smooha, Samy. *Israel: Pluralism and Conflict.* Berkeley: University of California Press, 1978.

Spiegel, Steven L., ed. *Conflict Management in the Middle East.* Boulder, Colo.: Westview Press, 1992.

Teveth, Shabtai. *Ben-Gurion and the Palestinian Arabs: From Peace to War* Oxford: Oxford University Press, 1985.

Vital, David. *Zionism: the Crucial Phase.* New York: Oxford University Press, 1987.

———. *Zionism: the Formative Years.* New York, Oxford University Press, 1982.

Canada-Quebec

Behiels, Michael D. *Prelude to Quebec's Quiet Revolution: Liberalism versus Neo-Nationalism, 1945–1960.* Kingston and Montreal: McGill-Queens University Press, 1985.

Chodos, Robert, and Eric Haimovitch. *Quebec and the American Dream.* Toronto: Between the Lines, 1991.

Coleman, William D. *The Independence Movement in Quebec, 1945–1980.* Toronto: University of Toronto Press, 1984.

Commission of Inquiry on the Position of the French Language and on Language Rights in Quebec (Gendron Commission). *Report.* 2 vol. Quebec City: Imprimerie Nationale, 1972.

Cook, Ramsay. *Canada, Quebec, and the Uses of Nationalism.* Toronto: McClelland and Stewart, 1986.

Dion, Leon. *Nationalismes et politique au Québec.* Montreal: Hurtubise HMH, 1975.

Grant, George. *Lament for a Nation.* Ottawa: Carleton University Press, 1978.

Guindon, Hubert. *Quebec Society: Tradition, Modernity, and Nationhood.* Toronto: University of Toronto Press, 1988.

Jacobs, Jane. *The Question of Separatism: Quebec and the Struggle over Sovereignty.* New York: Random House, 1980.

MacLennan, Hugh. *Two Solitudes.* New York: Duell, Sloan and Pearce, 1945.

McNaught, Kenneth. *The Penguin History of Canada.* London: Penguin Books, 1988 edition.

McRoberts, Kenneth, and Dale Posgate. *Quebec: Social Change and Political Crisis.* Toronto: McClelland and Stewart, 1980.

Pinard, Maurice. *The Quebec Independence Movement: A Dramatic Reemergence.* Montreal: McGill University Working Papers in Social Behavior, Spring 1992.

Royal Commission on Bilingualism and Biculturalism. *Report.* 5 vols. Ottawa: Queens Printer, 1967.

Russell, Peter H. *Constitutional Odyssey: Can Canadians Be a Sovereign People.* Toronto: University of Toronto Press, 1992.

Sales, Arnaud. *La bourgeoisie industrielle au Québec.* Montreal: Presses de l'Université de Montréal, 1979.

Trudeau, Pierre-Elliot. *Federalism and the French-Canadians.* New York: St. Martin's, 1968.

Vaillancourt, François. *Langue et disparités de statut économique au Québec.* Government of Quebec: Conseil de la Langue Française, 1988.

Index

DATE DUE